Happy Southern Cooking!
Drew W. Weeks

2ND EDITION

True Southern Family Recipes

The Joy of Home Cooking

DREW W. WEEKS

R & E Publishers • San Jose, California

D1377671

R & E Publishers
468 Auzerais Ave., Suite A
San Jose, CA 95126
(408) 977-0691

Book Design and Typesetting by Diane Parker

Cover by Kaye Quinn

SECOND EDITION

Library of Congress Card Catalog Number: 92-12345

ISBN 1-56875-094-3

CONTRIBUTIONS

A special thanks to R&E Publishers, who gave my first book a home and helped it along the way into your home.

Without the encouragement and understanding of my husband, Tom, and my two children, Shannon and Warren, the idea for this book would not have been conceived. I am deeply grateful for their assistance in testing, tasting, retesting, and rating so many recipes over the past years.

For the support of my sister, Mary, who had confidence that the recipes contained herein were worthy of printing and sharing with all of you, I am most appreciative.

The literary assistance of Vivian and Joanne helped translate my thoughts and ideas into words.

The assistance provided by Steve and Ramona was invaluable and sincerely appreciated. I am deeply indebted to my husband's secretary, Faye, who so cheerfully and graciously did all the little things that were so helpful.

To the many friends who inspired me to write this book and to those who so willingly tested and tasted the recipes, I am deeply grateful. Without their encouragement and support, this book would not have been written.

ACKNOWLEDGMENTS

Throughout the retesting of my recipes just prior to completing the manuscript for this book, I spent many hours cooking, cooking, cooking and my grocery bill skyrocketed. The cooperation I received when I contacted many food companies for samples or complimentary coupons was overwhelming.

I would like to thank the following companies who were generous enough to contribute their products for use in testing and retesting the many recipes in this book:

> Arrowhead Mills
> Borden Distribution Center
> Church & Dwight Co., Inc.
> Food Lion Stores, Inc.
> H. J. Heinz Company
> Hanover Foods Corporation
> Hidden Valley Ranch
> Hodgson Mill Enterprises, Inc.
> Idahoan Foods
> Knapp-Sherrill
> Kraft General Foods
> LaVictoria Foods, Inc.
> McCormick & Company, Inc.
> Morton Salt Co.
> National Fruit Product Company, Inc.
> Pet, Incorporated
> Pompeian, Inc.
> San-J International, Inc.
> Seaboard Farms, Inc.
> Shaffer, Clarke & Co., Inc.
> Specialty Brands
> T. W. Garner Food & Co.
> Thomas J. Lipton Company
> Tulkoff Products, Inc.
> U.S. Sugar Co., Inc.

DEDICATION

In memory of my loving parents,
Frances and Hunter Wright,
who taught me the joy of home cooking.

PREFACE

During my childhood and adolescent years in South Carolina, family mealtimes were special occasions when we gathered to discuss events of the day while everyone enjoyed a delicious home-cooked meal. Mealtime was a cherished time of family togetherness.

I truly believe that my grandmother was correct when she said, "Time and money spent on preparing good meals are time and money NOT spent at the doctor's office." Although restaurants and fast-food chains have a place in our busy society, nothing, *absolutely nothing*, replaces a good home-cooked meal.

This cookbook was written to help those of us who want quality meals, yet have a limited amount of time to spend cooking. Some recipes require more time in the kitchen than others; however, they can usually be prepared in advance. Most of the recipe ingredients are staples in the average kitchen.

These family recipes, which I have been using for the past 30 years, were created or adapted from a variety of sources, including many old-family recipes. They have been tested and enjoyed by those who like nothing and those who like everything! It is my wish that your family and friends will enjoy them as much as we have.

TABLE OF CONTENTS

TO YOUR HEALTH!
(SUBSTITUTIONS)

To help reduce your fat and sodium intake, the following substitutions can be made in most recipes in this book without any other recipe changes.

Instead of	*Use*
Egg	Egg substitute (liquid)
Sour Cream	No-Fat or Low-Fat Sour Cream
Cream Cheese	No-Fat or Low-Fat Cream Cheese
Milk (whole)	Skim Milk
Buttermilk	Non-Fat Buttermilk
Cottage Cheese	Low-Fat Cottage Cheese
Cheddar Cheese	Low-Fat Cheddar Cheese
Cooking Oil	Canola Oil
Salt	Omit entirely, except in recipes for baked goods (pies, cakes, biscuits, cookies, etc.)

- For sautéing, use non-fat cooking spray in place of oil

- If recipe calls for cooked **ground** beef, cook, rinse and drain all ground beef before mixing with other ingredients

- Eat smaller portions of meat and cheese dishes and desserts

- Eat larger portions of vegetable, pasta, fruits and grain dishes

- Buy **lean** cuts of meat and trim fat from meat before cooking

1

Appetizers

APPETIZERS

COLD APPETIZERS

HOT APPETIZERS

APPETIZERS

Over the last few decades, entertaining has become very casual, and cocktail parties have become more and more popular with both hostesses and guests.

If serving appetizers before a meal, select light ones that whet, rather than satisfy, the appetite. A good balance would be one hot appetizer and two or three cold ones.

When designed to satisfy the appetite, appetizers served at a cocktail party should include a variety of both hot and cold foods, ranging from light to hearty. For those guests with a sweet tooth, remember to include a dessert.

Although appetizers are generally eaten with one's fingers or with toothpicks, the thoughtful hostess should provide small plates, china or paper, on which guests may place an assortment of appetizers from the table. Serving appetizers on trays, which are frequently circulated among the guests, is another more formal serving method.

Most of these recipes are easy to prepare, and many can be prepared in advance. Use the following appetizers as a great beginning to a meal or a casual get-together, and you will be an appreciated host or hostess.

APPETIZERS - COLD

5-LAYER SEAFOOD APPETIZER

Makes 12 or more servings

Prepared in layers, this appetizer brings out that delicious shrimp flavor! It can be made a day ahead, covered with plastic wrap, and refrigerated.

Place each layer in a shallow, glass casserole dish or quiche pan.

First (bottom) Layer:

- 1   (8 ounce) package cream cheese
- 2   teaspoons horseradish
- 1/2   teaspoon worcestershire sauce
- 4   teaspoon low-calorie Miracle Whip salad dressing *or* low-calorie mayonnaise
- 2   teaspoons fresh lemon juice

Mix all ingredients together and spread in dish.

Second Layer:

- 1   (12 ounce) bottle chili sauce or seafood cocktail sauce

Evenly spread sauce over cheese mixture.

Third Layer:

- 1   large bunch spring onions with green tops, finely minced
- 2/3   cup peeled, chopped cucumber, well-drained

Remove seeds from cucumbers. Sprinkle onions and cucumbers over second layer.

Fourth Layer:

- 3/4   pounds shrimp, peeled and cooked

Dice shrimp and drain on paper towels. Place paper towel on top and gently press to remove excess moisture. Gently sprinkle shrimp over third layer.

Fifth Layer:

- 1   ounce (1/4 cup) grated cheddar cheese
- 1/4   cup sliced Jalapeno peppers (optional)

Sprinkle cheese around the edges. If you like hot dishes, place Jalapeno peppers in 4-inch circle in center; otherwise, omit them.

Cover and refrigerate. Serve with crackers and spreading knife.

VARIATION: Substitute 1 pound crab meat or 3 (6 1/4 ounces each) cans crab meat for the shrimp. Remove any shell or cartilage and drain as directed above.

BEEF SANDWICH SPREAD

Makes 48 to 56 quarters

Because the bread stays fresh and does not absorb the filling, this sandwich spread (contributed by Ginny Hodges) is perfect for any occasion: picnics, tailgating, cocktail parties, buffets, luncheons and teas.

- 1 (8 ounce) package cream cheese, at room temperature
- 6 tablespoons low-calorie mayonnaise
- 1 tablespoon prepared mustard
- 3 tablespoons dry minced onions
- 1/2 teaspoon San-J Szechuan Sauce
- 2 (2 1/2 ounces each) packages sliced smoked chopped beef
- 12-14 slices sandwich bread, white or multigrain bread

In medium bowl, add cream cheese, mayonnaise, mustard, onions, and Szechuan sauce. Mix well. Cut beef into small pieces. Add beef and stir to mix. Chill overnight.

Spread 3 tablespoons of mixture on each of the 6 slices of bread. Place another slice of bread on top of each filling. Cut sandwiches in quarters. If desired, cut each quarter in half to make bite-sized appetizers.

Serve on a platter and garnish with fresh parsley sprigs.

Any remaining beef filling may be placed in covered container and refrigerated. Use within 4 days.

VARIATION: Add 1 teaspoon poppy seeds to mixture. For more formal occasions, remove crust from bread before spreading filling.

BOURBON BALLS
Makes 72 balls

An old-family specialty served to guests during the Christmas holidays.

    1/2   cup (4 ounces) bourbon
  1 1/2   tablespoons light corn syrup
      1   (12 ounce) box vanilla wafers, crushed
      1   cup chopped pecans
      2   tablespoons cocoa
  1 1/2   cup confectioners' powdered sugar

Place vanilla wafers in food processor or blender, and process until wafers are the size of bread crumbs. Mix bourbon and corn syrup together. Add wafer crumbs, 1 cup powdered sugar, pecans and cocoa together, and mix until well blended.

Using lightly greased hands and 1 teaspoon of mixture, form into balls. Using 1/2 cup sifted powdered sugar, roll balls until well coated. Place uncovered balls on cookie sheet and let them dry in air for about 30 minutes. Then store in air-tight container.

Keep in cool place, but do not refrigerate. Serve on tray or place in candy dish and serve.

CHEESE POT
Makes 3 to 4 cups

My mother's creation which I have enjoyed throughout the years.

      1   pound (4 cups) grated sharp cheddar cheese
      1   (8 ounce) package cream cheese, at room temperature
    1/2   cup sour cream
      2   tablespoons skim milk
    1/2   teaspoon garlic salt
    1/8   teaspoon cayenne pepper
      1   tablespoon grated onion
           a few sprigs of parsley

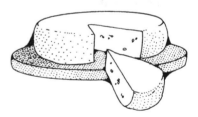

Mix cheddar cheese, cream cheese, sour cream, milk, garlic salt, cayenne pepper and onion. Stir until well blended. Chill in refrigerator several hours. Form into a large ball. Place on a plate.

Thirty minutes before serving, remove from refrigerator. Cheese Pot should be served at room temperature. Decorate with parsley sprigs and serve with crackers and a spreading knife.

VARIATION: Substitute 2 tablespoons beer, bourbon or dry white wine for the milk.

CHIPPED BEEF AND CHEESE SPREAD   *Makes 12 to 18 appetizer servings*

This can be served as a spread for crackers or used to make dainty sandwiches.

2   (2 1/2 ounces each) packages smoked, chopped beef, minced
2   tablespoons dry cooking sherry
5   ounces cream cheese
1   tablespoon low-calorie mayonnaise
1/4   cup chopped, stuffed green olives
1   teaspoon prepared horseradish sauce

Using a mixer, blend all ingredients together. Chill.

Serve cold with an assortment of crackers and a spreading knife.

VARIATIONS: Make sandwiches using small party rye bread or white bread. If using white bread, remove crusts and cut sandwiches into quarters.

CONFETTI CEREAL MIX   *Makes 10 to 12 cups*

Spicy, slightly hot and crunchy, this high-fiber mix is great for munching!

In a large bowl add:

2   cups Wheat Chex
2   cups Rice Chex
2   cups Corn Chex

Quantities of each cereal may vary, but be sure that you have at least 6 total cups of above cereals. Then add:

1   (12 ounce to 16 ounce) can peanuts or pecans
4   cups of any mixture of the following: Cheerios cereal, pretzels or cheese tidbits

Preheat oven to 250 degrees.

In a large pot or tall kitchen trash bag, add the Wheat Chex, Rice Chex, Corn Chex, nuts and other cereal mixture. Evenly sprinkle **Spicy Seasoning** (recipe follows) or pour mixture over cereals and nuts. Stir or shake to evenly coat cereal with spices. Pour seasoned cereal mix into two pans 9x13x2-inch and spread evenly in pans.

Bake uncovered for 2 to 3 hours, stirring every 30 minutes, until crisp and lightly browned. Cool completely.

Store in an air-tight container. This will keep for a month or more.

Spicy Seasoning

- 1/2   cup (1 stick) margarine or butter
- 2   teaspoons garlic salt
- 1   teaspoon onion salt
- 1/2   teaspoon chili powder
- 1/4   teaspoon cayenne pepper
- 1/4   cup worcestershire sauce

In a small sauce pan, add butter, garlic salt, onion salt, chili powder, cayenne pepper and worcestershire sauce. Heat on medium heat until butter is melted. Stir well.

CUCUMBER DIP   *Makes about 1 1/2 cups*

An unusual flavor combination that is so refreshing it keeps people coming back for more. This is equally good with chips or fresh vegetables. This is best when prepared and refrigerated several hours or overnight. This was shared by Fran Weeks.

- 1   (8 ounce) package cream cheese, at room temperature
- 1   tablespoon grated onion
- 1   tablespoon low-calorie mayonnaise
- 1   teaspoon worcestershire sauce
- 1   teaspoon lemon juice
- 1   cucumber, peeled and grated (about 1 cup)

In a small bowl, use an electric mixer to blend together cream cheese, onion, mayonnaise, worcestershire sauce, and lemon juice.

After measuring grated cucumber in a measuring cup, turn measuring cup upside down and press firmly to squeeze excess moisture from the cucumbers. Add well-drained cucumbers to cream cheese mixture, stirring with a spoon (do not use mixer) until well mixed.

Serve with chips or fresh, raw vegetables, using any attractive combination below:

broccoli florets	green pepper strips	carrot strips
mushrooms	cauliflower florets	radishes
celery strips	spring onions	cucumber strips
summer squash strips		

VARIATIONS: Add 1/4 teaspoon ground curry and 2 tablespoons catsup to the cream cheese.

CURRY DIP

Make about 2 1/2 cups

Let the flavors blend by making this dip several hours in advance.

2	cups low-calorie mayonnaise	1/4 cup chili sauce
2	tablespoons white vinegar	1 1/2 teaspoons curry powder
1/2	teaspoon salt	1 teaspoon paprika
1/4	teaspoon pepper	

Thoroughly mix all ingredients together; then chill. Serve with an assortment of the following fresh, raw vegetables: broccoli florets, carrot strips, cauliflower florets, celery strips, cucumber strips, green pepper strips, mushrooms, radishes, spring onions, or summer squash strips.

DEVILED EGGS

Makes 12 deviled eggs

Deviled eggs never tasted so good! Although a very popular appetizer, deviled eggs are also perfect for picnics, tailgating parties, and luncheons.

- 6 hard boiled eggs
- 1 tablespoon plus 2 teaspoons horseradish sauce (see insert below)
- 2 tablespoon pickle relish, well-drained
- 1 teaspoon prepared mustard
- 1/4 teaspoon Morton's Nature's Seasoning
- 1/4 teaspoon dried basil

Slice eggs in half lengthwise. Gently remove the cooked yolks and place in bowl. Add horseradish sauce, pickle relish, mustard, seasonings, and basil. Stir with a fork to mix well. With a knife, fill egg white hollows with egg yolk mixture, rounding into a slight mound.

To serve, lightly sprinkle with paprika.

VARIATIONS: Substitute mayonnaise for the horseradish sauce. To make fuller eggs, grate one half egg white into yolk mixture. This will make 11 deviled eggs.

Egg Salad

Grate all egg whites into egg yolk mixture. Add 1 teaspoon grated onion and 1 tablespoon finely diced celery. Stir to mix well. Spread mixture on bread slices, with or without crust. Cut into halves or quarters.

* * * * * * * * * *

How to Select Horseradish

Horseradish sauce is a mayonnaise-based sauce containing horseradish. **Cream-style prepared horseradish** is a horseradish preserved in vinegar and oil. Some brands of horseradish (sauce or prepared) are hotter than others, so try several brands until you find one that suits your taste.

FRESH VEGETABLE PIZZA   *Makes one 17x11-inch pizza or one 16-inch round pizza*

You've got to try it to believe how deliciously different this cold pizza can be! It is everyone's favorite appetizer. This is a modified version of a recipe which originated with the Service League of Hammond, Indiana.

    2   cans crescent rolls or 2 packages ready-made pizza crust
    1   (8 ounce) package cream cheese, at room temperature
  1/2   cup low-calorie mayonnaise
    1   (1 ounce) package Hidden Valley Ranch salad dressing mix (dry)
  1/2   head fresh broccoli, remove stems, finely chop tops
    1   bunch spring onions with green tops, thinly sliced
    1   large or 2 small tomatoes, peeled, seeds removed and diced
  1/2   cucumber, peeled, seeds removed, diced
    4   ounces (1 cup) grated cheddar cheese or shredded parmesan cheese

Preheat oven to 375 degrees. Lightly grease 17x11-inch rectangular cookie sheet or a 16-inch round pizza pan. Thoroughly mix cream cheese, mayonnaise and package of Ranch dressing mix. Set aside while preparing and baking crust.

Spread rolls or crust evenly over pan, pressing seams to seal. Bake for 12 minutes, until lightly golden brown. Cool completely. Spread cream cheese mixture evenly over the crust.

Prepare the vegetables by dicing finely, which will make slicing the finished pizza easier. Each vegetable should be placed in a separate container until ready to decorate the crust.

Tomatoes need special attention, so that the pizza will not get soggy. Peel tomatoes, remove seeds, and dice in small pieces. In a bowl, place 3 layers of paper towel, and then add tomatoes. Blot the top of the tomatoes with another paper towel, removing any excess liquid.

Over the cream cheese filling, evenly scatter the vegetables in the following order: cucumbers, onions, broccoli, tomatoes and cheese. Make sure that entire cream cheese layer is evenly covered with vegetables to make a decorative multicolored topping.

Cover with plastic wrap and gently press vegetables into filling.

Refrigerate until serving time. Cut into small squares or slices.

VARIATION: Any raw vegetables may be added or substituted for those used above, such as, olives, purple onions, celery, grated carrot, minced green pepper and diced summer squash.

HAM SALAD PUFFS *Makes 60 small puffs*

These are very light cream puffs filled with ham salad; however, they can be filled with a meat filling of your choice, such as chicken or tuna salad.

- 1 teaspoon salt
- 1 cup boiling water
- 1/2 cup shortening or margarine
- 1 cup flour
- 4 eggs
    Ham Salad (recipe follows)

Preheat oven to 400 degrees. Grease 9x13-inch cookie sheet.

In medium saucepan, combine salt, boiling water and shortening. Bring to a boil and then reduce heat to medium. Immediately add flour, stirring vigorously until dough forms a ball in the center of the pan. Cool slightly. Then add eggs, one at a time, beating after each addition until mixture is smooth and very stiff. Using a teaspoon, drop dough into balls, about 1-inch apart.

Bake 15 to 18 minutes until puffs are lightly golden brown. DO NOT UNDER-BAKE. Puffs are done when a toothpick inserted in the center comes out clean. Cool completely.

Cut top half from each puff and fill with **Ham Salad**. Replace each top and arrange on serving tray. Serve cold or at room temperature.

Ham Salad *Makes 6 1/2 cups filling*

- 4 cups ground cooked ham
- 4 ounces (1 cup) grated cheddar cheese
- 1 cup low-calorie mayonnaise
- 1/4 cup sour cream
- 1 teaspoon dry mustard
- 1/2 cup pickle relish, well-drained

In medium bowl, combine all ingredients and blend well. Use for filling **Ham Salad Puffs**.

VARIATION: **Chicken Salad**. Substitute equal amount of finely chopped chicken for the ground ham. Omit dry mustard. Add 1/2 teaspoon basil. **Egg Salad:** (see page 9) for a filling.

MARINATED APPLE SLICES
Makes about 1 quart

This marinade serves a dual purpose: It adds a delicious flavor and preserves the color of the apple slices for several days.

- 1/2 cup dry white wine
- 1 cup peach schnapps liqueur
- 1/2 cup cranberry juice
- 1 tablespoon lemon juice
- 3 large Winesap apples, unpeeled, sliced

Mix wine, peach schnapps, cranberry juice, and lemon juice. Slice apples and place in juices. Refrigerate and marinate overnight.

To serve, drain and place in a small bowl. Serve with crackers and an assortment of small cheese wedges.

MARINATED VEGGIES
Makes about 1 quart

A popular make-ahead appetizer that keeps for several weeks. It is a healthy substitute for a fresh vegetable and dip tray for picnics, tailgating, cocktail parties or casual get-togethers.

- 1/2 cup water
- 6 large peeled carrots, cut in 1/2-inch slices
- 1 head cauliflower, remove stem and use florets only
- 1 head broccoli, remove stem and use florets only
- 2 (4 1/2 ounce) jars whole button mushrooms, drained
- 2 (3 ounces each) jars small black olives, drained
- 1 large onion, cut into thin slices, separated into rings
  Zippy Vegetable Marinade (recipe follows)

In a large saucepan, add water and carrots. Bring to boil and gently boil for 2 minutes. Remove carrots and drain. Add cauliflower and broccoli to boiling water. Boil 1 minute. Remove cauliflower and broccoli and drain. Drain all vegetables. In a large glass jar or plastic bowl, add carrots, cauliflower, broccoli, mushrooms, olives, and onion. Pour marinade over vegetables. Cover. Refrigerate for at least 24 hours before serving to blend flavors.

To serve, drain vegetables and place in serving dish. For spearing vegetables, place a holder of toothpicks nearby.

VARIATIONS: Any balanced combination of the following can be substituted for (or used in addition to) the vegetables above: fresh zucchini, cut into 1/2-inch slices or green peppers, cut into bite-sized pieces or celery, sliced.

Zippy Vegetable Marinade

- 1/2 cup sugar
- 3 cups red wine vinegar
- 4 teaspoons salt
- 2 teaspoons dried basil
- 1/2 cup cooking oil

In saucepan, heat sugar, vinegar, salt and basil. Cook until sugar is dissolved. Remove from heat. Stir in oil. Pour over vegetable mixture. Chill for several hours or overnight.

VARIATIONS: Regular apple cider vinegar may be used. However, the flavor will be delicious, but different.

MEXICAN CHEESE SQUARES *Makes 81 one-inch squares*

Served at room temperature or chilled, it's simple and so deliciously Mexican!

- 1 (4 ounce) can chopped green chilies, well-drained
- 1/4 teaspoon cayenne pepper or red pepper
- 1 pound (4 cups) grated cheddar cheese
- 6 eggs, slightly beaten

Preheat oven to 350 degrees. Grease 9-inch square baking pan.

Spread peppers in prepared pan. Sprinkle with cayenne pepper. Cover with cheese. Pour beaten eggs over cheese.

Bake for 30 minutes or until firm in the center. Cool.

Cut into 1-inch squares and serve.

VARIATIONS: For green chilies, substitute 3 to 4 fresh jalapeno peppers. Remove seeds and finely chop. Spread in bottom of pan. Continue to follow directions above.

MEXICAN 6-LAYER DIP   *Makes 12 or more servings*

Having a great combination of flavors with eye-appeal, this appetizer is ideal for a picnic, tailgating party, a cocktail party, or casual entertaining. It is especially pretty when prepared in a round quiche pan.

- 1   (8 ounce) package cream cheese
- 1   can Jalapeno cheese dip
- 1   teaspoon San-J Szechuan sauce
- 1   tablespoon San-J teriyaki sauce
- 1   (16 ounce) can refried beans
- 1   (16) ounce jar LaVictoria HOT Ranchera Sauce, divided
- 1   (8 ounce) carton sour cream
- 1   stalk celery, diced (1/4 cup)
- 2/3 cup chopped cucumber, peeling and seeds removed
- 1   cup finely diced onion or 2 spring onions with tops, diced
- 2   tomatoes, peeled, seeds removed, chopped and well-drained

Bottom Layer

Mix cream cheese, Jalapeno cheese dip, Szechuan sauce, and teriyaki sauce. Spread in bottom of dish.

Second Layer

Mix refried beans and 6 tablespoons Ranchera sauce. Spread for second layer.

Third Layer

Spread sour cream over bean layer.

Fourth Layer

Pour 1 cup Ranchera sauce over sour cream.

Fifth Layer

Sprinkle celery, cucumber and onion over sauce.

Sixth Layer

Sprinkle drained tomatoes evenly on top.

Cover with plastic wrap and refrigerate. Serve with nacho chips, corn chips or crackers and a spreading knife.

VARIATION: Sprinkle 2 ounces (1/2 cup) grated cheddar cheese on top of tomatoes.

PECAN HARD CANDY *Makes 4 to 5 cups*

An appetizer for those people who have a sweet tooth.

- 4 cups pecans, mixed halves and pieces
- 1 cup sugar
- 1/2 cup water
- 1 teaspoon cinnamon
- 1 teaspoon salt
- 1 1/2 teaspoon vanilla flavoring

Preheat oven to 375 degrees. Grease two 9x12-inch pans. Grease the bowl of a wooden spoon. Heat nuts on ungreased 9x12-inch baking pan or cookie sheet for 15 minutes, stirring often.

In a large saucepan, mix sugar, water, cinnamon, and salt. Heat, without stirring until a temperature of 236 degrees on a candy thermometer is reached. Remove from heat. Stir in vanilla flavoring. Then add pecans. Stir with a greased wooden spoon until creamy. Pour out into prepared pans, separating into pieces as it cools. Cool completely.

Store candy in air-tight container.

VARIATIONS: 4 cups of walnut meats may be substituted for pecans.

PICKLED SHRIMP   *Makes about 1 quart*

Although this is best with fresh shrimp, it is also delicious with canned shrimp.

1 1/2	pound fresh, raw shrimp, peeled
2-3	stalks (1/2 cup) chopped celery leaves
1/4	cup whole mixed pickling spices
2	quarts boiling water
2	large sliced onions (2 cups)
5	whole bay leaves
1 1/2	cup cooking oil
1 1/2	cup white vinegar
1/4	cup (2 ounces) chopped pimentos
2	tablespoons capers with liquid
1 1/2	teaspoon celery seed
1 1/2	teaspoon salt
1/4	teaspoon Texas Pete hot sauce

Loosely tie celery leaves and pickling spices in a piece of cheesecloth, making a spice bag (see insert below). Place in boiling water and simmer for 10 to 15 minutes. Add shrimp and cook 5 minutes. Drain well. Discard contents of spice bag.

In large bowl, place sliced onions and shrimp in alternating layers. Add bay leaves. Combine oil, vinegar, pimentos, capers, celery seed, salt and hot sauce. Pour over the shrimp and onions. Cover and chill for at least 6 hours or overnight.

With a slotted spoon, remove shrimp and onions. Place them in a serving bowl, with toothpicks available for spearing shrimp.

VARIATION: For the fresh shrimp, substitute 4 (6 ounces each) cans shrimp, drained. Add shrimp to boiling water, but let sit for 5 minutes rather than cooking for 5 minutes.

* * * * * * * * *

How to Make a Spice Bag

An inexpensive man's handkerchief may be used, instead of cheesecloth, for making a spice bag. Be sure to wash the new handkerchief before using it, and also wash it after each use as a spice bag.

PIMENTO CHEESE *Makes 1 1/2 cups*

Commercial pimento cheese never tasted this good! This pimento cheese is equally good made into sandwiches or used to stuff celery. This recipe can easily be doubled.

- 2   cups (8 ounces) grated sharp cheddar cheese
- 1/4   cup low-calorie mayonnaise
- 1   (4 ounce) jar Dromedary chopped pimentos
- 1/4   teaspoon cayenne pepper
- 1   tablespoon vinegar or red wine vinegar

In small bowl, mix cheese, mayonnaise, pimentos, cayenne pepper and vinegar. Stir until well blended OR place ingredients in food processor and process about 1 minute until pimento and cheese are in tiny pieces.

VARIATIONS: Substitute 1 tablespoon LaVictoria Hot Ranchera sauce for vinegar. (If you like it hot!)

Add 1/4 teaspoon chili powder

Stuffed Celery

- 8   stalks celery, washed and cut into 3-inch pieces

Stuff celery with pimento cheese. Place on serving plate and sprinkle with paprika.

Pimento Cheese Sandwiches

- 12   slices bread, with or without crust

Spread pimento cheese on one side of 6 slices of bread. Spread mayonnaise on one side of remaining 6 slices of bread. Place mayonnaise side of each slice of bread on pimento cheese. For a meal, cut sandwiches in half. For appetizers, remove crust from bread and cut each sandwich into quarters.

SALMON PARTY BALL   *Makes 18 to 24 servings*

An inexpensive meat spread that everyone loves! This is a modified version of my mother's recipe.

1	(8-ounce) package cream cheese, at room temperature
1	tablespoon lemon juice
1	tablespoon grated onion
1	teaspoon cream-style prepared horseradish
1/4	teaspoon salt
1/4-1/2	teaspoon hickory flavored liquid smoke (adjust to your taste)
3	tablespoons grated green pepper
1/3	cup grated unpeeled cucumber, drained
1	(14 3/4 ounce) can salmon, skin and large center backbone removed
1/2	cup finely chopped, fresh parsley

After measuring cucumber, turn measuring cup upside down and press to remove excess moisture. Measure onion and then turn measuring spoon upside down and press onion to drain and remove excess moisture.

In small bowl, using electric mixer, mix cream cheese, lemon juice, grated onion, horseradish, salt, liquid smoke, and green pepper about 1 minute until creamy. Add salmon and mix another 30 seconds. Chill mixture 2 or more hours until firm.

While salmon mixture is chilling, very finely chop fresh parsley and place in single layer on waxed paper or plastic wrap. When salmon/cheese mixture is firm, form into a ball and gently roll in parsley to cover the ball.

To serve, place in center of large plate and surround with crackers and a spreading knife.

VARIATIONS: Use 1/2 cup finely chopped pecans instead of parsley.

SHRIMP MOLD
Makes about 3 3/4 cups

This unusual shrimp appetizer has a delicate flavor and a creamy texture with a delightful little crunch. This is best when fresh shrimp are used.

- 1 envelope unflavored gelatine
- 1/2 cup water
- 1 (8 ounce) package cream cheese
- 1 (8 ounce) bottle Thousand Island salad dressing
- 1/4-1/2 teaspoon Old Bay seafood seasoning
- 1 teaspoon lemon juice
- 1 teaspoon worcestershire sauce
- 2 tablespoons grated onion
- 1 tablespoon grated green pepper
- 1 pound (2 cups) cooked chopped shrimp, fresh, canned or frozen
- 2-3 stalks (1/2 cup) diced celery

Grease 1 quart gelatine mold.

In top of double boiler, place gelatine, water and cream cheese and heat until melted. Mix well and remove from heat. Cool slightly. Add salad dressing, seafood seasoning, lemon juice, worcestershire sauce, onion, green pepper, shrimp, and celery. Stir to mix well. Pour into prepared mold and refrigerate several hours until completely set (2 to 3 hours or overnight). Unmold on a bed of crisp lettuce. Serve with crackers and a spreading knife.

VARIATION: Add 1 tablespoon diced pimentos.

Substitute 1 bottle chili sauce or seafood cocktail sauce for Thousand Island salad dressing.

Substitute 1 bottle horseradish sauce for Thousand Island Dressing.

* * * * * * * * *

How to Buy Shrimp

Shrimp range in size from small to jumbo and are priced according to their size or count. When buying fresh shrimp, look for shrimp that have either no odor or a mild odor and a firm texture. About 2 to 2 1/2 pounds of de-headed shrimp in the shell will yield about 2 pounds of shelled shrimp. Usually allot about 1/2 pound of shelled shrimp per person. About 40-50 large shrimp in the shell will yield about two (2) cups of peeled shrimp.

Fresh raw shrimp can be stored in the refrigerator for up to three days. If you are going to cook them later, it is best to freeze them in the shells immediately after purchase. Shrimp should have their heads removed and be thoroughly washed before freezing.

SPICY CHEESE BITES   *Makes 4 dozen*

A cheese cookie with a light crunch. These are habit-forming!

      4   ounces (1 cup) grated sharp cheddar cheese, at room temperature
    1/2   cup (1 stick) margarine or butter, at room temperature
      1   cup flour
    1/4   teaspoon salt
    1/4   teaspoon cayenne pepper or red pepper
      1   cup Rice Crispies cereal
     48   pecan halves

Preheat oven to 325 degrees.

In large bowl, mix cheese and margarine. Add flour, then salt and cayenne pepper. Blend well. Stir in cereal.

Using a teaspoon, drop dough from the spoon onto an ungreased cookie sheet, placing dough about 1/2-inch apart. Slightly flatten dough by pressing a pecan half on top of each ball of dough.

Bake 15 to 18 minutes until cookies just start to brown. Do not brown. Cool. Serve at room temperature.

Store in air-tight container. These will keep for weeks.

VARIATIONS: Instead of placing pecans on top, chop pecans and add to the batter when the cereal is added.

For a spicier cookie, add 1/4 teaspoon chili powder.

For a hotter cookie, increase cayenne pepper to 1/2 teaspoon.

BEER CHEESE FONDUE   *Makes 4 servings*

Fondue cooking creates a relaxed, social atmosphere with stimulating conversations which makes an ideal meal for entertaining. Prepare ahead and let each dinner member have fun cooking or dipping his own bread cubes in the fondue sauce (see insert below).

1	(10 3/4 ounce) can cheddar cheese soup, undiluted
5-9	ounces of beer
12	ounces (3 cups) grated natural Swiss cheese
1 1/2	teaspoon fresh minced garlic
1	teaspoon dry mustard
1/2-3/4	teaspoon cayenne pepper
1	teaspoon Morton Nature's Seasoning or seasoned salt
1	loaf unsliced French bread, cut into 1-inch cubes

Place soup in sauce pan on medium high heat. Heat 5 minutes. Add beer, cheese, garlic, mustard, cayenne, and seasoning. Reduce heat to medium-low. Stir with wire whisk and continue to heat until cheese is melted and texture is creamy.

Pour cheese mixture into a warm fondue pot. Keep fondue warm, but not bubbling hot, during the meal. Use fondue forks or bamboo skewers for spearing bread.

Serve with a basket of French bread cubes and a green salad. A bottle of dry, white wine will compliment the flavor of the cheese fondue.

VARIATIONS: Substitute equal amount of cheddar cheese for the Swiss cheese.

Apple slices may also be served for dunking into the fondue sauce.

* * * * * * * * * *

How To Eat Cheese Fondue

Each person should have a dinner fork and bamboo skewers or a fondue fork, which has a long metal handle and small tines. Each person should be responsible for preparing his dinner by spearing the bread cubes, one at a time. The cubes should then be submerged in the cheese for a few seconds to coat the cubes well and then drained for a few seconds before placing hot cheese-coated bread on plate. Be careful with the hot cheese and hot fork to avoid burning your mouth.

BROCCOLI AND CHEESE PIZZA   *Makes about 4 dozen squares*

    1   refrigerated pizza crust OR 1 package crescent rolls
    2   tomatoes, peeled, chopped and well-drained
    1   (10 ounce) package frozen, chopped broccoli, thawed and drained
    2   tablespoons margarine or butter
    1   medium (1/2 cup) finely diced onion
    2   tablespoons biscuit baking mix
  1/2   teaspoon salt
  1/4   teaspoon pepper
    1   cup skim milk
    4   hard boiled eggs, grated or coarsely chopped
    2   ounces very thinly sliced, fully cooked ham, diced
    4   ounces (1 cup) grated cheddar cheese

Preheat oven to 425 degrees.

Spread pizza crust or crescent rolls in bottom of 9x12 shallow, greased, metal pan, spreading crust up sides. Bake crust for 10 to 12 minutes or until crust is browned. Reduce oven temperature to 350 degrees.

Press paper towels over broccoli and tomatoes to remove any excess moisture. Heat margarine and onion in 2-quart saucepan until bubbly. Stir in baking mix, salt, and pepper until smooth. Slowly stir in milk and cook, stirring constantly until thickened. Remove from heat and gently stir in eggs, broccoli, ham and cheese. Spread mixture evenly over pizza crust. Sprinkle tomatoes on top.

Bake at 350 degrees for 20 to 25 minutes until egg mixture is set. Let set 5 minutes. Cut into small squares. Remove gently and place on serving plate.

VARIATION: If you like spicy foods, add 1 teaspoon cayenne pepper.

               Add 1/2 teaspoon basil when salt and pepper are added.

BUFFALO-STYLE CHICKEN WINGS   *Makes 24 drumettes*

A very spicy, and slightly hot, appetizer which is usually served with celery sticks and blue cheese dressing for dipping.

Cut wings at each of the two (2) joints. Discard the tip of the wing and use the remaining 2 pieces of each wing (see page 31). Fry in hot deep fat about 5 to 8 minutes until they float to the top of the oil. Remove and place on paper towels to drain well.

Before serving, place wings and either version of **Hot Wings Sauce** (recipes follow) in air-tight bowl and shake well to cover each wing. Remove wings from sauce and place on serving plate. Place celery strips on side of plate and a small bowl of **Blue Cheese Supreme** (page 219) dressing or **Cucumber Dip** (page 8) in center of serving plate.

Wing Hot Sauce - Version 1

12	chicken wings
1/2	cup (1 stick) margarine
1	cup vinegar
1	teaspoon cayenne pepper (add more to taste)
2	teaspoon Texas Pete hot sauce
1	teaspoon worcestershire sauce
2	teaspoon prepared mustard
1/4	cup catsup
3	stalks celery, cut into 2-inch pieces

Wing Hot Sauce - Version 2

1/4	cup Texas Pete hot sauce
1/4	cup taco sauce, mild, medium or hot
1/4	Maurice's barbecue sauce
1/4	cup French dressing
1	tablespoon soy sauce

Mix sauce ingredients and simmer 5 minutes. Cook and dip chicken according to instructions above.

VARIATION: If either sauce is too hot for your taste, reduce the amount of Texas Pete hot sauce or cayenne pepper.

CHAFING DISH BROCCOLI APPETIZER

Makes 20 to 24 cocktail servings

This is an inexpensive party pleaser.

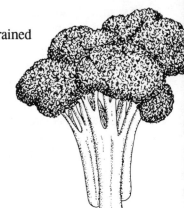

2	(10 ounces each) packages frozen chopped broccoli, cooked and drained
1/2	cup grated onion
2	(4 ounces each) jars sliced mushrooms, drained
1/2	cup (1 stick) margarine or butter
1/4	teaspoon fresh minced garlic
1	(10 3/4 ounce) can cream of mushroom soup
6	ounces of processed cheddar cheese, at room temperature
1/8	teaspoon Texas Pete hot sauce
2	teaspoons lemon juice
1	teaspoon worcestershire sauce
24	miniature pastry shells, baked OR 1 bag of jumbo corn chips

Cook broccoli as directed on package and drain well. In large frying pan over medium-high heat, saute onions, mushrooms, and garlic in margarine. Add soup, cheese, hot sauce, lemon juice, and worcestershire sauce. Reduce heat and cook, stirring constantly, until cheese is melted. Then stir in broccoli and cook until hot.

Pour into chafing dish and serve hot. Let guest serve themselves by spooning mixture into pastry shells or use corn chips for dipping.

VARIATION: Substitute 6 ounces of grated Swiss Cheese for the cheddar cheese.

CRAB CHEESE PUFFS   *Makes 40 appetizers*

A quick hot appetizer which can be kept in the freezer for several months, ready to be cooked on a moment's notice.

- 1/2 cup (1 stick) margarine or butter
- 2 teaspoons low-calorie mayonnaise
- 1/4 teaspoon garlic salt
- 1 jar Kraft Olde English sharp cheese or cold pack sharp cheese
- 1 cup fresh crab meat or 1 (6 1/2 ounce) can crab meat, drained
- 5 English muffins, separated into 10 halves

Place margarine, mayonnaise, garlic salt, and cheese together. Cool slightly. Gently stir in crab. Spread mixture evenly on top of English muffins. Cut each muffin into quarters, forming 4 wedges. Place on cookie sheet.

Broil muffins until slightly browned on top. Serve hot. These may be frozen, uncooked, and broiled just before serving.

TO FREEZE: Place muffins on cookie sheet. Cut into quarters, cover and freeze up to 3 months. When ready to serve, remove from freezer. Broil frozen, until hot and lightly browned.

VARIATIONS: An equal quantity of tuna, salmon or ground ham may be substituted for the crab.

FAJITA CHICKEN CHUNKS   *Makes 16 appetizer servings*

- 2 pounds boneless, skinless chicken breasts
- 1 jar fajita sauce
- 1/2 teaspoon fresh minced garlic
- 1/2 cup water
- 2 teaspoons sugar
- 2 tablespoons olive oil

Mix fajita sauce, garlic, water and sugar. Cut chicken breasts into bite-sized cubes. Marinade for about 4 hours. Drain.

In frying pan, heat olive oil on medium-high. Add a little chicken at a time and stir-fry about 2 minutes. Remove and place in large bowl. Repeat process with remaining chicken. When all chicken has been browned, reduce heat and return chicken to frying pan. Add 1 cup of reserved marinade. Cover and cook on simmer about 20 to 30 minutes until tender. Drain.

Place in bowl and serve with toothpicks or spear each cube of chicken with a toothpick and place on tray, with toothpick in vertical position.

HOT CHEESE PUFFS   *Makes about 180 puffs*

This inexpensive appetizer tastes great and can be prepared in advance and frozen.

    1   loaf unsliced bread, French or Italian
    1   (3 ounces) package cream cheese
    4   ounces (1 cup) grated sharp cheddar cheese
  1/2   cup (1 stick) margarine or butter
    2   egg whites, stiffly beaten

Preheat oven to 400 degrees. Line two 9x13-inch cookie sheets with aluminum foil.

Trim crust from bread, and cut into 1-inch cubes. In a double boiler, melt cream cheese, cheddar cheese and margarine. Heat until well blended, stirring frequently. Remove from heat and stir in whipped egg whites.

Dip bread into cheese mixture until well-coated. Place each cube on prepared pan. Do not let them touch each other. Cover with plastic wrap and refrigerate overnight. The puffs may be frozen at this point.

Uncover and bake for 12 to 15 minutes until hot and slightly golden brown. Keep a close watch, as they will burn quickly once they begin to brown.

TO FREEZE: Freeze unbaked puffs on cookie sheet. When solidly frozen, remove puffs and place in sealable freezer bag. Immediately return to freezer. When ready to cook, place on cookie sheet and bake as directed above, adding 1 to 2 minutes to cooking time.

HOT CRAB MEAT SPREAD
Makes 12 servings

This hot crab spread is equally delicious when made with canned tuna fish.

- 1 (8 ounce) package cream cheese
- 1 tablespoon milk
- 2 tablespoons chopped onion
- 1/2-1 teaspoon cream-style prepared horseradish
- 1/4 teaspoon salt
- 1 (6 1/2 ounce) can crab meat, drained
- 1/3 cup sliced almonds, toasted

Preheat oven to 375 degrees. Grease small casserole dish.

In medium-sized bowl, mix cream cheese, milk, onion, horseradish and salt. Stir in crab meat. Pour mixture into casserole dish. Sprinkle almonds on top and pat gently to press almonds lightly into top of mixture.

Bake about 15 to 20 minutes until the top becomes lightly browned.

Serve hot with crackers and a spreading knife.

VARIATION:Substitute one (6 1/2 ounce) can of small shrimp or tuna fish, drained, for the crab meat.

HOT MEATBALLS IN BOURBON BBQ SAUCE
Makes 18 to 24 servings

Meatballs have never tasted so scrumptious! The aroma of the sauce is tantalizing.

- 2 cups catsup
- 1 cup grape jelly
- 1/2 cup bourbon
- 1/4 cup brown sugar
- 1/2-1 teaspoon hickory flavored liquid smoke
- 2 teaspoons soy sauce
  double meatball recipe (see **Spicy Meatballs in Sauce** page 30)

In large pot, heat catsup, jelly, bourbon, sugar, liquid smoke, and soy sauce over medium-high heat until all ingredients are well-blended and hot. Add meatballs and simmer for 1 hour, stirring occasionally, being careful so that meatballs stay whole.

To serve, fill electric (or sterno) fondue pot or chafing dish with hot meatballs. Keep warm on low setting. Have a container of toothpicks available for retrieving meatballs from the sauce.

PARTY CHEESE ROUNDS   *Makes about 40 appetizers*

These can be prepared in advance, frozen and broiled just before serving.

    1   egg
    1   medium onion, grated
  1/2   teaspoon salt
  1/4   teaspoon chopped dried chives
  1/8   teaspoon seasoned pepper
  1/2   teaspoon cream-style prepared horseradish
    2   ounces (1/2 cup) grated cheddar cheese
    1   (4 ounce) package cream cheese
    1   box of onion melba rounds
    4   teaspoons caraway seeds

Cream together egg, onion, salt, chives, seasoned pepper, horseradish, cheddar cheese and cream cheese. Refrigerate mixture until ready to bake.

Spread mixture on melba rounds to 1/8-inch thickness. Sprinkle with caraway seeds. Place melba rounds on cookie sheet.

Broil about 4 inches from broiler for 3 to 5 minutes or until lightly browned on top. Serve hot.

VARIATION: For a spicier taste, add 1/8 teaspoon cayenne pepper.

TO FREEZE: After spreading mixture on rounds and placing on cookie sheet, these may be frozen and then baked as needed. Do not thaw before broiling; however, the broiling time may need to be increased by a minute or two.

SAUSAGE PINWHEELS
Makes about 32 to 40 appetizers

Make in advance and keep in the freezer. They will be ready for a spur-of-the-moment party.

    1   package crescent rolls
    1   pound hot bulk sausage, at room temperature

Unroll crescent rolls, separating into rectangles, using two rolls for each rectangle. Spread sausage on each rectangle, spreading to the edges. Roll up, jelly-roll fashion. Gently wrap in plastic wrap and freeze. Use within two months.

About 1 hour before baking, remove from freezer and let slightly thaw, about 20 minutes. Slice into thin rounds, about 8 to 10 slices per roll, and place on an ungreased cookie sheet.

Turn oven to broil. Broil 3 to 4 inches from heat, until browned. Using a spatula, turn and brown on other side. Watch these carefully while broiling, as they will burn easily once browned. Remove from oven and drain on paper towels.

Serve warm with a bowl of mustard sauce for dipping.

VARIATIONS: Use 1/4 cup prepared mustard. Spread on rectangles before spreading sausage. Continue as directed above.

SPICY MEATBALLS IN SAUCE
Makes 36 small meatballs

Cooking in the microwave makes these meatballs quick and easy to prepare. The liquid smoke in the Spicy Sauce (recipe follows) is the secret ingredient that makes this appetizer unforgettably delicious.

Meatballs

1	pound ground beef, round or chuck
1/2	cup finely chopped onion
2	tablespoons finely chopped green pepper
1	egg, slightly beaten
2	tablespoons skim milk
1/2	cup bread crumbs
1	teaspoon garlic salt
1/2	teaspoon pepper
	Spicy Sauce (recipe follows)

In a large bowl, combine beef, onion, green pepper, egg, milk, bread crumbs, garlic salt and pepper. Toss lightly until well mixed. Form into about 3 dozen small meatballs.

Place meatballs in a single layer in a 9x12x2-inch glass microwave proof dish. Microwave, uncovered, on about 70% power for 3 to 5 minutes. Remove from microwave, and gently stir to rearrange, moving the meatballs on the outside of the dish into the center of the dish. Return to microwave and continue to cook on 70% power for 2 to 3 additional minutes until almost done. Cover with foil and let stand 5 to 10 minutes. (Some meatballs may still be slightly pink, but they will finish cooking upon standing). Remove meatballs. Discard any juices in dish. Return meatballs to dish.

After **Spicy Sauce** has been cooked, pour the sauce over the meatballs. Microwave on 70% power for 3 to 5 minutes, stirring once.

Pour into a chafing dish and serve hot. Place a holder of toothpicks near to use for spearing meatballs.

Spicy Sauce

1 1/2	cups catsup
1	tablespoon prepared mustard
2	tablespoons vinegar
1	tablespoon worcestershire sauce
2-3	teaspoons hickory flavored liquid smoke

Combine all sauce ingredients in a microwave proof dish. Microwave on 100% power for 3 to 4 minutes.

SWEET AND SOUR CHICKEN WINGS   *Makes 30 drumettes*

This can be served as an appetizer or a meal. Prepare 4 drumettes per person as an appetizer and 10 drumettes as a meal.

30	chicken wing drumettes	1/4	cup grape jelly
3	tablespoons worcestershire	1/4	cup vinegar
3	tablespoons soy sauce	1/4	teaspoon ground ginger
1	envelope dry onion soup mix	3	tablespoons dark corn syrup
		1	tablespoon prepared mustard

Preheat oven to 300 degrees.

Mix worcestershire sauce, soy sauce, soup mix, grape jelly, vinegar, ginger, corn syrup, and mustard. Stir until well blended. Place drumettes in a large casserole dish. Pour sauce over drumettes.

Cover with aluminum foil and bake for 30 minutes. Remove casserole from oven and drain sauce from pan, reserving sauce for basting. Increase oven temperature to 400 degrees.

Leaving casserole uncovered, bake another 20 minutes, basting with reserved sauce, until chicken drumettes are browned. Turn each piece over and cook an additional 10 minutes. If you like these really browned and crispy, place under broiler for 1 to 2 minutes before serving.

VARIATION: For a meal, this may be prepared with any meaty chicken pieces, such as, breasts, thighs or drumsticks. Increase cooking time to make sure chicken is done. If needed, double sauce ingredients for the larger quantity of chicken.

* * * * * * * * *

How to Cut Chicken Drummettes

Chicken wings cut into drumettes are available at most grocery stores; however, if you want to cut your own, buy whole chicken wings. Cut off tips of each wing at the joint and discard, then separate wing into two pieces by cutting between remaining joint.

SWEET AND SOUR COCKTAIL FRANKS   *Makes 16 servings*

A quick and easy appetizer that pleases everyone. Contributed by Fran Weeks.

- 1   cup catsup
- 1   cup grape jelly
- 3   tablespoons lemon juice
- 3   tablespoons prepared mustard
- 1   (20 ounce) can pineapple chunks, drained
- 2   (16 ounce each) packages of franks (hot dogs), cut into one-inch pieces

Over low heat, simmer catsup, jelly, lemon juice and mustard together in sauce pan for about 3 minutes. Stir well to mix all ingredients well. Add franks and pineapple and continue to simmer for about 15 minutes.

Transfer the franks, pineapple and sauce to a fondue pot or chafing dish. Keep warm and serve with cocktail picks or toothpicks. Replenish the fondue pot as needed during the party.

TO FREEZE: Any franks, pineapple or sauce which have not been put in the fondue pot can be frozen for later use. To serve, thaw, reheat, and serve as suggested above.

VARIATIONS: Add 1 teaspoon hickory flavored liquid smoke.

Substitute 4 (7 ounces each) packages cocktail franks for regular franks.

Substitute 24 to 32 cooked meatballs for franks.

2
Barbecues, Marinades & Sauces

BARBECUES, MARINADES AND SAUCES

BARBECUES, MARINADES AND SAUCES

Want chicken, beef, pork, seafood or vegetables to taste deliciously different? Marinate it. Cook it in a sauce. Serve it with a sauce. The possibilities are endless.

Barbecue sauces are designed to be (1) poured over the meat before baking, (2) brushed on the meat while grilling, or (3) mixed with the cooked meat.

Marinades are used to tenderize and add flavor to meats before cooking. To intensify the flavors, marinades are often used to baste the meat while it is cooking.

Sauces are served either in a separate dish or poured over cooked meats, poultry, seafood, or vegetables.

BARBECUE SAUCES

PRIME TIME BARBECUE SAUCE   (For Chicken or Pork)   *Makes about 2 quarts sauce*

This original recipe was created by Mrs. Cullum, a dear friend of Ella Weeks, my mother-in-law. Ella shared the secret recipe with me about 25 years ago. You'll never want to be without a batch of this delicious mustard-based sauce.

1	quart vinegar
5	teaspoons salt
5	teaspoons pepper
2 1/4	cups prepared mustard
1 3/4	cups catsup
1/2	cup sugar

Heat vinegar and sugar over low heat until sugar dissolves. Cool slightly.

Mix catsup, mustard, salt and pepper together until well blended. Gradually pour in sugar & vinegar mixture, stirring with a wire whisk to form a creamy mixture.

Pour into glass bottles, cover and store at room temperature. This keeps unrefrigerated indefinitely. It can be used immediately; however, it is better if it ages for a week or more before using.

Use as a baste when grilling any cuts of chicken or pork.

VARIATIONS: To make sauce a little hotter, add 5 teaspoons cayenne pepper.

Add 1 tablespoon hickory flavored liquid smoke.

Alternate Version

This sauce is a little spicier, but not hotter. To the recipe above, add the following:

1/4	teaspoon hickory flavor liquid smoke
1/4	cup honey
1/4	cup corn syrup
1/2	cup soy sauce

TARGET BARBECUE SUPREME (for chicken, pork and beef)
Makes 1 1/2 cups

This is a deliciously sweet, hickory smoke-flavored barbecue sauce which is excellent for baby back ribs or any other cut of beef. It is also good for barbecuing chickens. This is a tomato-based sauce.

1/4	cup molasses
1	cup catsup
1/2-3/4	cup brown sugar
4	teaspoons hickory liquid smoke
1/2	teaspoon onion salt
1/2	cup + 2 tablespoons vinegar
1/2	teaspoon dry mustard
1/2	teaspoon garlic powder, not garlic salt

Mix molasses, catsup, 1/2 cup brown sugar, liquid smoke, onion salt, vinegar, mustard and garlic powder. Simmer for 20 minutes. Taste, add additional 1/4 brown sugar, if desired, and cook another 5 minutes. Mix 1 1/2 teaspoons corn starch with 1 tablespoon water. Stir to mix well. Pour into hot mixture, stirring constantly, and cook until slightly thickened, about 5 minutes. Cool.

MARINADES

SUPER-SUPER TENDERIZING MARINADE

Makes about 1/2 cup

An excellent tenderizer for beef, chicken or pork, especially when using it for a stir-fry recipe. This will give meat a delicious flavor and tenderize it at the same time.

- 1 tablespoon cornstarch
- 1 tablespoon dry sherry or dry white wine
- 2 tablespoons soy sauce
- 1 teaspoon sugar
- 1/2 teaspoon baking soda
- 1/4 cup cold water
- 1/2 teaspoon salt (optional)

Mix cornstarch, sherry, soy sauce, salt, sugar, baking soda and water. Add thinly sliced beef, chicken or pork. Cover and let sit in refrigerator from 1 hour to overnight.

VARIATION: Add 1 teaspoon of garlic salt.

Add 1 teaspoon hickory flavored liquid smoke.

VERSATILE MEAT MARINADE

Makes about 1 1/2 cups sauce

This tangy marinade can be used for shrimp, fish, chicken, pork, beef or venison.

- 1/4 cup bourbon
- 1 teaspoon minced fresh garlic
- 1/2 cup water
- 1 teaspoon Texas Pete Hot Sauce
- 1/4 cup catsup
- 1/4 cup packed brown sugar
- 2 tablespoons teriyaki sauce
- 1 teaspoon coarse-ground black pepper
- 1/2 teaspoon baking soda

Mix all ingredients together and marinate selected meat or seafood several hours or overnight. Use for stir-fry or grilling.

Stir Fry

Cut beef into thin strips, chicken or pork into 1 1/2-inch cubes, or peel & devein shrimp before marinating.

Grilling

Grill cut-up chicken, whole roasts or pork chops. OR cut boneless chicken, beef and pork into cubes. Cut cubed venison into 2x4-inch strips. Place beef, chicken, pork shrimp or venison on skewers, which have been soaked in water for 30 minutes. While grilling, turn meat often and baste with reserved marinade after each turning.

Place fish fillets in wire fish grilling basket. Grill about 10 to 12 minutes, turning fish only once.

When grilling, cooking times will vary depending upon the temperature of the grill. Times below are listed for a "hot" grill.

COOKING TIMES

Chicken (pieces)	1 hour
Roasts:	
Beef—any size 2 inches thick	45 minutes
Pork—4 pounds	1 to 1 1/2 hours
Beef skewers	5 to 7 minutes
Chicken skewers	7 to 10 minutes
Pork skewers	7 to 10 minutes
Shrimp skewers	4 minutes
Cubed Venison skewers	4 minutes
Pork Chops	25 to 35 minutes

SAUCES

BLENDER MAYONNAISE

Makes 1 1/4 cups

This tastes even better than commercial mayonnaise. When it isn't convenient to go to the store and you run out of mayonnaise, blend a batch of this mayonnaise in under 1 minute.

1	egg
1/2	teaspoon dry mustard
1/2-1	teaspoon salt
2	tablespoons vinegar
1	cup cooking oil

Place egg, dry mustard, salt, vinegar and 1/4 cup of oil in blender. Turn on low for 2 to 3 seconds. Turn blender off and scrape sides if necessary. Turn blender on and add remaining 3/4 cups oil all at once. Blend a few seconds until the consistency of mayonnaise.

Refrigerate. Use in place of commercial mayonnaise.

VARIATIONS: For variety, add 1/4 teaspoon seasonings of your choice, such as, basil or tarragon, parsley or garlic salt.

BLENDER SALAD DRESSING

Makes 2 cups

1	egg
1/2	teaspoon dry mustard
1	teaspoon salt
2	tablespoons sugar
1/16	teaspoon paprika (a dash)
2	tablespoons lemon juice
2	cups cooking oil

Put egg, mustard, salt, sugar, lemon juice, and paprika into blender and mix on low for 2 to 3 seconds. Turn blender on and add oil all at once. Blend a few seconds until the consistency of mayonnaise.

Refrigerate. Use in place of commercial salad dressing.

VARIATION: Use olive oil, peanut oil or canola oil in place of cooking oil.

CHINESE RED SWEET AND SOUR SAUCE   *Makes about 1 1/2 cups sauce*

It's the best sweet and sour sauce this side of China Town! This recipe originated after my visit to a family-style Chinese restaurant in San Francisco. While trying to re-create their delicious sauce, I mixed, tasted, threw out sauces and started again many times, until I finally captured that same great taste. Give it a try!

    1/2   cup catsup
    1/2   cup apple cider vinegar
      1   tablespoon red wine vinegar
    1/4   cup orange juice
    1/4   cup + 2 tablespoons sugar (6 tablespoons)
    1/4   teaspoon dry mustard
    3/4   teaspoon Texas Pete Hot Sauce
  1 1/2   tablespoons cornstarch
      2   tablespoons water

Combine cornstarch and water and mix well.

In saucepan heat catsup, vinegars, orange juice, sugar, mustard, and hot sauce until sugar is dissolved. Slowly add cornstarch mixture, stirring constantly until mixture thickens, about 1 minute. Remove from heat. If sauce is a little too thick, add 2 more tablespoons water and stir well.

Serve hot over rice with **Chinese Sweet and Sour Chicken Dinner** (page 140).

COCKTAIL SAUCE EDISTO   *Makes about 1 cup sauce*

Whether a purchase at a local seafood store or the catch of the day, fresh seafood is always served at our beach house with a bowl of this slightly spicy sauce.

    3/4   cups catsup
      2   teaspoons lemon juice
      2   teaspoons worcestershire sauce
  2 1/2   teaspoons Tulkoff hot cream-style prepared horseradish

Mix catsup, lemon juice, worcestershire sauce, and horseradish together. Serve immediately or chill and serve.

Serve this sauce with seafood or fried mozzarella cheese sticks.

VARIATION: For a hotter version, add 1/2 teaspoon Texas Pete hot sauce.

Substitute 3 1/2 teaspoons Kraft cream-style prepared horseradish. (see page 41)

EASY HOLLANDAISE SAUCE
Makes about 1/2 cup sauce

An easy sauce which is delicious served over steamed broccoli or over easy **Eggs Benedict** (page 106).

- 1/4 cup low calorie mayonnaise
- 2 tablespoons lemon juice
- 1 egg, slightly beaten
- 1/4 teaspoon dry mustard
- 1 teaspoon prepared mustard
- 3-4 tablespoons skim milk

Add mayonnaise, lemon juice, egg, dry mustard, prepared mustard, and skim milk. Cook over low heat, stirring constantly, until sauce is hot and thickened. Serve immediately.

HORSERADISH SAUCE
Makes 1 1/4 cups

This sauce is delicious with seafood or as a dip for fried cheese sticks or fried mushrooms.

- 1 egg
- 1/2 teaspoon dry mustard
- 1/2-1 teaspoon salt
- 1 tablespoon sugar
- 5 tablespoons cream-style prepared horseradish
- 1 cup cooking oil

Place egg, dry mustard, salt, sugar, horseradish and 1/4 cup of oil in blender. Turn on low for 2 to 3 seconds. Turn blender off and scrape sides if necessary. Turn blender on and add remaining 3/4 cups oil all at once. Blend a few seconds until the consistency of mayonnaise.

* * * * * * * * *

How to Select Brands of Horseradish

Different brands of cream-style prepared horseradish vary in degree of hotness. Kraft brand is milder than Tulkoff Extra Hot Horseradish.

HOT MUSTARD SAUCE   *Makes about 3/4 cups sauce*

When a spicy, VERY hot sauce is desired for dipping appetizers, this is a good choice.

    1/4   cup dry mustard
    2-4   tablespoons sugar
    1/4   teaspoon salt
    1/4   cup cider vinegar
    1/2   cup low-calorie mayonnaise
      1   egg, slightly beaten

In small saucepan, combine mustard, sugar and salt. Stir to mix. Then add vinegar and egg and cook, stirring constantly, until mixture thickens. Remove from heat and let sit for 5 minutes. Stir in mayonnaise and chill. Keep refrigerated.

Serve as a dip with Chinese won tons or egg rolls, boneless fried chicken strips or sliced ham.

FIRE-ENGINE SWEET MUSTARD SAUCE

Slightly sweet and very hot!

    1   (4 ounce) can dry mustard   1   cup sugar
    1   cup vinegar   1/4   teaspoon salt
    2   eggs

Mix dry mustard and vinegar. Cover and let stand for 4 hours. In double boiler, add eggs and sugar and stir to mix well. Add salt and mustard mixture and heat over medium heat, stirring constantly for about 10 minutes or until mixture is the consistency of custard.

VARIATION: If mustard sauce is too hot, let it cool thoroughly and then add 1/2 cup of low-calorie mayonnaise.

JEZEBEL SAUCE   *Two versions*

Although these classic recipes have an unusual combination of ingredients, the flavor is delicious: sweet, tangy and hot!

VERSION 1   **(Makes 3 1/2 cups)**

    12   ounce jar pineapple preserves
    10   ounce jar apple jelly, at room temperature
   1/4   cup Dijon mustard
     2   tablespoons cream-style prepared horseradish

VERSION 2   **(Makes 4 1/4 cups)**

    16   ounce jar pineapple preserves
    16   ounce jar apple jelly, at room temperature
     1   (1 ounce) can dry mustard
     1   (5 ounce) jar cream-style prepared horseradish

Using either version, mix all ingredients together until well blended. Store in air-tight container (nonmetallic) and refrigerate.

To serve, place a 3-ounce or 8-ounce block of cream cheese on plate and pour some of sauce over it. Serve with crackers and a small spreading knife.

WINE SAUCE

Makes about 1 1/2 cups sauce

This is good with either chicken, beef, or pork.

Use the following for all sauces:

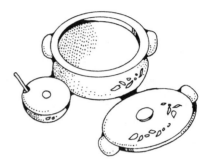

2	tablespoons margarine or butter
2	tablespoons flour
1	teaspoon finely chopped dried parsley
1/2	teaspoon garlic powder
1/4	teaspoon pepper
1	cup skim milk
1/4	cup dry white wine

Beef Version: Add 1 teaspoon beef bouillon granules
                    1 teaspoon basil

Pork Version: Same as beef version

Chicken Version: Add 1 teaspoon chicken bouillon granules
                    1/4 teaspoon poultry seasoning

Melt margarine in frying pan. With wire whisk, stir in flour and bouillon to make a paste. Add parsley, garlic powder and seasonings. Slowly add milk, stirring constantly until mixture boils and thickens.

VARIATIONS: For a tasty change, add the following to margarine and saute for 2 minutes: 1 (4 ounce) jar sliced mushrooms.

3

Beef, Pork & Venison

BEEF, PORK AND VENISON

In these times of cholesterol and fat consciousness, beef and pork can still be a delicious, yet healthy, addition to your weekly menus.

With improved methods of raising leaner beef and pork, these meats can be wise choices of protein. Select the leanest cuts of beef and pork. Cooking techniques can further lower the fat content of foods prepared with beef and pork.

When selecting ground beef, you get more edible meat for your money by selecting ground chuck, ground round or ground sirloin tip, instead of ground beef. If available, ground venison is exceptionally lean and can be substituted for ground beef in many dishes.

Want a meal that will delight everyone from the very young to the very old? Serve **Oven Porcupines** (page 65), **Texas Hash** (page 70) or **Best-Ever Meat Loaf** (page 50)! Having weekend guests? Try quick and easy **Hot Reuben Sandwiches** (page 61)! Want to impress your guests? Serve **Perfect Roast** (page 66) or **Honey Grilled Roast** (page 60)!

BEEF, VENISON AND PORK

Beef

Pork

Venison

BEEF

BARBECUED SKEWERED BEEF   *Makes 4 servings*

1-1 1/4   pounds tender lean beef, sirloin tip, London broil, etc.
1   tablespoon fresh minced garlic
3/4-1   cup **Target Barbecue Sauce** (page 36)
1   cup water
2   tablespoons vinegar
12-16   skewers 5-inch long

Cut beef into 1-inch cubes. Place in saucepan. Add garlic, 1/4 cup barbecue sauce, water and vinegar. Simmer 1 hour. Drain meat and cool slightly. Preheat oven to 350 degrees. Thread meat on skewers. Place in single layer in casserole dish. Pour remaining 1/2 cup barbecue sauce over skewered meat. Bake 20 to 30 minutes until sauce is slightly browned.

Serve with **Holiday Potatoes** (page 184)**,** a vegetable, and **Crunchy Seasoned Bread** (page 89)**.**

VARIATION: **Barbecue Sandwiches**

Cut meat into thin strips. Cook 1 hour as directed above on top of stove. Drain water and sauce from saucepan. Add 1/2 cup barbecue sauce to meat and simmer 30 minutes, stirring frequently. Place meat in hamburger buns.

BEEF ENCHILADAS

Makes 6 servings

   1   recipe **Flour Tortillas** (recipe follows) or 12 purchased tortillas
 1/4 cup cooking oil

In a hot frying pan, add a little of the cooking oil for each tortilla. Fry each tortilla until lightly browned on both sides.

Enchilada Sauce

   1   can cream of chicken soup
   1   (10 ounce) can Ro*tel diced tomatoes and chilies
   1   medium onion, diced (1/2 cup)
   1   (4 ounce) can chopped green chilies

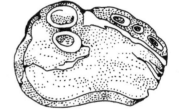

Mix all sauce ingredients together and set aside.

Enchilada Filling

   1   medium onion, diced and sauteed
1 1/2 pounds lean ground beef, browned and drained (page 55)
 12 ounces (3 cups) Monterey Jack cheese

Mix all filling ingredients together. Place a little of this mixture on each tortilla. Roll up tortillas in jelly-roll fashion and place each in a shallow lightly greased baking pan.

Preheat oven to 350 degrees. Pour all of sauce over rolled tortillas. Pour any remaining beef mixture or cheese over sauce.

Bake uncovered until hot and bubbly, about 30 minutes.

A green salad, with **KC Sweet and Sour Dressing** (page 219), and **Curried Fruit** (see page 249) are great accompaniments to Beef Enchiladas.

Flour Tortillas

Makes 12 tortillas

2	cups flour	3	tablespoons shortening
1	teaspoon salt	1	teaspoon baking powder
1	teaspoon powdered milk	1/4	cup lukewarm water (more if needed)

Mix flour, salt, milk, shortening and baking powder together. Add water and mix well. Shape into balls. Place balls between sheets of waxed paper, and roll until very thin (1/8-inch thick).

VARIATION: As a dessert, serve tortillas warm with butter and jam.

BEST-EVER MEAT LOAF

Makes 4 to 6 servings

This meat loaf, loaded with fiber and nutrition, will become a favorite of your family.

1 1/2	cups tomato-based barbecue sauce
1	teaspoon Morton's Nature seasoning
1 1/4	cups quick (not instant) oatmeal
1	tablespoon wheat germ
3	tablespoons diced onion
1	egg
2	pounds extra-lean ground chuck or ground round beef
	No-stick cooking spray
1/2	cup **Target Barbecue Supreme** sauce (page 36) or Bull's Eye barbecue sauce

Preheat oven to 350 degrees. Spray a 9x9-inch glass or metal baking pan with no-stick cooking spray.

Place the first 7 ingredients in a 2-quart bowl and stir with a large fork to mix well.

Shape the mixture into a loaf and place in the prepared pan, leaving space around outside of loaf. Using the blunt end of a knife, poke about 12 holes (1-inch deep) into the top of the loaf. Spread **Target Barbecue Supreme** on top of the meat loaf, allowing sauce to run into the knife holes.

Bake uncovered for about 1 hour until the meat loaf is browned on the outside.

Remove with slotted spatula, drain well and place on serving platter or plate. Cut into 1/2-inch slices and serve with **Twice-Baked Stuffed Potatoes** (page 188) and **Lime Grapefruit Pineapple Salad** (page 213).

VARIATIONS: 1/2 cup diced green pepper can be added to mixture.

Tomato sauce can be substituted for 1 1/2 cups tomato-based barbecue sauce.

MEAT LOAF SANDWICHES

Meat loaf is excellent leftover and used for sandwiches. To serve on a hoagie bun or hamburger bun, spread both sides of bun with low-calorie mayonnaise. Slice meat loaf 1/2-inch thick and place slices on bottom bun. Place 1 tablespoon of **Target Barbecue Supreme** sauce on top of sliced meat loaf. Cover with top bun. Serve cold or microwave each sandwich 30 seconds on Reheat (80% power). Add a slice of lettuce, if desired.

BILL'S ITALIAN SPAGHETTI AND MEATBALLS

Makes 6 generous servings

This real Italian spaghetti contains meatballs rather than browned ground beef. It has a thick, zesty tomato sauce. Bill Perdue's original.

Sauce

1	(6 ounce) can tomato paste
3	(15 ounces each) cans tomato sauce
1	(28 ounce) can crushed tomatoes
1	(4 1/2 ounce) can sliced mushrooms
1	medium onion, whole
5	whole bay leaves
1	teaspoon basil
1/2	teaspoon garlic salt
2	teaspoons fresh minced garlic
2	teaspoons Italian seasoning
1	teaspoon crushed red pepper

1   recipe **Meatballs** (recipe follows)

1   (16 ounce) box of vermicelli or spaghetti noodles, cooked according to package instructions, well-drained

1/2 cup grated parmesan cheese or fresh grated Romano cheese

In large pot, add tomato paste, tomato sauce, crushed tomatoes, mushrooms, whole onion, bay leaves, basil, garlic salt, minced garlic, Italian seasoning and crushed red pepper. Add meatballs and simmer, covered, for several hours. Uncover and simmer 1 hour longer.

Serve hot over cooked vermicelli (spaghetti) noodles. Sprinkle grated parmesan cheese on top. A green salad and **Crunchy Seasoned Bread** (page 89) complete a delicious Italian meal.

Meatballs

Makes 18 to 20 meatballs (1 1/2 -inch diameter)

2	slices of white bread, toasted	1 1/2	teaspoons Italian seasoning
2	eggs	1	teaspoon garlic salt
2	pounds very lean ground beef, round or chuck		

Cover counter with waxed paper. Put meat on paper and spread until meat is in a thick layer. Crack eggs on top of meat. Sprinkle with garlic salt, garlic, and Italian seasoning. Rub toast together over top of meat, making tiny bread crumbs. Fold meat over and over until thoroughly mixed. Put a small amount of meat mixture into hands and roll into 1 1/2-inch meatballs. Do not cook before adding to sauce above.

CORNED BEEF BRISKET DINNER   *Makes 6 to 8 servings*

    3-4   pound corned beef brisket
       1   (12 ounce) can beer or 12 ounces dry white wine
       6   large potatoes, peeled and cut in half
    4-5   pounds cabbage, cut into wedges
 1-1 1/2   cups water

Place brisket in crockpot and add beer. Cook on High for 5 to 6 hours or Low 10 to 12 hours or until meat is very tender.

About 45 minutes before serving, add water to a large pot (not the crockpot). Add potatoes and place cabbage on top of potatoes. Bring to boil, reduce heat and gently steam for about 20 minutes or until potatoes are done and cabbage is tender but not overcooked.

Remove corned beef from crockpot and remove all visible fat. Slice across the grain and place on end of large platter. Drain potatoes and cabbage and place these on other end of platter.

VARIATIONS: This sliced corned beef can be used to make delicious **Hot Reuben Sandwiches** (page 61)

CORNED BEEF QUICHE

Makes 4 to 6 servings or
about 30-appetizer servings

A delicious, yet easy, main course for breakfast, brunch, midnight snack, or ladies' luncheon. It can be made ahead and baked in the oven an hour before serving. This recipe was shared by Hallie Townsend.

First Layer Ingredients

- 1 can (15 ounces) corned beef hash
- 1/4 teaspoon seasoned salt
- 1/4 cup grated onion
- 1 deep dish pie crust

Mix corned beef hash, onion and salt together. Press into pie shell.

Topping Ingredients

- 2 eggs
- 1/4 teaspoon seasoned pepper
- 4 ounces whipped cream cheese with chives
- 1 cup creamed cottage cheese or small curd cottage cheese

Preheat oven to 350 degrees.

Mix Topping ingredients together and pour over first layer. Bake for 50 minutes or until filling on top is set and firm.

Cut into wedges and serve hot with fresh fruit or fruit salad.

VARIATIONS: Use a refrigerated pastry rolls and place in large rectangular baking dish. Follow directions above for filling and topping. When cooked, cut into squares to make an unusual and delicious party appetizer.

This can be frozen baked or raw for later use. Adjust baking time if frozen raw. If frozen cooked, reheat at 300 degrees until hot in center.

CREAMED DRIED BEEF ON TOAST   *Makes 4 servings*

A salty dish which is good served over toast or noodles with poached eggs.

2 1/2	tablespoons butter
2 1/2	tablespoons flour
1 1/4	cup milk
1/2	teaspoon soy sauce
5	ounces sliced dried beef, cut in small square pieces
4	slices bread, toasted

In frying pan, melt butter over low heat. With wire whisk, stir in flour to make a paste. Gradually add 1/2 cup of the milk, stirring briskly to make a smooth thick paste, adding more milk to thin sauce to consistency of gravy. Add soy sauce and stir well.

With heat on low, add dried beef and stir well. Let simmer about 5 minutes, adding more milk if needed to keep the sauce a medium-thick consistency.

Serve hot on toast or noodles.

VARIATION: For a late night supper, after adding the beef and stirring well, add 1/2 can of green peas, drained. Stir gently. Simmer 5 minutes and serve over noodles. Cook 4 to 6 ounces noodles according to package directions. Drain well. Substitute noodles for toast or English muffin.

DOUBLE-DUTY MEAT SAUCE

Makes 12 cups of sauce

This recipe takes advantage of the fact that the main ingredients and beginning cooking steps for chili and spaghetti are identical. This basic sauce is made and then divided into two (2) pots: one seasoned as **Quick Spaghetti** (page 68) while the other is seasoned as **Quick Chili** (page 67). However, the entire recipe can be made into 12 servings of either chili or spaghetti.

This sauce can be prepared in advance, refrigerated, and then used the next day. To reduce fat and calories, be sure to check insert below.

Meat Sauce

3	pounds ground lean beef or ground venison
1	(28 ounce) can crushed tomatoes
2	(16 ounce) cans stewed tomatoes
1	cup thick catsup
4	stalks celery, diced (1 cup)
1	large onion, diced (1 1/4 - 1 1/2 cups)

In a heavy 4 quart pot, brown meat, separating into small pieces as it browns, until meat is no longer pink. Drain as directed below (see inset). Return to pot and add crushed tomatoes, stewed tomatoes, catsup, celery and onions, and simmer for 15 minutes.

Sauce is now ready to be seasoned to make chili and spaghetti OR a pot of each. Use this Double Duty Meat sauce in preparing **Quick Chili** or **Quick Spaghetti**. I usually remove 4 cups (1/3 recipe) of sauce and make **Quick Chili**, and season the rest (8 cups or 2/3 recipe) to make **Quick Spaghetti**.

* * * * * * * * *

How to Drain Ground Beef

This is an easy method of removing extra calories and fat from COOKED ground beef. While beef is hot, pour into a colander, rinse under hot water for 30 seconds. Drain for 3 minutes.

FRENCH CROCKPOT BEEF STEW   *Makes 6 to 8 servings*

An extremely flavorful and tender stew, which cooks unattended and makes a hearty meal.

2	pounds lean beef
2	medium onions
4	medium carrots, peeled
3	stalks celery, sliced
1	cup tomato juice or 1/4 cup catsup (omit sugar if using catsup)
1	tablespoon sugar
1	teaspoon Morton's Nature's Seasoning or seasoned salt
1	tablespoon worcestershire sauce
1/4	teaspoon pepper
1/2	teaspoon basil
1	teaspoon fresh minced garlic
1	package dry onion/mushroom soup mix
1/2	cup water
1/4	cup cooking sherry

Cut beef, onions, and carrots into bite-sized pieces. Place beef, onions, celery, and carrots in crockpot. Pour tomato juice and sugar (or catsup) over beef. Add seasoned salt, worcestershire sauce, pepper, basil, garlic and soup mix. Pour water and sherry over seasonings. Stir to mix well. Cook on high for 6 hours or low for 8 to 10 hours. Mix 1 tablespoon corn starch and 2 tablespoons water. Pour into crockpot, stirring until thickened, about 2 minutes.

Serve with boiled potatoes or over rice or noodles.

VARIATIONS: At beginning of cooking time, add 2 medium potatoes, pared and cut into large pieces.

Add dumplings to top: Mix 1 cup biscuit baking mix and 1/3 cup milk. Do not thicken liquid in crockpot. Turn crockpot on high and make sure that liquid is boiling. Drop teaspoonsful of dough over boiling liquid. Cover and cook 15 minutes **AND DO NOT OPEN LID** during this time.

When stew is thickened, add 8 ounces of sour cream. Turn crockpot off. DO NOT let sour cream come to a boil.

Substitute dry white wine, beer or water for the cooking sherry.

If you have a large 4-1/2 quart crockpot, you can double the ingredients and increase cooking time to 8 hours. This will serve 12 to 16 people.

GREAT SUPER-EASY CHILI   *Makes 8 to 10 servings*

This will become a favorite winter-time meal! This version makes a medium-hot chili; however, both mild and hot versions are given below. This can also be prepared in a crockpot (see insert below).

    2   pounds lean ground chuck or ground round
    1   large onion, diced
    1   green pepper, diced or 2 tablespoons chopped dried green pepper
    3   (16 ounce each) cans stewed tomatoes, undrained
    2   (10 ounces each) Ro*tel diced tomatoes and chilies
    4   (16 ounces each) cans chili beans, undrained
    1   tablespoon chili powder

In frying pan, cook ground beef over high heat, stirring to break meat into small pieces, until no longer pink. Pour meat into a colander and rinse under warm water for 30 seconds. Drain well.

Pour meat into a 4 quart pot. Add all other ingredients, stir to mix well. Simmer on low for 1 to 2 hours, stirring occasionally.

Serve with **Leafy Lettuce with Feta Cheese** (page 213) salad and crackers.

VARIATION: Pour chili into bowls. Sprinkle with grated cheddar cheese.

Mild Version	**Hot Version**
omit 1 can Ro*tel	delete 1 can stewed tomatoes
add 1 can tomatoes	add 1 jar LaVictoria Hot Ranchera Sauce
use only 1/2-2 teaspoons chili powder	add 1/2-1 teaspoon cayenne pepper

* * * * * * * * *

How to Plan Ahead with Crockpot

Crockpot cooking is designed to cook unattended for a long while. Before leaving for work, start this dinner in the crockpot by browning and draining beef (see page 55). Place meat and other ingredients in crockpot and turn on temperature designated in recipe. Recipes usually cook from 4 to 6 hours on high and 8 to 10 hours on low.

To prepare in advance, brown meat the night before and drain. Refrigerate. Chop vegetables, such as pepper and onion and place in sealable plastic bags or containers. This leaves less than 5 minutes preparation time for the next morning. Place all prepared ingredients in crockpot.

HAMBURGER STEAKS SUPREME   *Makes 3 to 4 servings*

Turn plain ground beef into a special meal: seasoned hamburger steaks with a delicious mushroom gravy.

1	tablespoon soy sauce
1	tablespoon prepared mustard
1/2-1	teaspoon chili powder (to your taste)
1/2	teaspoon oregano
1	teaspoon fresh minced garlic
1	pound lean ground beef (ground chuck, ground round, or ground sirloin tip)
6	large or 10 medium fresh mushrooms, washed, drained and sliced
1	large onion, cut in 12 to 16 wedges or cut into 1/4-inch slices
1	package dry onion/mushroom soup
1	cup water
1	teaspoon worcestershire sauce
1	teaspoon beef bouillon granules
2	tablespoons dry white wine
2	teaspoons corn starch

Mix soy sauce, mustard, chili powder, oregano, garlic and ground beef together. Form into 4 patties about 3/4 to 1-inch thick. In a frying pan set on high temperature, fry patties until browned, turning to brown both sides (about 2 minutes on each side). Remove patties from skillet and place on a plate.

In same frying pan, over medium-high heat, saute mushrooms and onions until crisp tender (slightly wilted), about 3 to 5 minutes. Place vegetables in colander and rinse under warm water for 30 seconds. Drain for 1 minute. Wash frying pan to remove all grease.

Add dry soup and water to clean frying pan, and stir to mix well. Cook over medium-high heat until mixture is boiling (about 1 minute). Turn to low heat, add worcestershire sauce and bouillon. Add cooked burgers. Spoon mushrooms and onions on top, cover and cook about 15 to 20 minutes. Remove burgers and place on serving dish.

To make gravy, mix cornstarch and wine, stirring well. Stir cornstarch mixture into frying pan and continue cooking, stirring constantly until gravy is thickened.

Serve with cooked white rice, noodles, or mashed potatoes and a bowl of gravy.

HOME-STYLE SHORT RIB DINNER   *Makes 4 to 6 servings*

If partially prepared ahead, this meal can be started before leaving home. It is great for a very busy day and provides a wholesome, well-balanced meal.

  3-4   pounds lean short beef ribs, cut into small pieces
  4-5   medium potatoes, peeled and cut into quarters
  4-5   large carrots, peeled, pared and cut into 2-inch pieces
    1   large onion, chopped (1 cup)
    2   stalks of celery, chopped (1/2 cup)
  1/2   cup water
    1   tablespoon beef bouillon granules
    1   tablespoon worcestershire sauce
    1   tablespoon soy sauce
    1   teaspoon dried crushed basil
    1   package of dried onion/mushroom soup mix

For Gravy

  2-3   tablespoons corn starch
  1/4   cup water

Place ribs in a large crockpot. Add onions and celery. Place carrots and potatoes around and on top of ribs. Mix water, beef bouillon, worcestershire sauce, soy sauce, basil and soup mix. Pour over vegetables and ribs. Cover with lid.

Cook on high for 4 to 6 hours or low for 8 to 10 hours.

Turn crockpot heat to high. With slotted spoon, remove carrots, potatoes and ribs from crockpot. Arrange on large platter. In small jar or bowl, add corn starch. Gradually add water until cornstarch is dissolved. Pour this into hot crockpot liquid, stirring constantly until thickened. Serve as gravy with ribs and vegetables.

VARIATION: Substitute 3 pounds of boneless lean beef, cut into large pieces for the ribs.

To Prepare the Night Before

Prepare carrots and potatoes and store in bowl of water, with carrots on top. Make sure that potatoes are completely covered with water. Prepare celery and onions, place in sealable plastic bag or other container. Store both containers in refrigerator. In small jar, mix water, bouillon, worcestershire sauce, soy sauce, basil and soup mix.

In the morning, assemble and cook as directed above.

HONEY GRILLED ROAST   *Makes 4 to 6 servings*

This is a family favorite which was shared by Beth Lynn, Aiken, SC. Even chuck roast turns out tender and perfectly cooked—well-browned on the outside and medium-rare on the inside.

    1   beef roast: chuck, sirloin tip, shoulder, eye of round (see tip below)

Marinade

    2   gloves garlic, mashed
    2   teaspoon salt
    1   cup chicken bouillon
  1/4 cup soy sauce
  1/4 cup honey
  1/4 cup catsup
  1/2 teaspoon baking soda

Pour marinade over roast and marinate in covered pan for 6 to 8 hours or overnight, turning several times. Tougher cuts of meat should be marinated overnight. Remove from marinade.

Cook on hot grill, either charcoal or gas, for 45 minutes, turning often to prevent charring, basting with reserved marinade each time roast is turned. Roast will be medium-rare on the inside and well browned on the outside.

Remove roast from grill. Place on serving platter and cover with the **Glaze** (recipe follows). Glaze should melt over roast. Slice roast across the grain into thin (1/4-inch) slices and serve, leaving juice in platter.

VARIATION: Marinate spare ribs (3/4 pound per person). Bake in oven at 450 degrees for 10 minutes, then at 350 degrees for 1 hour 20 minutes until done. If desired, place on hot outdoor grill for about 10 minutes to brown. Glaze as directed above.

Glaze

  1/4 cup honey
  1/2 teaspoon dry mustard

Preparation Tip

You can use any size and weight of roast, but the thickness should be between 2 1/2 - 3 inches for the roast to be medium rare. If roast is thicker, increase cooking time accordingly, adding 8 to 10 minutes for each 1/2-inch increase in thickness.

HOT REUBEN SANDWICHES   *Makes 4 servings*

These sandwiches can be made several hours ahead, covered, refrigerated and then cooked just before serving.

> 8   slices of rye bread
> 3   tablespoons Thousand Island Dressing
> 3   tablespoons prepared mustard or coarse ground mustard
> 8   ounces of thinly sliced corned beef
> 4   slices of Swiss cheese
> 1   small (8 ounce) can of sauerkraut, well-drained
> 3-4   tablespoons margarine or butter

Spread 4 slices of bread with Thousand Island dressing. On each slice of bread place 2 ounces of corned beef, 1 slice of Swiss cheese, and 1/4 of sauerkraut.

Spread the other 4 slices of bread with mustard. Place each slice, mustard side down, over the sauerkraut. Spread the top of each sandwich with margarine.

Choose between the following two (2) methods of cooking:

(1)   Heat a 10 to 12-inch skillet, or griddle, on a medium-high heat. Add the remaining butter until melted. Place the unbuttered side of each sandwich in the skillet or on the griddle. Cook until golden brown. Turn each sandwich and continue cooking until the other side is browned and cheese is melted.

(2)   Place sandwiches on nonstick cookie sheet. Bake at 350 degrees for about 20 minutes until cheese is melted and bread is lightly browned on both side. Turn sandwiches over, if necessary, to brown both sides. Whether or not you need to turn these will depend upon your particular oven. If using this cooking method, you may omit all margarine to reduce calories.

Place each sandwich on a plate and cut in half. Serve with dill pickle strips and potato chips or hot **German Potato Salad** (page 182).

VARIATION: Use small party-rye bread and make small appetizer-sized sandwiches as directed above, adjusting quantity of ingredients for each small sandwich.

Preparation Tip

You may use packages of corned beef, canned corned beef, or slices of corned beef from leftover **Corned Beef Brisket Dinner** (page 52).

MEATBALL STROGANOFF   *Makes 4 to 6 servings*

An inexpensive meal with an elegant taste, it's just right for that special occasion.

    8   ounces wide noodles, cooked according to package directions, drained

Meatballs

    1   pound lean ground beef, chuck, sirloin or round
    1   egg
    1   tablespoon dried parsley flakes
  1/2   cup finely minced onion
    2   tablespoons Italian bread crumbs
    1   tablespoon parmesan cheese
    1   teaspoon fresh minced garlic
    1   teaspoon Morton's Nature Seasoning or seasoned salt

Mix ground beef, egg, parsley, onion, bread crumbs, cheese, garlic and Nature Seasoning. Mix well. Form into firmly packed meat balls about 2-inches in diameter. Place in single layer (with meat balls not touching) in microwave proof dish; cover with plastic wrap. Microwave on high (100% power) about 8 minutes. Let stand about 5 minutes, while you prepare sauce. Drain.

Stroganoff Sauce

  1/2   cup water
  10   large mushrooms, sliced or 1 (4 ounce) jar sliced mushrooms, drained
    1   can cream of mushroom soup
    1   tablespoon beef bouillon granules
    1   (8 ounce) carton sour cream

Preheat oven to 300 degrees. In frying pan, over medium heat, mix water, mushrooms, soup and beef bouillon granules, stirring to mix well, and cook until hot. Remove from heat and add sour cream, stirring to mix well.

In large bowl, add hot drained noodles and warm sour cream mixture. Stir to mix well. Add hot drained meatballs, and gently stir until well mixed. Pour into deep-dish 3-quart casserole. Cover. Serve immediately or reheat in oven about 25 minutes until hot, not boiling.

* * * * * * * * *

How to Heat Sour Cream

Sour cream should be heated gently and never allowed to boil, as boiling will change its consistency.

MONGOLIAN BEEF
Makes 3 to 4 servings

Without any doubt, this is the best stir-fry beef this side of a Chinese restaurant. It is very tender and full of flavor.

- 4   cups hot cooked white rice
- 1   pound flank steak, sirloin tip or beef tenderloin
- 1/2   cup oil, olive, corn, peanut or canola

Cut meat into 2-inch wide strips. Stack strips and cut across the grain in 1/4-inch thick slices.

Marinade

1 tablespoon cornstarch	1/2 teaspoon pepper
2 tablespoon dry sherry	1 teaspoon sugar
1 tablespoon light olive oil	1/2 teaspoon baking soda
2 tablespoons San-J Tamari soy sauce	

Combine all ingredients for **Marinade** in bowl and mix. Add beef and toss to coat each piece of meat. Cover and marinate in refrigerator 1 1/2 hours or overnight. Stir to separate pieces of beef.

Spicy Sauce

- 1   tablespoon light olive oil
- 1   tablespoon fresh minced garlic or minced garlic packed in water
- 1   tablespoon fresh minced ginger or 1 teaspoon ground ginger
- 8   spring onions with green tops, cut into thin 2-inch strips
- 2   dried chilies, chopped
- 1/2   teaspoon crushed red peppers (for those who like it HOT)
- 1-2   tablespoon Hoisin sauce
- 10-12   fresh mushrooms, sliced OR
    - 1   (4 ounce) jar sliced mushrooms
- 1   large green pepper, cut into 1-inch x 1/4-inch strips

Heat remaining oil in wok or skillet until very hot. Add beef and chopped chilies, a small quantity at a time, and stir-fry about 2 minutes until beef turns light brown. Remove and drain well. Continue with remaining beef strips. Discard all except 1 tablespoon oil.

In the remaining 1 tablespoon oil, add all **Spicy Sauce** ingredients. Stir-fry for 2 minutes. Stir in **Seasoning Sauce** (recipe follows—next page) and cook, stirring until sauce thickens. Return the beef to the wok and mix well. Serve immediately over hot cooked rice.

MONGOLIAN BEEF (continued)

Seasoning Sauce

1	tablespoon corn starch
3	tablespoons soy sauce
1	teaspoon vinegar
2	teaspoons sugar
1/2	teaspoon salt
1/4	cup chicken bouillon

Combine all ingredients for **Seasoning Sauce** in small bowl. Cover and set aside.

VARIATION: Substitute 1 pound broccoli florets, cut into bite-sized pieces, in place of, or in addition to, the green peppers.

OVEN PORCUPINES   *Makes 4 to 6 servings*

Rice gives these meatballs a light texture, and the sauce adds a scrumptious flavor which appeals to both young and old, and everyone in between. It is important to use only very lean ground beef for this recipe.

Porcupines

1 pound ground beef, round or chuck	1/2 teaspoon celery salt
1/2 cup instant white rice, uncooked	1 teaspoon salt
1/2 teaspoon fresh minced garlic	1/3 cup chopped onion
1 1/2 tablespoons diced green pepper	1/8 teaspoon pepper
1/4 cup water	**Sweet and Sour Sauce** (recipe follows)

Preheat oven to 350 degrees.

In large bowl, mix meat, rice, garlic, green pepper, water, celery salt, salt, onion, and pepper and stir until well mixed. Using a tablespoon of mixture for each porcupine, shape mixture into balls and place in an 8x8x2-inch baking dish. Pour **Sweet and Sour Sauce** over porcupines. Cover casserole dish. Bake 45 minutes. Uncover and bake 15 minutes longer.

Sweet and Sour Sauce

1 (15 ounce) can tomato sauce	1 cup water
2 teaspoons worcestershire sauce	1/4 cup brown sugar
1 tablespoon prepared mustard	

Stir tomato sauce, worcestershire sauce, mustard, water and brown sugar together to make a sauce.

VARIATION: Substitute long grain white rice for instant rice. Bake 1 hour covered, and 15 to 20 minutes uncovered.

Stuffed Peppers in Microwave

Cut 3 large carrots into strips. Microwave 5 minutes. To porcupine meat mixture, add 1/2 cup raw, long-grain white rice. Prepare **Sweet and Sour Sauce**. Mix 1/2 cup sauce into meat mixture. Stuff 4 large green peppers with the meat mixture. Place peppers in 8x8-inch square baking dish. Place carrots around peppers. Pour remainder of sauce over peppers and carrots. Cover with plastic wrap. Microwave on HIGH for 8 minutes. Let sit for 5 minutes. Then microwave on 50% power for 10 minutes. Let sit 5 minutes before serving. Or follow oven baking instructions for Porcupines.

PERFECT ROAST

Any thick-cut roast of tender, boneless beef, such as sirloin tip roast, eye of the round, standing rib roast or London broil. The perfect way to cook any size roast at least 3 inches thick. It is <u>very important</u> to know the **exact weight** of the roast to be cooked, so check the label carefully.

Heat oven to 500 degrees.

Cut all visible fat from meat. Rub entire outside of roast with generous amount of salt and ground black pepper, or any other seasoning that you prefer.

Place roast in roasting pan with sides at least 2 inches deep. Bake according to the following:

RARE	3 minutes per pound
MEDIUM RARE	3 1/2 minutes per pound
MEDIUM	4 minutes per pound
MEDIUM WELL	4 1/2 minutes per pound
WELL DONE	5 minutes per pound

Turn oven OFF. DO NOT OPEN OVEN DOOR FOR AT LEAST 1 1/2 HOURS. You can wait as long as 2 hours. Let stand 5 minutes. Slice rare and medium rare meat on platter with recess where juices can drain. Then place slices on serving platter.

Pour drained juice into roasting pan. Loosen pan drippings. If juice is too strong, add a small amount of warm water. Serve roast with juice or gravy (see inset below).

* * * * * * * * * *

How to Make Gravy

For each cup of liquid or pan juices, add the following:

1 1/2 teaspoons corn starch mixed with 1 tablespoon water

Add corn starch mixture to hot liquid, stirring constantly with a wire whisk until liquid is thickened. The wire whisk will make a creamy gravy without any lumps.

If broth or pan juices are not available, make broth by using 1 1/2 teaspoons granulated beef or chicken bouillon dissolved in 1 cup of hot water.

QUICK CHILI *Makes 4 to 6 servings*

4   cups (1/3 recipe) **Double-Duty Meat Sauce** (page 55)
2   (16 ounce each) cans chili beans, undrained
1   tablespoon chili powder
4   ounces (1 cup) grated cheddar cheese

For HOT chili, also add the following:

1   (10 ounce) can Ro*tel tomatoes and chilies
1/4-1/2   teaspoon cayenne

Place meat sauce in saucepan, add chili beans and chili powder (and other ingredients, if making Hot chili), reserving cheese. Simmer for 1 hour, stirring occasionally.

Serve hot chili in bowls and sprinkle with grated cheddar cheese, so that cheese melts on top. Serve with saltine crackers, **Crunchy Seasoned Bread** (page 89), or **Sour Cream Corn Bread** (page 91). and a salad.

If making chili to serve on hot dogs, beans may be omitted. This makes enough chili for 2 dozen hot dogs.

VARIATION: **Makes 12 Servings:**

1   recipe (12 cups) **Double-Duty Meat Sauce**
6   (16 ounce each) cans chili beans, undrained
3   tablespoons chili powder

For 12 servings HOT chili add:

1   (10 ounces each) cans Ro*Tel tomatoes and chilies
3/4-1 1/2   teaspoons cayenne pepper

QUICK SPAGHETTI   *Makes 4 to 6 servings*

    1   medium green pepper, diced OR 1 tablespoon dried diced green pepper
  1/2   teaspoon oregano
    1   teaspoon basil
    2   whole bay leaves
    1   teaspoon fresh minced garlic
    8   cups (2/3 recipe) **Double-Duty Meat Sauce** (page 55)
    8   ounces vermicelli, cooked according to package directions

Place **Double-Duty Meat Sauce** in pan. Add green pepper, oregano, basil, bay leaves, and garlic.
Simmer for 1 hour.

Serve Spaghetti sauce over cooked vermicelli. Garnish with grated parmesan cheese.

VARIATION: **Makes 12 Servings**:

    1   recipe (12 cups) **Double-Duty Meat Sauce**   3   whole bay leaves
    1   large green pepper, diced   1 1/2   teaspoon fresh minced garlic
    1   teaspoon oregano   12   ounces vermicelli, cooked and drained
 1 1/2 teaspoons basil

SUCCULENT CROCKPOT ROAST BEEF   *Makes 4 to 6 servings*

A well-done roast that is so tender and moist that it melts in your mouth.

    1   (3 pound) lean beef roast, sirloin tip or chuck
    1   envelope dry onion/mushroom soup mix, uncooked
    1   cup water
    4   large carrots, peeled and cut into 3 pieces
    6   medium potatoes, peeled

In crockpot, place roast. Pour dry soup mix over roast. Add 1 cup of water. Add carrots and potatoes.
Cook on high for about 6 hours or low for 8 to 10 hours. Remove roast, carrots and potatoes and place
on large platter.

Slice roast across grain and place on platter. If desired, thicken gravy (see page 66). Serve with
Overnight Layered Salad (page 215).

VARIATION: Substitute 1/2 cup dry white wine or beer and 1/2 cup water for the 1 cup water.

TACO SALAD   *Makes 4 servings*

A delicious, easy and quick meal that everyone enjoys. It is especially good when ripe tomatoes are abundant and summer schedules are hectic.

1   pound lean ground beef
1   (16 ounce) jar LaVictoria Medium Salsa Suprema OR mild taco sauce
1/2 teaspoon tumeric
2   teaspoons cumin
2   cup shredded lettuce
1   cup grated cheddar cheese
2   tomatoes, diced
1   cup sour cream
1   medium onion, minced
4-5 ounces Tortilla chips, slightly crushed

Brown beef in saucepan, stirring frequently to break meat into small pieces, until meat is no longer pink. Pour meat into colander and drain (page 55). Return to saucepan. Add Salsa Suprema and simmer for 15 minutes. Serve either in large bowls or on large plates.

Put each ingredient in a separate bowl, place on the table. Let each person assemble a salad starting with a layer of lettuce, then crushed chips, meat sauce, cheese, diced tomatoes, onions and sour cream. Each person should assemble his salad either at the table or a serving bar.

Use LaVictoria Hot Ranchera sauce or a mild taco sauce as a salad dressing.

TEXAS HASH   *Makes 4 to 6 servings*

A great meal for a cold-winter day. It has an excellent blending of flavors that everyone enjoys.

2	pounds lean ground chuck
2	medium onions, diced (1 1/2 cups)
2	green peppers, diced (1 1/2 cups)
2	(16 ounces each) cans tomatoes
2	teaspoon worcestershire sauce
1	cup uncooked long-grain white rice
1 1/2	teaspoon chili powder
2 1/2	teaspoon salt
1/2	cup water

Brown ground chuck in skillet, breaking meat into small pieces. Cook until pink disappears from meat. Pour into colander and drain (see page 55).

Place cooked meat and all other ingredients in crockpot. Stir thoroughly. Cover & cook on Low for 6 to 8 hours or High for 4 hours.

Great served with a salad and **Homemade French Bread** (page 95).

VARIATIONS: Add 1 teaspoon cayenne pepper.

Add 2 (16 ounce) cans chili beans when meat is added to crockpot. Sprinkle with 4 ounces (1 cup) grated cheese. Cover and let stand for 5 minutes until cheese melts.

For a spicier version, substitute 1 can Ro*Tel tomatoes and chilies for 1 can tomatoes, OR 2 cans Ro*tel for 2 cans tomatoes.

To Serve 8 to 10 people

For a 4 1/2 quart crockpot, use 1 1/2 times all recipe ingredients.

To Serve 2 to 3 people

Use one-half of ground chuck, onion, peppers, tomatoes, worcestershire sauce, rice and cayenne pepper. Use 1 teaspoon salt and 2 teaspoon chili powder in place of the seasonings listed above.

PORK

BBQ PORK ROAST

Makes 4 to 6 servings

4   pound lean pork roast
3   cups **Prime Time Barbecue Sauce** (page 35)
1   cup water

Remove all visible fat from roast and discard fat. In large, heavy pot, add roast, water and 2 cups of barbecue sauce. Cover pot. Over high heat, bring liquid to a boil. Lower heat and simmer 1 1/2 hours or until tender and meat is easily removed from bone (190 degrees or more on meat thermometer).

Slice roast, removing any remaining fat, and place on platter. Serve with remaining cup of barbecue sauce.

Crockpot Method

Place ingredients, as instructed above, in a crockpot. Cover and cook on high for 6 to 8 hours until meat is done and very tender.

Barbecue Sandwiches

When roast is tender, remove all fat. Chop pork into small pieces. Place in colander and drain well (see insert page 55). Place chopped pork in saucepan with 1/2 to 1 cup **Prime Time Barbecue Sauce**, stirring frequently. Simmer just until pork is hot and sauce is evenly distributed.

Place a generous amount of barbecued pork in each hamburger bun. Serve with chips and dill pickle. Serve with a pitcher of barbecue sauce.

FAVORITE BABY BACK PORK RIBS *Makes 3 to 4 servings*

These ribs are every bit as good as those served at most rib-specialty restaurants. Although it can be made with regular pork ribs, it is much, much better when made with baby back ribs, which are leaner.

- 3 pounds baby back pork ribs
- 1 bottle Bull's Eye barbecue sauce OR
- 1 recipe **Target Barbecue Supreme** (page 36)
- 6 cups water

Cut ribs between each bone (see tip below). Place in large pot in layers and add water until almost covered. Bring to boil. Reduce heat so that water is slowly boiling and continue to cook for 1 to 1 1/2 hours, until meat is tender but still attached to the bones.

Remove ribs from pot. Drain and place in roasting pan in single layer. Cover ribs with 1-1/2 cups of barbecue sauce.

Bake uncovered in 350 degree oven for 45 minutes to 1 hour until ribs are browned on top and very, very tender, but still attached to bones.

Serve with **Marinated Topped Salad** (page 214) and **Scalloped Potato Casserole** (page 186).

Preparation Tip

You may want to have your butcher cut whole slab of ribs into individual rib pieces.

GRILLED PORK CHOPS *Makes 4 to 6 servings*

- 6-8 lean pork chops, with or without bone
- 1 cup **Prime Time Barbecue Sauce** (page 35)

Pour barbecue sauce over pork and let marinate for 30 minutes to 1 hour. Remove chops from sauce and cook over **HOT** grill for about 7 to 10 minutes per side until browned, basting often with marinade.

Serve with **Holiday Potatoes** (page 184) and a salad, either fruit or green.

PORK CHOPS   *Makes 4 servings*

- 1/2 cup **Seasoned Bread Crumbs** (recipe follows)
- 1/2 teaspoon Morton's Nature's seasoning
- 1/2 teaspoon garlic salt
- 1/2 teaspoon basil
- 1/4 teaspoon dill weed
- 1/4 teaspoon onion salt
- 4 lean pork chops
- 1 tablespoon cooking oil

Trim all fat from pork chops. Mix bread crumbs and all seasonings together in shallow bowl. Coat each side of chops with seasoned bread crumbs. Cook in one of the following ways:

Cooking Method 1

Put oil in frying pan and heat to medium-high temperature. Add coated pork chops and fry until lightly golden brown. Turn each pork chop over and brown on second side. Turn heat to low and simmer, uncovered, for 20 minutes until pork chops are completely done but still juicy.

Cooking Method 2

In baking pan, place pork chops on a broiling rack. Drizzle with the oil. Bake at 350 degrees for 35 to 45 minutes, until chops are golden brown and completely done.

Seasoned Bread Crumbs

Take about 3/4 cups of **Crunchy Croutons** (page 221) or 3 slices of **Crunchy Seasoned Bread** (page 89). Break bread into pieces. Place either bread or croutons in mini-food processor and process for about 30 seconds.

* * * * * * * * *

How to Make Bread Crumbs

Select any type of stale white or whole grain bread, such as hot dog buns, hamburger buns, loaf bread, hoagie buns and rolls.

Break bread into pieces and place in food processor or mini-food processor. Process until bread is in crumbs. Pour crumbs onto a cooking sheet, making a thin layer. Use as many baking pans as needed. Place in oven and bake on 250 degrees until bread crumbs are dried out and very, very lightly browned. Cool. Store in an air-tight container. These may be frozen.

If crumbs are not completely dried-out, they will mold.

HAM ROLL-UPS   *Makes 6 servings*

Serve for lunch or as an appetizer for a casual get-together.

8	ounces cooked ham, chopped
8	ounces cheddar cheese, cubed
2	eggs, boiled and chopped or grated
3	tablespoons low-calorie mayonnaise
1	medium onion, chopped
1	cup chili sauce
1/2	cup (1 stick) margarine
1	(4 ounce) jar green olives, diced
6	hot dog buns

Preheat oven to 350 degrees.

Mix ham, cheese, eggs, mayonnaise, onion, and chili sauce.

Spread margarine on each hot dog roll on both sides. Place 1/6 of ham and cheese mixture on each roll. Wrap each roll in aluminum foil, drug-store fashion, sealing well.

Bake for 30 minutes or until hot and cheese is melted.

VARIATION: To serve as an appetizer, cut each filled hot dog roll into 5 pieces before wrapping in foil.

* * * * * * * * * *

How to Grate Eggs

When a recipe calls for grated hard boiled egg, use a vegetable grater. Grate eggs just before using so they will not discolor.

Grated eggs are good placed on top of fresh cooked spinach and salads. They are good stirred into mixed salads such as ham salad, chicken salad, and potato salad.

They are excellent made into **Egg Salad** (page 9).

PORK LOIN & CABBAGE CASSEROLE   *Makes 4 to 6 servings*

So easy: preparation time is under 15 minutes. This makes a complete meal in a dish!

    6   thick, boneless pork loin slices, 3/4-inch thick, browned on both sides in 1 tablespoon oil
    6   potatoes, peeled and thinly sliced
    1   onion, peeled and thinly sliced
    1   head cabbage, sliced in 1-inch wedges
    1   can cream of chicken soup
    1   cup skim milk

Place ingredients in 9x12-inch casserole dish in the following order:

    Bottom layers: cabbage
                       potatoes
                       onions

    Top layer: pork chops

    Sauce: Mix soup and milk together. Pour over top layer.

Preheat oven to 350 degrees. Cover casserole and bake in oven for 45 minutes. Uncover and bake an additional 15 to 20 minutes.

VARIATION: Add 1/2 teaspoon Italian seasoning.

VENISON

VENISON TERIYAKI
Makes 4 servings

A specialty at many Chinese restaurants, this teriyaki is made with lean venison instead of beef. The marinade is the secret to its mouth-watering tenderness.

- 1 pound cubed venison, cut into 1 1/2-inch wide strips
- 1 dozen 5-inch wooden skewers

Marinade

- 1/4 cup San-J teriyaki marinade
- 1/4 cup soy sauce
- 1/4 cup honey
- 1/4 cup water
- 3 tablespoons cooking sherry
- 1/2 teaspoon baking soda
- 1/2 teaspoon minced garlic
- 1/4 teaspoon ground ginger or 1/2 teaspoon fresh grated ginger
- 1/2 teaspoon cayenne pepper
- 1/2 teaspoon dry mustard

Cut strips into pieces about 4 inches long, and place in a sealable plastic container. Mix teriyaki marinade, soy sauce, honey, water, sherry, soda, garlic, ginger, cayenne and mustard together. Pour sauce over venison, seal and shake well to cover all pieces of venison. Marinate for at least 3 hours or overnight, but not more than 2 days.

Remove venison from marinade and thread on skewers. Grill over highest heat for 1 to 2 minutes on each side, basting frequently. Turn and cook 1 more minute. Cooking times will very with different grills. Do not over cook, as this will cause venison to be dry. Remove from grill and brush venison with **Honey Glaze** (recipe follows)

Honey Glaze

- 1/4 cup honey
- 1/2 teaspoon dry mustard

Make glaze, by stirring honey and mustard together.

4

Beverages

BEVERAGES

Virgin

Spirits

BEVERAGES

Although this section is small, it provides recipes that will become favorites in your collection. All "virgin" recipes are at the beginning, and recipes containing alcohol complete the section.

Koolaid Punch and Holiday Punch are both delightful flavor combinations enjoyed by children and adults alike. Use both of these recipes to experiment and create your own variations.

The Irish Creme, Amaretto, and Coffee Liqueur recipes are inexpensive adaptations of these expensive commercial brands available at your local liquor or package store. These recipes are best when made in advance. They make great holiday gifts for those who have "everything"!

VIRGIN BEVERAGES

COFFEE PUNCH *Makes 12 servings*

- 3/4 cups instant coffee
- 3 quarts cold water
- 1/4 cup sugar
- 1/2 gallon vanilla ice cream or ice milk

Heat water, sugar and coffee until dissolved. Place ice cream in punch bowl and pour hot coffee over it. Stir until it looks like coffee with cream. Let the rest of ice cream float on top.

HOLIDAY PUNCH *Makes 16 small servings*

This is a colorful punch with a refreshing taste - perfect to serve during the Christmas season or on Valentine's Day.

- 1 quart cranberry juice
- 1 quart orange juice
- 1 pint lemon juice
- 2 quarts gingerale, chilled

Mix cranberry juice, orange juice and lemon juice together and chill several hours or overnight. Chill ginger ale.

Just before serving, pour chilled mixture into punch bowl. Add chilled gingerale. Ladle into small punch cups or glasses.

MICROWAVE TEA

Makes 1/2 gallon

6   tea bags
2   quarts water
1   cup sugar

In pitcher or bowl, add 3 cups water and tea bags. Microwave on high for 5 minutes. Cover and let steep for about 10 minutes. Add sugar and stir to dissolve. Add remaining 5 cups water, filling pitcher line to 8 cups or 2 quarts. Chill.

VARIATIONS: Slice one lemon. Add to tea before steeping.

REFRESHING KOOLAID PUNCH

Makes 18 large servings

2   packages lemon-lime Koolaid, unsweetened
1   large can unsweetened pineapple juice
2   cups sugar
2   quarts water
1 or 2   one-liter bottles ginger ale
     lemon, orange or lime slices or cherries

Mix first 4 ingredients together until sugar is dissolved. Chill several hours or overnight.

Pour some of the above mixture into a mold. Add some orange, lemon or lime slices and cherries, cut in half. Freeze.

Just before serving, add above mold to bowl, pour punch into bowl and add ginger ale.

RUSSIAN TEA

Makes 12 quarts liquid or 4 cups dry mix (36 cups reconstituted)

Although I have not seen it for years, this classic recipe is so refreshing it should be shared. Although not certain, I believe it originated with the manufacturers of Tang orange drink mix.

1   jar (18 ounces) instant breakfast drink
1 1/4   cups sugar
3/4   cups instant tea mix (without lemon)
1   teaspoon cinnamon
1/2   teaspoon ground cloves

Combine breakfast drink, sugar, tea, cinnamon, and cloves. Store dry mix in air-tight container for later use, OR mix with 3 quarts boiling water, stirring to dissolve. Taste. Add additional boiling water to adjust taste. Serve hot in cups or mugs.

To make one serving, place 1 heaping tablespoon of mix in a cup and add boiling water.

SPIRITED BEVERAGES

AMARETTO LIQUEUR

This almond-flavored liqueur, contributed by Joyce Grimes, Barnwell, SC, is quite delicious.

- 1   tablespoon dry instant coffee
- 2   cups boiling water
- 3   cups sugar
- 1   ounce almond extract
- 1/8   teaspoon bitters (5 dashes)
- 3-4   cups vodka

Dissolve coffee in 1/4 cup boiling water. Add remaining 3/4 cup boiling water. Add sugar and dissolve. Add almond extract, bitters and vodka. Add last cup of water. Stir to mix all ingredients. Pour into decorative decanters and store for 1 month before serving.

This will keep indefinitely.

CITRUS SLUSH   *Makes 16 generous servings*

A great drink to keep on hand during the sweltering summer months.

- 1   (6 ounce) can frozen orange juice, undiluted, thawed
- 2   (6 ounce) cans frozen lemonade concentrate, undiluted, thawed
- 2   (6 ounce) cans frozen limeade concentrate, undiluted, thawed
- 3 1/2   cups water
- 1   cup sugar
- 1   quart (4 cups) vodka
- 2   (28 ounces each) bottles of 7-up or ginger ale

Combine orange juice, lemonade and limeade concentrates, water, sugar and vodka. Stir to mix thoroughly. Place in a large plastic freezer container. Freeze at least 48 hours, stirring several times.

To serve: Spoon mixture into tall glass until glass is 3/4th full. Fill glass to top with 7-up or gingerale. Stir well and serve immediately.

COFFEE LIQUEUR *Makes 1/2 gallon*

This makes a great White Russian or Black Russian cocktail. Pour into a decorative decanter and give as a holiday gift.

- 4 cups sugar
- 3/4 cups freeze dried coffee granules
- 3 cups boiling water
- 1 quart of 100 proof vodka
- 1 6-inch vanilla bean or 2 teaspoons vanilla flavoring

Dissolve sugar in water. Stir in coffee. Heat a few minutes to dissolve coffee granules. Add vanilla bean or flavoring. Mix well.

Cool thoroughly. Add vodka. Using two (2) 1-quart bottles, place half of a vanilla bean in each bottle. Fill with cooled coffee/vodka mixture.

Store at least 3 weeks before serving, shaking bottles occasionally.

VARIATION: Add 1/4 cup chocolate syrup when coffee is added.

White Russians

(Mix coffee liqueur and vodka in 2 to 1 proportions)

In each 8 ounce glass, add 1 ounce (2 tablespoons) coffee liqueur and 1/2 ounce (1 tablespoon) vodka. Add ice and fill with milk. Stir to mix well and serve.

Black Russians

A White Russian without the milk!

Fill each 4 ounce glass with ice. Pour 1 ounce coffee liqueur and 1/2 ounce vodka over ice. Stir to mix well and serve.

COFFEE LIQUEUR DESSERT
Makes 6 servings

These are commonly called "Angel Tips".

> 1 cup **Coffee Liqueur** (page 81)
> 6 large scoops French vanilla ice cream
> 2 cups crushed ice
> 3 tablespoons chocolate syrup
> 3 tablespoons chopped pecans
> 6 sherbet glasses

Place coffee liqueur, ice cream, ice, and chocolate syrup in blender. Cover and blend on high speed until thickened, about 8 to 10 seconds. Serve in stemmed glasses. Top with 2 teaspoons chocolate syrup. Sprinkle each glass with 1 teaspoon of chopped pecans.

IRISH COFFEE
Per Serving

In an 8-ounce coffee mug, mix the following:

> 4 ounces (1/2 cup) hot coffee OR 1/2 cup hot water and 2 teaspoons instant coffee
> 2 teaspoons sugar
> 2 tablespoons **Irish Creme Liqueur** (page 83)
> 1 ounce (2 tablespoons) bourbon or Irish whiskey

Serve immediately. Top with a dollop of whipped cream, if desired.

IRISH CREME LIQUEUR

A smooth, creamy liqueur that melts in your mouth—a blending of coffee, chocolate, and cream. I have kept this for as long as 6 months, and it was still delicious!

    4   eggs
    2   tablespoons freeze-dried coffee granules
    2   tablespoons chocolate syrup
    2   tablespoons vanilla flavoring
  1/2   cup boiling water
1 1/2   cup Irish Whiskey or good brand bourbon
  1/2   pint (1 cup) Half and Half cream
    1   can (14 ounces) condensed milk

Using electric mixer, whip eggs in large mixing bowl. Dissolve coffee granules in boiling water. Add coffee and remaining ingredients to egg mixture. Mix well. Strain if desired.

Store in refrigerator up to one month. Serve as an after-dinner drink.

Irish Creme Dessert   *Makes 4 to 6 servings*

    1   pint ice cream, vanilla or coffee flavored
    1   cup Irish Creme Liqueur, chilled
  1/2   cup chocolate fudge sauce
  2-3   tablespoon chopped pecans

In each stemmed glass, add ice cream. Pour chilled liqueur over top of ice cream. Pour fudge sauce over liqueur and sprinkle with pecans. Serve with a spoon.

NEW YEAR'S SUNRISE   *Mixture per glass*

In each stemmed glass, mix equal parts of orange juice and champagne.

Garnish with a lemon slice, pineapple chunk or other fresh fruit.

SANGRIA   *Makes 6 to 8 servings*

A light refreshing drink!

- 1   bottle (24 ounces) red wine
- 1   shot (1/4 cup) brandy or cognac (can use gin)
      Juice of 2 oranges (1/2 cups)
      Juice of 2 lemons   (1/3 cups)
- 1/2-3/4 cup sugar
- 1/2   bottle (14 ounces) sparkling water

Mix all ingredients together, adding sparking water just before serving. Serve over ice in stemmed glasses.

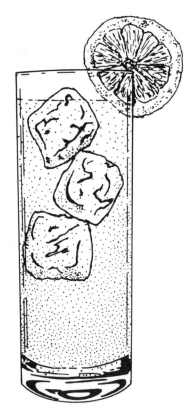

5

Breads

BREADS

BREAD

Does the aroma of bread baking in the oven remind you of your childhood? Homemade bread creates a down-home, comfy atmosphere like a fire crackling in the fireplace on a cold winter night.   Re-create this childhood nostalgia for your family by baking some breads in this section.

Quick breads are leavened with baking powder and/or baking soda, while yeast breads become light and airy by using the rising power of yeast. Quick breads are just that: quickly mix ingredients together and "pop" the loaf into the oven. Preparation and cooking time are usually under one hour.

Although yeast breads are not difficult to prepare, they require more time and patience. However, yeast breads, the Royal family of breads, are usually the lightest and most cherished breads.

Wheat gluten in yeast breads causes higher rising, improves shape, enhances flavor, increases protein and extends freshness. It is basically wheat flour with the starch removed. Yeast breads and rolls are a good choice when you are spending a relaxed day or afternoon at home.

Breads fall into two other categories: (1) breads and (2) sweet breads. Biscuits, rolls, loaf bread and cornbread fall under the first category, which is the emphasis of this section. Cinnamon rolls and Cream Cheese Bread fall under the second category. You will find varieties of both in this section.

Tired of garlic bread? Try new Crunchy Seasoned Bread for a flavor that is excellent served with almost any meal. For a special occasion try Aunt Nell's Spoonbread, a classic dish from the early 20th century. It might become a family favorite! Perhaps the recipes in this chapter will inspire your own creations.

QUICK BREADS

AUNT NELL'S SPOONBREAD

Makes 8 servings

For more than 50 years, my Aunt Nell cooked this Virginia recipe. A Southern classic, spoonbread is delicious served with seafood or any country-cooked meal.

1	cup corn meal	1/2	teaspoon baking soda
2	cups boiling water	2	eggs
2	teaspoons salt	1	cup nonfat buttermilk
1 1/2	teaspoons baking powder		

Preheat oven to 350 degrees. Lightly grease a 1 1/2 quart casserole.

Place corn meal in large saucepan. Pour boiling water over meal and cook over low heat for about 5 minutes, stirring frequently. Remove from heat. Add salt, baking powder, baking soda, eggs and buttermilk. Stir to mix well. Pour into prepared casserole.

Bake about 50 minutes to 1 hour until done and set in center.

Serve with fried shrimp or fish and cole slaw or baked ham, collards, black-eye peas and stewed tomatoes.

10-MINUTE BISCUITS

Makes 16 biscuits

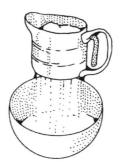

- 2 cups self-rising flour
- 1 cup plain flour (used for kneading)
- 1 teaspoon baking soda
- 1/2 teaspoons salt
- 1 cup skim milk
- 1 package yeast (2 1/2 teaspoons)
- 1 cup margarine or shortening
- 3/4 cup nonfat buttermilk

Blend dry ingredients together. Cut in shortening until the mixture resembles coarse crumbs. Add milk and buttermilk, all at once, and stir until well blended.

Preheat oven to 425 degrees. Spread 1/2 cup flour in circle on large board or clean counter surface. Turn out dough onto prepared surface. Place a little flour on top of dough and knead just 3 times. The less the dough is kneaded and handled, the more tender the biscuits will be.

Roll out to 1/2-inch to 3/4-inch thick and cut 3" biscuits and place on ungreased cookie sheet. Cover with cloth. Let rise for 1 hour.

Bake on medium-high rack for 12 to 15 minutes until golden brown on top.

For Appetizers: Cut smaller biscuits. Reduce cooking time to 8 to 10 minutes.

CHEESE ROLL-UPS   *Makes 24 to 30 roll-ups*

Terri Anderson, Barnwell, SC, graciously shared this recipe with me.

- 8   ounces (2 cups) grated sharp cheddar cheese
- 1   cup (2 sticks) margarine or butter, at room temperature
- 2   loaves thin sandwich bread
- 1   tablespoon Morton's Nature's Seasoning OR garlic salt

Remove crusts from bread. Spread margarine on each slice of bread. Sprinkle with cheese and seasoned salt. Roll-up each slice bread and press seam to seal. Chill about 2 hours.

Preheat oven to 300 degrees. Bake for 30 minutes. Serve hot.

VARIATION: Use 2 cans asparagus spears. Place one spear on each slice of bread before rolling it up.

Use 2 cans of crescent rolls instead of loaf bread.

CORN BREAD   *Makes 6 to 8 servings*

Because yellow corn meal gives color to corn bread, some people prefer it to white corn meal; however, the flavors are very similar.

- 1   cup flour
- 1   cup yellow corn meal
- 3   tablespoons sugar
- 1   tablespoon baking powder
- 1/2 teaspoon salt
- 1   egg
- 1   cup skim milk
- 1/4 cup salad oil

Preheat oven to 350 degrees. Grease 9x9-inch square pan.

In large bowl, add flour, corn meal, sugar, baking powder and salt. Stir to mix well. Add egg, milk and oil. Stir, by hand, to mix well. Pour into prepared pan.

Bake for 15 to 20 minutes until edges are golden brown and top is lightly browned.

Cut into squares and serve hot with margarine or butter.

VARIATION: Substitute nonfat buttermilk for skim milk and add 1/2 teaspoon baking soda.

CRUNCHY SEASONED BREAD   *per serving*

This bread is crunchy throughout and well-seasoned.

 1   slice bread: English muffin, Italian bread, 1/2 half hamburger bun, French bread, or other sliced bread
 1   teaspoon margarine or butter
1/8   teaspoon Morton's Nature Seasoning OR garlic salt

Preheat oven to 250 degrees.

Spread margarine on one side of bread. Sprinkle with seasoning. Bake about 20 to 25 minutes, adjusting cooking time to thickness of bread selected. Turn oven to Broil. Broil, about 3-inches from heat, until lightly golden brown on top. Immediately remove from oven and place on serving plate.

VARIATIONS: Do not bake. For soft toasted bread, broil buttered side up, about 3 inches from heat until golden brown. Immediately remove from oven and serve.

HUSH PUPPIES EDISTO   *Makes 8 to 10 servings*

3/4   cup self-rising flour
3/4   cup self-rising corn meal
 1   medium onion, finely minced or grated
 1   teaspoon baking soda
 3   tablespoons sugar
 1   egg
3/4-1 cup skim milk or buttermilk
1/2   teaspoon salt (optional)

Mix flour, corn meal, soda, salt and sugar together. Stir in onion and egg. Mix well. Add milk, stirring until mixture is the consistency of soft biscuit dough. Let rest 5 minutes. Stir.

Dip small spoon in glass of cold water, then scoop out spoonful of hush puppy mix. Gently lower spoon into medium hot, deep fat oil, turning spoon so that the batter gently falls out of the spoon into the oil. Continue with remaining batter, cooking about 8 to 10 puppies at one time. Do not overcrowd. Turn with spoon to brown evenly. Fry about 2 to 3 minutes until golden brown.

Left over batter may be refrigerated and used within a week.

VARIATION: Increase corn meal to 1 1/2 cups. Decrease flour to 1/2 cup. Use 2 teaspoons baking powder instead of 1 teaspoon baking soda.

JOYCE'S HUSH PUPPIES

Makes 3 dozen

- 1   box Jiffy corn bread mix
- 2   tablespoons grated green pepper (1/3 medium pepper)
- 1/2 cup grated onion with juice (1 medium or 1/2 large onion)
- 2   tablespoons skim milk
- 1   egg, slightly beaten
- 2   tablespoons flour
- 1   teaspoon salt
- 1   teaspoon pepper

Pour corn bread mix into medium-sized bowl. Add green pepper, onion, milk, egg, salt and pepper. Stir to mix well. Let sit for 5 minutes. Cook as directed in inset on page 120.

VARIATION: Substitute nonfat buttermilk for skim milk and add 3/4 teaspoon baking soda.

* * * * * * * * *

How to Cook Hush Puppies

To cook hush puppies, have grease temperature on medium-high so that hush puppies will cook completely on the inside before getting too brown on the outside. Hush puppies should float to top of hot grease when they are done.

To lower hush puppies into grease, first dip clean spoon in cold water. Then fill spoon with mix and lower into hot grease, turning spoon to let hush puppy float out of spoon.

SOUR CREAM CORN BREAD

Makes 6 to 8 servings

A corn bread that actually melts in your mouth! It's soft instead of crumbly.

   1   cup self-rising corn meal
1/2   cup cooking oil
   1   (8 ounce) carton sour cream
   1   cup canned cream-style corn
   2   eggs

Preheat oven to 425 degrees. Lightly spray 8x8-inch or 9x9-inch square casserole with nonstick cooking spray.

Mix all ingredients together. Pour into prepared dish.

Place casserole dish on shelf in lower 1/3 of oven. Bake for approximately 25 minutes until set in the middle and lightly golden brown on top.

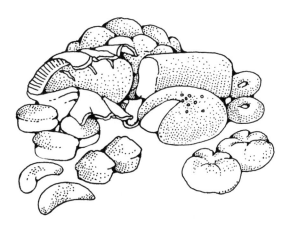

SOUTHERN BUTTERMILK BISCUITS   *Makes 24 biscuits*

        3   cups self-rising flour
        1   cup (2 sticks) margarine or butter
        1/2 teaspoon baking soda
        1   cup buttermilk
        1/2 cup self-rising flour (to flour surface for kneading)

Preheat oven to 450 degrees. Spread 1/2 cup of flour on a smooth surface, such as a pastry cloth or a clean, dry counter top. This flour will be used for kneading dough.

In large bowl add 3 cups flour and baking soda. Using a pastry blender or a knife and fork, cut margarine into flour until pieces are smaller than green peas. Pour in buttermilk. Mix well and form a soft dough.

On surface prepared with flour, gently knead dough until no longer sticky. Sprinkle a little flour from surface on top of dough. Roll dough to 3/4 inches thick. With a round cookie cutter, cut biscuits from dough, leaving as little uncut dough between biscuits as possible. Place biscuits on ungreased 9x12-inch cookie sheet. Gently knead remaining dough and roll out again. Cut additional biscuits and place on cookie sheet.

Bake biscuits for about 8 to 10 minutes until browned on the bottom and lightly browned on top. If biscuits brown too quickly on the bottom, move the cookie sheets up one rack in the oven.

Remove biscuits from oven and serve hot with butter.

* * * * * * * * * *

How to Handle Biscuit Dough

The less biscuit dough is handled the more tender it will be. Therefore, flour a large surface and roll all of biscuit dough at one time. Cut biscuits and place on baking sheet. Then re-roll scraps from between biscuits. Biscuits cut from the first rolling of the dough will be the most tender.

YEAST BREADS

ANGEL BISCUITS
Makes 2 to 3 dozen

This recipe has appeared in so many cookbooks that it has become a classic. The originator of this recipe is unknown; however, it is so delicious that this section would be incomplete without it.

1	package yeast	2	tablespoons very warm water
1	teaspoon baking soda	1	cup (2 sticks) margarine or butter
3	teaspoons baking powder	5	cups flour
1 1/2	teaspoons salt	2	cups non-fat buttermilk
		2	tablespoons sugar, optional

Dissolve yeast and sugar in warm water. Stir all dry ingredients together in large bowl. Using pastry blender or food processor, cut margarine into dry ingredients until particles are the size of green peas. Add buttermilk and then yeast mixture, stirring until thoroughly moistened.

Turn dough onto floured board and knead 1 minute. On floured surface, roll out to 1/2 -inch thickness and cut into 2 or 2 1/2-inch rounds, placing biscuits on an ungreased cookie sheet. Let rise 1 hour.

Preheat oven to 400 degrees. Bake about 12 to 15 minutes until lightly golden brown on top. Biscuits freeze beautifully.

* * * * * * * * *

How to Make-Ahead Biscuits

Refrigerate biscuit dough in an air-tight container or sealable plastic bag for several days. Leave head room in container so dough can expand. Biscuits can be made ahead and covered with plastic wrap.

For yeast biscuits, about 2 hours before baking, remove dough or biscuits from refrigerator. Allow dough to return to room temperature and rise before baking. For baking powder biscuits remove pan from refrigerator and immediately place in hot oven.

BEST-GUEST MORNING BREAD   *Makes 1 bundt cake*

As a family tradition, this sweet cheese-filled bread, is served to Santa Claus on Christmas Eve. This can be frozen, thawed, and re-heated in the microwave or oven.

Dough

2	packages yeast (5 teaspoons)	3	eggs, slightly beaten
6	tablespoons sugar	1	(8 ounce) carton sour cream
1/2	cup (1 stick) butter	5	cups flour (bread flour)

In large bowl, add yeast and sugar and stir. Add butter, eggs and sour cream and mix with electric mixer until well blended. Gradually add flour until a stiff dough forms. Place in well greased bowl and let rise until double in bulk.

Lightly grease a tube or bundt pan. Punch down and place on floured surface. Knead bread about 1 minute. Roll out dough to an 18 -inch circle. Cut an "X" in the center of dough, making a hole to fit over center of tube or bundt pan. Gently place dough in prepared pan. Place one of the following **Sweet Creamy Filling** recipes (recipes follow) in a circle around dough. Then fold the center pieces outward and the outside edge over filling to gently seal filling inside of dough. Decorate with candied fruit or other decorations, such as pecan halves. Let rise until double in bulk.

Bake at 350 degrees for 35 to 40 minutes until golden brown. Drizzle **Glaze** (recipe follows) over bread while it is still warm. Serve warm or at room temperature.

Sweet Creamy Filling # 1

2	(8 ounces each) packages cream cheese	1/2	cup sugar
2	eggs	1	tablespoon vanilla

Sweet Creamy Filling # 2

4	egg yolks	1/2	cup + 2 tablespoons sugar
4	(8 ounces each) packages cream cheese	4	teaspoons vanilla

Mix cream cheese, eggs, sugar and vanilla until mixture is very creamy.

VARIATION: Melt 1 ounce unsweetened baking chocolate (see page 120). Drizzle in a decorative pattern over the glaze.

Substitute 2 teaspoons vanilla and 2 teaspoons lemon extract and 1 teaspoon dried lemon peel for the vanilla in either version.

Glaze

Place 1 to 2 cups powdered sugar in bowl. Add water, 1 tablespoon at a time, until mixture is slightly thinner than cake frosting.

ENGLISH MUFFINS

Makes about 1 dozen

1 recipe **Mother's White Bread** (page 96)

Follow directions for making white bread until bread is kneaded the second time. At this point, make muffins as follows:

On a surface covered with corn meal, roll dough to a thickness of 3/8-inch. Using a sharp-edged 3-inch round object, cut dough and place circles on prepared baking sheet. Top each circle with another circle. Let rise until double in bulk.

In a frying pan with a little oil, fry English muffins on medium-low until lightly golden brown on both sides and done, about 20 minutes. Remove from pan and cool on a baking rack.

HOMEMADE FRENCH BREAD

Makes 1 large or 2 regular loaves

Because this bread does not contain eggs and has a negligible amount of sugar and fat, it is a low-calorie, low-cholesterol bread. It makes a very light, tender bread.

2 1/2	teaspoons dry yeast (1 package yeast)	1 1/2	teaspoons light olive oil
3	cups bread flour	1 1/2	cups warm water
1 1/2	teaspoons salt	2 1/2	teaspoons gluten (optional)
1 1/2-2	teaspoons sugar		

Lightly grease a cookie sheet.

Mix all dry ingredients together. Heat 1/4 cup water and olive oil to boiling. Pour hot mixture into 1 1/4 cups warm water. Pour this into dry ingredients and mix to make a dough, scraping sides of bowl. Let dough rise until double in bulk, about 1 to 1 1/2 hours.

Press dough down and scrape sides of bowl. Let rise again until double in bulk. Press dough down and remove from bowl. Place dough on floured surface (use about 1/2 cup flour). Knead dough about 5 minutes working in enough dough to prevent dough from being sticky.

Divide dough in half. Shape into long narrow loaves and place the two (2) loaves side by side, but about 6 inches apart, on a lightly greased cookie sheet. Let rise again until double in bulk.

Bake about 30 to 35 minutes until lightly golden brown and crusty on top. Cool at least 15 minutes. Slice with a serrated bread knife.

VARIATION: Omit salt and add 1 tablespoon Morton's Nature's seasoning or garlic salt to dough.

MOTHER'S WHITE BREAD   *Makes 2 loaves of bread*

This makes enough dough to bake into two loaves of bread or a loaf of bread and several dozen rolls!

>   2   packages of yeast (5 teaspoons)
> 2 1/2 cups warm water
>   1/4 cup plus 2 teaspoons sugar
>   2   eggs
>   1/2 cup cooking oil
>   1/2 teaspoon salt
>   1   cup plus 7 cups flour

Put 2 teaspoons sugar and yeast in large bowl. Pour hot water over yeast and stir to mix. Add 1 cup flour and mix well with whisk to make a smooth batter. Cover with a cloth and let rise for thirty minutes.

Mix 1/4 cup sugar, eggs, oil and salt together. Add this mixture to the yeast mixture and stir to mix well. Stir in 6 cups flour and mix well. Add enough of the remaining cup of flour to make a stiff dough.

Form into a ball and place in a large greased bowl. Cover with a cloth and allow to rise until double in size (see note below). Punch down.

Preheat oven to 350 degrees. Lightly grease and flour two loaf pans or spray pans with Baker's Joy. Gently shape into loaves and place into prepared pans. Let rise again until doubled in bulk.

Bake 45 minutes to 1 hour until golden brown and hollow sounding when thumped. Remove from oven and brush top of loaves with melted butter or take a stick of butter and rub the top of each loaf until well coated. Cool on a rack.

VARIATION: **To make rolls:**

> Instead of shaping into loaves, break off small hunks of dough, fold ends under and place on ungreased cookie sheet. Repeat with remaining dough, letting dough just barely touch. Let rolls rise until double in bulk. Bake about 25 to 30 minutes until lightly golden brown. Brush tops of rolls with butter.

* * * * * * * * *

How to Rise Yeast Dough

Use warm, not hot, water to dissolve yeast. Hot water will kill yeast. When yeast breads are rising, they should be placed in a draft-free location. Either cover bread with a clean dish towel or leave uncovered and place in a microwave oven.

MULTIGRAIN BREAD OR ROLLS

Makes 1 loaf or 24 rolls

    2 1/2 teaspoons yeast (1 package)
        2 eggs
        1 tablespoon wheat germ
      3/4 cup buttermilk, scalded
      1/4 cup cooking oil
      1/4 cup brown sugar
        1 tablespoon molasses
      1/2 teaspoons salt
    1 3/4 cups bread flour or plain flour
      1/4 cup rye flour
      1/4 cup whole wheat flour
      1/4 cup oat bran
    2 1/2 teaspoons wheat gluten (optional)

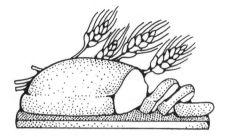

Lightly grease and flour 1 loaf pan. To scald buttermilk, place in glass measuring cup or bowl and microwave 1 minute on HIGH. Alternate method: Heat in pot on medium high heat until it just starts to boil. Do not boil. Remove from heat immediately. Cool.

In a large bowl, stir yeast into 1/4 cup buttermilk (scalded and cooled). Stir until yeast is dissolved. Add remaining buttermilk, sugar, salt, cooking oil, molasses, wheat germ, and eggs. Mix well. Stir in flour until well blended.

Let rest 5 minutes. Remove from bowl and knead on floured surface for 5 minutes. Place in lightly greased bowl and cover with clean dish towel. Let rise about 1 hour. (see page 96).

Remove dough from bowl and place on lightly greased surface. Knead an additional 5 minutes. Place in prepared loaf pan. Let rise until double in bulk again.

Preheat oven to 350 degrees. Place loaf pan in lower 1/3 of oven and bake for 40-50 minutes or until golden brown on top and a hollow sound is made when bread is thumped lightly on top.

Remove from oven and let sit for 10 minutes. Remove from loaf pan and cool on a rack.

VARIATION: **To Make Rolls**

At this point, pull dough into a piece about 12 inches long. With a sharp knife, cut off dough into pieces about the size of a golf ball. Flatten slightly with hand, and place on prepared baking sheet, placing dough pieces about 1-inch apart. Let rise until double in bulk. Bake in preheated oven for about 12 minutes until golden brown on top and bottom.

WHITE BREAD   *Makes 1 large loaf or 24 rolls*

2 1/2	teaspoons yeast (1 package)
2	eggs
1	tablespoons wheat germ
3/4	cup buttermilk, scalded
1/4	cup cooking oil
1/4	cup sugar
1/2	teaspoons salt
2 1/2	cups white bread flour
2 1/2	teaspoons wheat gluten (optional)

Grease and flour 1 loaf pan. To scald buttermilk, place in glass measuring cup or bowl and microwave 1 minute on HIGH. Alternate method: Heat in saucepan on medium high heat until it just starts to boil. Do not boil. Remove from heat immediately. Cool.

In a large bowl, stir yeast into 1/4 cup buttermilk (scalded and cooled). Stir until yeast is dissolved. Add remaining buttermilk, sugar, salt, cooking oil, wheat germ, and eggs. Mix well. Stir in flour until well blended.

Let rest 5 minutes. Remove from bowl and knead on floured surface for 5 minutes. Place in lightly greased bowl and cover with clean dish towel. Let rise until double in bulk - about 1 hour (See page 96).

Remove dough from bowl and place on lightly greased surface. Knead an additional 3 to 5 minutes. Place in prepared loaf pan. Let rise until double in bulk again.

Preheat oven to 350 degrees. Place loaf pan in lower 1/3 of oven and bake for 40-50 minutes or until golden brown on top and a hollow sound is made when bread is thumped lightly on top.

Remove from oven and let sit for 10 minutes. Remove from loaf pan and cool on a rack.

VARIATION: **To Make Rolls**

At this point, pull dough into a piece about 12 inches long. With a sharp knife, cut off dough into pieces about the size of a golf ball. Flatten slightly with hand, and place on greased baking sheet, placing dough pieces about 1-inch apart. Let rise until double in bulk. Bake in preheated oven for about 12 minutes until golden brown on top and bottom.

WHOLE WHEAT BREAD

Makes 1 loaf

This bread has lots of flavor and nutrition!

1 1/2	cups warm water or nonfat buttermilk
2	tablespoons sugar
2	tablespoons cooking oil
1	package dry yeast
1	teaspoon salt
1	tablespoon wheat germ
1	cup whole wheat flour
1 1/2-2	cups white flour
2 1/2	teaspoons wheat gluten (optional)

Grease and flour a 9-inch loaf pan.

In a large bowl, mix water, sugar, oil, yeast, salt and wheat germ. Let stand 10 minutes. Add wheat flour and 1 cup of white flour and mix with a whisk.

With a wooden spoon, mix enough white flour to make a medium stiff dough. Turn out dough onto a floured board and knead about 3 to 5 minutes. Place in a greased bowl and turn to grease all over. Let rise (see page 96) until doubled in bulk. Push down from sides and let rise again.

Turn out onto a greased platter, and knead about 1 minute. Press out with hands and then roll up, jelly-roll fashion, and put into a prepared loaf pan. Preheat oven to 325 degrees. Let dough rise until about 1/2 - inch over the top of the loaf pan.

Bake about 35 to 40 minutes or until golden brown. If bread browns too quickly, make a little tent of foil and loosely cover the top of the loaf. Remove from pan and place on cake rack to cool.

6

Brunches

BRUNCHES

BRUNCHES

Brunch is a combination of **Br**eakfast and L**unch**, served as a late, late breakfast or as an early, early lunch. It is usually served between 9:00 am and 12:00 pm. Many dishes can be prepared the night before, so the cook can sleep late too!

Since Brunch usually replaces breakfast and lunch, many families subsequently have only one other meal during the day: dinner or supper.

Brunch menus may contain almost any breakfast, lunch or light supper dishes. Brunches probably allow the most creativity in planning, as almost any well-balanced, flavor-coordinated combination of foods may be served.

A brunch buffet for entertaining should contain some breakfast foods, such as Eggs Benedict or Muffin-Waffles, and other lunch or dinner items, such as **Corned Beef Quiche** (page 53), **Tom's Favorite Crab Cakes** (page 230), or **Slow Cooked Creamy Grits** (109). Something sweet, such as dessert, or a fruit tray is often served.

Many foods in this section are equally suitable for supper or dinner.

BRUNCH CASSEROLE   *Makes 6 to 8 servings*

    1   pound hot bulk sausage
    1   (8 ounce) can crescent rolls
    8   ounces (2 cups) grated mozzarella or cheddar cheese
  1/4   teaspoon salt
  1/8   teaspoon pepper
    4   eggs, beaten
  3/4   cups skim milk

Preheat oven to 425 degrees. Lightly grease 13x9-inch casserole dish.

Brown sausage. Pour into colander and rinse with hot water for 1 minute. Drain well. Place crescent rolls in prepared dish and spread to cover bottom. Press perforations to seal together. Sprinkle sausage over crescent rolls. Sprinkle cheese over sausage. Mix eggs and milk together until well blended. Pour mixture over cheese.

Bake for 15 to 20 minutes or until set. Let stand for 5 minutes before cutting into squares. Serve hot.

VARIATION: In place of mixing 4 eggs with milk, prepare in the following manner:

Break 8 eggs, spaced evenly, over the cheese. Pour 1/2 cup skim milk over eggs, sausage and cheese. Bake as directed above, making sure that eggs are set (no runny egg whites).

CITRUS SAUCE SUPREME   *Makes 4 servings*

A delightfully different sauce to serve over pancakes. Or cool and serve over a **Leaf Lettuce with Feta Cheese** salad (page 213).

- 3 tablespoons sugar
- 3 oranges
- 1 grapefruit
    grape jelly, as needed
- 3 kiwifruit, peeled and sliced
- 5 teaspoons corn starch
- 2 tablespoons water

Place colander over large bowl. Peel grapefruit and oranges and cut into sections. Place sections into colander and let drain for 5 minutes, reserving juice. Pour juice into measuring cup and add enough grape jelly to measure 3/4 cup.

Pour juice and jelly into saucepan and heat until melted. Mix corn starch and water. Pour corn starch mixture into saucepan and continue to heat, stirring constantly, until mixture thickens, about 2 minutes. Remove from heat. Gently stir in orange sections, grapefruit sections and kiwifruit slices.

Serve warm over pancakes or crepes, or cool and serve as a dressing for a lettuce salad.

CRISPY FRIED SALT HERRING
Makes 6 to 8 servings

When my mother was very young, her father used to purchase a year's supply of herring from an Indian Chief in Virginia. This supply was preserved by placing it in a keg with lots of salt. These herring were then eaten throughout the year. When I was growing up, it became a special breakfast treat. Because of its high sodium content, I save this recipe for very special occasions. If you like salty foods, you must give this a try!

1	(16 ounce) package salt herring
1	cup corn meal
1/4	cup cooking oil
2	quarts water

Place water in large bowl. Rinse each piece of herring under water and place in bowl. Soak overnight.

The next morning, remove herring pieces from water and rinse. Place herring in corn meal and turn to cover evenly with corn meal. Over medium-high heat, add oil and cook herring, skin side down, for about 1 minute. Reduce heat to medium and continue to cook until the top of each fish dries out and the skin side is lightly golden brown, about 10 minutes. Turn fish and lower temperature. Continue cooking on other side until lightly golden brown and crispy, about another 10 to 15 minutes. Remove and place on a double-layer of paper towels to drain.

Serve warm or at room temperature. Serve with toast and prepared mustard or butter.

VARIATIONS: Salt mackerel may be substituted for the salt herring.

Cooking Tip

The secret to cooking salt herring is cooking slowly so that the bones are thoroughly cooked and edible. If the salt herring is cooked properly, you will not be aware that you are eating the bones; however, they are a good source of calcium.

EGGS BENEDICT   *Makes 2 servings*

What a delicious breakfast! A gourmet breakfast entree on most restaurant menus.

    2   English muffin halves, toasted
    2   slices Canadian bacon, microwaved for 20 seconds
    2   slices processed American cheese
    2   eggs, poached, fried, or microwaved (see note below)
    1   recipe **Easy Hollandaise Sauce** (page 41)

For each serving, starting at the bottom, assembling ingredients in the following order:

        toasted English muffin half
        Canadian bacon
        cheese

Place under broiler until cheese is melted. Top with egg. Pour half of hot hollandaise sauce over each serving.

Cooking Tip

Whether poached or fried, it is preferable to have the egg yolk slightly runny for Eggs Benedict.

NOTE

For a really quick-fix breakfast, a microwave egg cooker is currently available in many retail stores. It microwaves 2 "poached" eggs in about 80 seconds plus about 5 minutes sitting time.

GRILLED TOMATO SANDWICHES   *Makes 2 servings*

A delightfully delicious summer sandwich.

    2   very ripe tomato, thinly sliced
    4   ounces cheddar cheese, sliced
    1   medium onion, peeled, very thinly sliced
    3   tablespoons low-calorie mayonnaise
    4   slices bread, white, wheat or multigrain

Place each slice of bread of a cookie sheet. Broil on one side until bread is toasted. Turn bread over. Spread each slice of bread with mayonnaise. Then divide tomato slices evenly between the bread. Evenly place cheese over tomatoes. Place 1/4 of onions on each sandwich.

Broil until cheese melts and bread is slightly toasted. Let sit for 1 minute before serving.

GRITS CASSEROLE
Makes 8 servings

This casserole lets you prepare grits in advance and cook 1 hour before serving. Contributed by Fran Weeks and modified as follows.

- 2   cups hot cooked grits
- 2/3 cup skim milk
- 1/2 cup (1 stick) margarine
- 2   eggs
- 4   ounces (1 cup) grated cheddar cheese
- 1/2 cup crumbled crisp cooked bacon

Preheat oven to 375 degrees.

Add eggs to milk and then mix with grits. Put into greased casserole dish. Set casserole into pan of water or place pan of water on shelf below grits casserole. Bake 1 hour.

During last 10 minutes of cooking add 1 cup (4 ounces) grated cheddar cheese. Crumble 1/2 cup bacon on top after removing from oven.

Before serving, sprinkle with a little paprika. Serve with **Tom's Favorite Crab Cakes** (page 230).

VARIATION: Add 1/2 cup diced onion, sauteed.
             Add 1/4 cup diced green pepper, sauteed.

MAPLE SYRUP
Makes 2 cups

When you run out of pancake syrup at a critical moment, this is a good substitute for the commercial pancake syrup.

- 2   cups sugar
- 1   cup water
- 1/2   cup corn syrup
- 1/4   teaspoon vanilla flavoring
- 1/2-1 teaspoon maple flavoring
- 1   tablespoon corn starch
- 1   tablespoon water

Over medium-high heat. Cook sugar, water, corn syrup, vanilla and maple flavoring for about 10 minutes. Mix corn starch and water. Add corn starch mixture to syrup mixture, stirring constantly, until mixture thickens, about 1 minute.

Serve warm or at room temperature over waffles or pancakes.

ORANGE AND GOLDEN RAISIN SAUCE   *Makes 1 cup*

A deliciously different sauce to serve over tortillas, pancakes, waffles or crepes.

- 2   tablespoons sugar
- 1   tablespoon corn starch
- 1/8   teaspoon ground nutmeg
- 1   cup orange juice
- 1/4   cup golden raisins

In small saucepan, combine sugar, corn starch, nutmeg and raisins. Stir in the orange juice and cook over medium heat, stirring constantly, until mixture boils and thickens.

QUICK MUFFIN WAFFLES   *Makes 4 to 6 servings*

If you love fruit-flavored waffles, this is an easy way to get them without all the fuss.

- 4   packages (7 ounces each) flavored muffin mix: Honey Pecan, Apple Cinnamon or Blueberry
- 3   cups skim milk
-     nonstick cooking spray

Pour muffin mix into bowl, add milk and stir. Preheat waffle maker according to manufacturer's instructions. Pour 1 heaping cup of batter evenly over bottom surface of waffle maker. Immediately shut lid and cook waffles according to manufacturer's instructions, usually about 5 to 7 minutes. Remove waffles when lightly golden brown. When waffles are done, the top of the waffle maker should open easily.

Serve hot with a syrup of your choice, such as **Maple Syrup** (page 107) **Citrus Sauce Supreme** (page 104), or **Orange and Raisin Sauce** (page 108).

SLOW-COOKED CREAMY GRITS

4 to 6 servings

Properly cooked grits should have the consistency of mashed potatoes.

1   cup quick (not instant) grits
3   cups water
1/2   teaspoon salt
1   cup skim milk
1   tablespoon flour, if needed

In a 2-quart sauce pan, add grits, water and salt. Stir. Heat on low heat about 20 minutes, stirring every 5 minutes. When grits become too thick, start adding a little milk until grits are the consistency of pancake batter. As they continue to cook, they will thicken again, and may need more milk.

After a total cooking time of 30 minutes, grits will be done. If grits are too thick, add a little more milk, stir, and cook about 5 minutes until the consistency of mashed potatoes. If grits are too thin, sprinkle 1 tablespoon flour over grits, stir well, and cook an additional 5 minutes. Spoon into a bowl and serve hot.

Serve with margarine, which should be placed on top of hot grits. Grated cheddar cheese is delicious sprinkled on top of hot, buttered grits, as it will melt and can be mixed into the grits.

Cooking Tip

When grits are done, they can continue to cook for up to 1 hour or more, if you continue to add more milk or water to keep them the consistency of mashed potatoes. The longer they cook the creamier they become.

Store any left over grits in a square pan large enough for grits to make a layer about 3/4-inches thick. Chill grits overnight. To cook, cut grits in squares. Place about 2 tablespoons of oil in frying pan and heat to medium high. Fry grits squares until brown on both sides and warm inside.

TOASTED ROAST BEEF SANDWICHES   *Makes 1 sandwich*

    2   slices bread
    1   tablespoon Horseradish sauce
    2   ounces very thinly sliced **Perfect Roast** (page 66)
    1   tablespoon pickle relish, drained
    1   slice Swiss cheese

Spread both slices of bread with horseradish sauce. Place roast beef on sandwich. Sprinkle relish over beef. Add cheese. Cover with second slice of bread, plain side up.

Toaster Oven—Cooking Method

Place sandwich in toaster oven and toast until golden browned.

Oven—Cooking Method

Place sandwiches on cookie sheet. Broil until browned on one side. Carefully turn sandwiches over and return to broiler. Broil until second side is browned.

Serve with **Grandmother's Potato Salad** (page 183) or **Zesty Macaroni Salad** (page 180), and **Deviled Eggs** (page 9) and a dill pickle.

7
Cakes & Frostings

CAKES AND FROSTINGS

CAKES AND FROSTINGS

Is someone having a birthday? Do you need a dessert for a covered-dish supper? Bake a scrumptious cake! Because cakes can be made in advance and can serve many people, they are one of the most popular desserts for all occasions - from casual to elegant.

Although some cakes, such as pound cakes, have no frosting, most cakes are glazed or frosted. The 7-Minute Frosting is so light and creamy that it is worth the few extra minutes of cooking. This is a classic recipe that is delightful!

Accurately measuring ingredients for a cake is important, as each ingredient plays a special part in the finished cake. Flour gives body; sugar and shortening provide tenderness, flavor and richness; leavening agents, such as baking powder and baking soda, control the height and texture; eggs add flavor and increase volume; liquid dissolves the sugar and allows the starch and gluten in the flour to develop. All recipes in this section were tested with large eggs, skim milk or buttermilk, double-acting baking powder, unsifted flour, and margarine.

Since correct oven temperature and baking time are critical to perfect cake results, use an oven thermometer and follow instructions for oven temperature and baking time. All cake pans should be greased and then lightly floured or sprayed with Baker's Joy. Cool cakes before removing from baking pans.

CAKES

APPLE COFFEE CAKE

Makes 4 to 6 servings

- 1   teaspoon vanilla flavoring
- 1   teaspoon almond flavoring
- 1   egg
- 1/2   cup skim milk
- 1/4   cup orange juice, reserved
- 1/4   cup margarine or butter
- 1/2   cup sugar
- 2   cups biscuit baking mix
- 3   cups apples, Winesap, Golden Delicious or other firm-textured, tart apple, cored, peeled & sliced
  Cinnamon Topping (recipe follows)

Preheat oven to 375 degrees. Spray a 9-inch round spring form or bundt pan with no-stick cooking spray.

Mix vanilla flavoring, almond flavoring, egg, milk, and orange juice. Add sugar and baking mix and stir until well blended. Pour batter into prepared pan. Add apple slices and press gently into top of dough, overlapping apples as needed. Pour **Cinnamon Topping** over apples.

Bake for 40 minutes or until lightly golden brown and a toothpick inserted into cake comes out clean. Let cool slightly before removing from pan. To serve with a dollop of nondairy whipped topping.

Cinnamon Topping

- 1/4   cup sugar
- 1   teaspoon cinnamon
- 4   tablespoons (1/4 cup) margarine, melted

Mix the ingredients together.

BOARDING HOUSE PINEAPPLE CAKE (No Oil)   *Makes 12 servings*

So easy and moist.

2	eggs
1	(20 ounce) can crushed pineapple, undrained
2	cups flour
1	cup sugar
1	cup (packed) brown sugar
2	teaspoons baking soda
1	cup chopped pecans

Preheat oven to 350 degrees.

In large bowl, beat eggs until light and fluffy. Add pineapple, flour, sugar, brown sugar and baking soda. Mix by hand until well blended. Stir in pecans. Spread in ungreased 9x13x2-inch baking dish.

Bake for 40 to 50 minutes or until toothpick inserted in center comes out clean. Cut into 12 squares.

Serve warm. A scoop of vanilla ice cream on top is delicious.

CHOCOLATE CREME DE MENTHE CAKE   *Makes one 2-layer Cake*

A beautiful double-frosted cake.

1	two-layer white cake mix
7	tablespoons creme de menthe
1	(8 ounce) carton nondairy topping
1	can Hot Fudge Topping

Make cake mix according to package directions for a 2-layer cake, except substitute water with 1/4 cup creme de menthe. Bake cake according to package directions. Cool cake.

Stir fudge topping before using. Frost cake with fudge topping. Let set for 10 minutes. Add remaining 3 tablespoons creme de menthe to the nondairy topping and stir to mix well. Use this mixture to frost cake a second time. Refrigerate cake.

Preparation Tip

Creme de menthe is a vivid green liqueur with a minty flavor.

FAVORITE APPLESAUCE CAKE

One 8-inch loaf

My favorite applesauce cake!

1/2	cup margarine, butter or shortening
1	cup sugar
2	eggs, well beaten
1	cup chopped pecans
1 1/2	cups golden raisins
2	cups flour
1	teaspoon baking soda
1/2	teaspoon nutmeg
1	teaspoon cinnamon
1 1/4	cups unsweetened applesauce

Preheat oven to 325 degrees. Grease and flour one 8x4x2-inch loaf pan.

Cream margarine for about 1 minute. Gradually add sugar and continue to beat until fluffy. Add eggs, 1/3 of mixture each time, beating after each addition. Stir in pecans and raisins.

Mix flour, baking soda, nutmeg and cinnamon together. Alternately stir flour mixture and applesauce into the creamed egg mixture until well blended. Pour batter into prepared pan.

Bake for 1 to 1-1/2 hours, until a toothpick in center comes out clean.

VARIATION: Bake in 2 nine-inch layer cake pans. Frost with **No-Fail Boiled Frosting** (page 129).

Cooking Tip

If the top of the cake browns before the cake is done, place a piece of aluminum foil over the top to prevent further browning.

FRESH APPLE LOVER'S CAKE   *Makes 1 large bundt cake or one 15x11-inch sheet cake*

A very moist cake that is chock full of taste and healthy goodness. It provides abundant fiber and nutrition from the large quantity of fresh apples and raisins.

    6   cups chopped apples, without peeling
    3   cups sugar
    3   eggs
  3/4   cup cooking oil
    3   teaspoons vanilla
    3   cups flour
    3   teaspoons baking soda
    3   teaspoons cinnamon
  1 1/2 teaspoon salt
  1 1/2 cup chopped pecans
  1 1/2 cup golden raisins

Preheat oven to 350 degrees. Grease and flour cake pan.

Combine apples and sugar and stir to coat apples. Let stand while preparing batter.

Beat eggs lightly. Add oil and vanilla and beat to mix well. In large bowl, mix flour, baking soda, cinnamon and salt. Alternately add flour mixture and apples to the egg mixture, beating until well mixed. Stir in pecans and raisins. Batter will appear a little thin.

Bake for approximately 1 hour or until a toothpick inserted in center comes out clean.

VARIATION: Leave peeling on apples and chop apples in food processor.

FROSTED PINEAPPLE CAKE (No Oil)   *Makes one 13x9-inch cake*

    2   eggs, well beaten
    2   cups sugar
    1   teaspoon vanilla
    2   teaspoons baking soda
  1/8   teaspoon salt
    1   (20 ounce) can crushed pineapple in heavy syrup, do not drain
    2   cups flour
    1   cup chopped pecans
    1   recipe **Cream Cheese Frosting** (recipe follows)

Preheat oven to 350 degrees. Grease and flour a 13x9 -inch pan.

In large bowl, add eggs, sugar, vanilla, baking soda, salt, and pineapple and mix well. Add pecans to flour. Add flour mixture to egg mixture and stir until well-blended. Pour into prepared pan.

Bake for 35 to 40 minutes. Cool. Spread **Cream Cheese Frosting** over baked cake.

Cream Cheese Frosting

    1   (8 ounce) cream cheese, at room temperature
  1/2   cup (1 stick) margarine or butter
1 1/2   cups confectioners' powdered sugar
  1/4   cup chopped pecans

Mix cream cheese, butter and powdered sugar until well blended. Pour over cooled cake. Sprinkle with chopped pecans.

KENTUCKY WHISKEY CAKE   *Makes 1 bundt cake*

This recipe was given to me by Helen Killion, a good friend of my mother.

8	ounces golden raisins
1	pound (16 ounces) candied red cherries (cut in half)
1	pint (2 cups) bourbon
6	eggs, separated into yolks and whites
1	pound (2 cups) sugar
1 1/2	cups (3 sticks) margarine or butter
5	cups flour
1	pound (4 cups) chopped pecans
2	teaspoons nutmeg
1	teaspoons baking powder

Preheat oven to 300 degrees. Grease and flour a large bundt or tube cake pan.

In bourbon, soak cherries and raisins overnight. In medium-sized mixing bowl, beat egg whites until stiff. Set aside.

In small bowl, mix chopped nuts and 1/2 cup of flour. In large mixing bowl, cream sugar and butter until fluffy. Add yolks of eggs and beat well. Add soaked fruit and soaking liquid. Gradually add remaining flour to egg yolk mixture, beating until well mixed. Fold in beaten egg whites. Add floured pecans and stir to mix well. Pour into prepared bundt or tube pan.

Bake 3 to 4 hours (watch baking time).

Cool. Soak cheesecloth in bourbon. Stuff in center of cake. Place in air-tight container. Refrigerate or freeze. If frozen, thaw before slicing.

VARIATION: Bake in 3 prepared loaf pans for 2 hours at 250 degrees. Wrap loaves in bourbon-soaked cheesecloth and store in air-tight container.

MINIATURE CHERRY CHEESECAKES   *Makes 48 small pastries*

Because it's bite-sized and lightly flavored, this makes a perfect appetizer to serve at a cocktail party or ladies' tea.

Graham Cracker Crust

      2 1/2   cups graham cracker crumbs
      1/2   cup sugar
      2/3   cups margarine

Prepare crust according to directions on package of graham cracker crumbs. Pat a small amount into each muffin pan. It works well to use paper liners in very small mini-muffin pans.

Cream Cheese Filling

      2   (8-ounces each) packages cream cheese, at room temperature
      1/2   teaspoon vanilla
      1/2   teaspoon mace
      1   cup sugar
      3   eggs, slightly beaten

In electric mixer bowl, add cream cheese, vanilla, mace, sugar and eggs. Mix until well blended and creamy. Pour mini-muffin pans 2/3 full of filling over the prepared crust.

Preheat oven to 350 degrees. Bake about 20 to 25 minutes or until set and lightly browned on top.

Cool and then remove from muffin pans. Serve without topping or place a little cherry or blueberry pie filling on top of each cheesecake.

MIRACLE WHIP CHOCOLATE CAKE   *Makes one double-layer 8-inch cake*

When frosted with peppermint **Seven-Minute Frosting**, this chocolate cake was my favorite birthday cake. It's still outrageously delicious.

- 2   eggs, divided into whites and yolks
- 2   cups flour
- 1   cup sugar
- 2   teaspoon baking soda
- 1 1/2   teaspoon baking powder
- 4   tablespoons (1/4 cup) cocoa
- 1   cup Miracle Whip salad dressing
- 1   cup non-fat buttermilk
- 2   teaspoons vanilla flavoring

Preheat oven to 300 degrees. Spray two 8-inch cake pan with Baker's Joy cooking spray.

Place egg whites in small mixing bowl and mix on high until stiff but not dry. Mix flour, sugar, baking soda, baking powder and cocoa together. Add salad dressing, water, buttermilk, vanilla flavoring and egg yolks. Mix until well blended. Gently fold in egg whites. Bake as directed below

Layer Cake	two 8-inch layers	Bake 40 minutes
Cup Cakes	24 cup cakes	Bake 12-15 minutes
Bundt Cake	one large	Bake 1 to 1-1/2 hrs

Cake is done when toothpick inserted in center comes out clean. Let cake cool completely before frosting.

Frost with **Creamy Chocolate Frosting** (page 126) or **Seven-Minute Frosting** (page 130), either peppermint or chocolate flavor. Drizzle melted chocolate over frosting. Let frosted cake sit open to the air until dry to the touch and no longer sticky. Place in air-tight cake container.

* * * * * * * * *

How to Melt Chocolate

To melt 1 ounce (1 square) unsweetened baking chocolate, place in glass cup. Microwave on 30% power for 1 to 2 minutes. Microwave another minute if needed.

MOIST JELLY COFFEE CAKE   *Makes 36 servings*

A very, very moist cake which is suitable for breakfast, brunch or a snack.

Batter

1	egg	1/2	teaspoon cinnamon
1/2	cup sugar	1/8	teaspoon ground ginger
1/2	cup skim milk	2	teaspoon baking powder
3	tablespoons margarine, melted	1	cup flour
2	tablespoons packed brown sugar	1	cup chopped pecans
1/2	teaspoon salt	1/2	cup light raisins
	Topping (recipe follows)		

Preheat oven to 350 degrees. Grease 8-inch square pan.

In large bowl, using electric mixer, beat egg, sugar, milk, margarine, brown sugar, salt, cinnamon, ginger and baking powder until creamy. Add flour and mix well. By hand, stir in pecans and raisins. Pour batter into prepared pan. Spread **topping** over batter.

Bake about 25 to 30 minutes or until batter is set and knife inserted in center comes out clean. Remove from oven and evenly spread 1/2 to 3/4 cups strawberry preserves on top of cake to form a glaze, while cake is still hot.

Cool slightly, cut into 2-inch squares and serve. If desired, a little nondairy topping or whipped cream can be served on top of each square. Store 2 days, unrefrigerated, or several days in refrigerator.

VARIATIONS: Substitute orange marmalade for strawberry preserves.

Topping

1/4	cup brown sugar	2	tablespoons margarine,
1/2	teaspoon cinnamon		at room temperature
1	tablespoon flour	3	tablespoons sour cream
1	tablespoon skim milk		

Make topping by mixing brown sugar, cinnamon, and flour. Add margarine, sour cream and milk and blend well.

OLD AIKEN POUND CAKE   *Makes 1 bundt cake*

A much cherished recipe which originated in Aiken, South Carolina, many years ago.

- 1   cup (2 sticks) margarine or butter, at room temperature
- 1/2 cup shortening, at room temperature
- 3   cups sugar
- 5   large eggs
- 3   cups flour
- 1   teaspoon baking powder
- 1   teaspoon mace
- 1/8 teaspoon salt
- 1   teaspoon vanilla
- 1   cup skim milk

Cream margarine, shortening and sugar until light and fluffy. Add eggs, one at a time, beating well after each addition.

In a bowl, mix flour, baking powder, mace and salt. Add vanilla to milk. To shortening mixture, alternately add flour mixture and milk mixture.

Spray heavy-duty bundt or tube pan with Baker's Secret. Pour batter into cake pan.

Place cake pan in COLD OVEN. Be sure that the temperature of your oven in accurate. Turn oven to 350 degrees and bake 1 hour and 10 minutes. Turn on oven light. DO NOT OPEN oven door while baking. When cake is done, it should be golden brown on top and a toothpick inserted in center of cake should come out clean.

VARIATIONS: Substitute rum or brandy flavor for the vanilla flavoring.

OLD-FASHIONED BUTTERMILK LAYER CAKE *Makes 1 nine-inch double layer cake*

This deliciously light cake originated with my great-aunt Phil in Richmond, Virginia, more than 60 years ago.

1	cup + 2 tablespoons (1 1/4 sticks) margarine or butter
1 1/2	cups sugar
1	teaspoon baking soda
1	cup nonfat buttermilk
3	eggs
1	teaspoon cream of tartar
2	cups flour
1	teaspoon vanilla

Preheat oven to 350 degrees. Grease and flour two (2) nine-inch cake pans.

Place cream of tartar and flour in bowl and mix well. In another bowl, beat butter and sugar together until light and fluffy. In another bowl, mix soda and buttermilk until well blended. Add eggs, one at a time, to the sugar mixture and beat after each addition. Then add buttermilk mixture and mix well. Gradually add flour mixture and beat until batter is very creamy. Pour evenly into the prepared pans.

Bake 30 to 35 minutes until cake springs back when touched lightly in center.

VARIATION: Add 1 teaspoon brandy extract and 1 teaspoon dried orange peel.

SOUR CREAM CHEESE CAKE   *Makes one large cheesecake*

Created by Kitty Windham, Aiken, SC, this scrumptious cheesecake is sinfully delicious. A small serving is enough. One bite will make you appreciate its creamy texture and delightful flavor.

Crust

    2 1/2   cups graham cracker crumbs
      1/4   cup sugar
      1/2   cup margarine, at room temperature

In medium bowl, with a fork, mix graham cracker crumbs with sugar and softened margarine until well combined. Press mixture on bottom and sides of large spring form pan, building up sides to form a rim around. Refrigerate until needed.

Filling

        5   packages (8 ounces each) cream cheese, room temperature
    1 3/4   cups sugar
        3   tablespoons flour
      1/4   teaspoon salt
      1/4   teaspoon grated lemon peel
        5   eggs (about 1 cup)
        2   egg yolks
      1/4   cup heavy cream
      1/2   cup sour cream

Preheat oven to 500 degrees. In large bowl of electric mixer, combine cream cheese, salt, sugar, flour, lemon peel and vanilla. Beat on high speed just until blended. Beat in eggs and egg yolks, one at a time. Add cream, beating just until well combined. Pour into prepared crust.

Bake 10 minutes at 500 degrees. Reduce temperature to 250 degrees and bake 1 hour longer. Top with sour cream and let cool in pan on wire rack. Cut and serve. Refrigerate any leftovers.

STRAWBERRY CAKE DELIGHT   *Makes 1 two-layer cake*

This cake is beautiful and delicious, yet easy to make! A perfect Valentine's Day dessert.

    1   box strawberry cake mix
    1   (12 to 16 ounce) strawberry jam
    1   can prepared sour cream frosting
    6   fresh strawberries, washed, drained, and sliced
        powdered sugar

Bake cake as directed in 8-inch round pans. Cool cake. Melt jam in microwave until spreading consistency, about 2 minutes on 40% power. Spread half of jam on first layer. Top with second cake layer. Spread frosting on all sides of cake. Spread remaining jam on top of cake.

Place sliced strawberries on top cake. Sprinkle with sifted powdered sugar. Slice and serve.

STREUSEL COFFEE CAKE   *Makes 24 servings*

Serve this for dessert or breakfast.

      1   package yellow cake mix
    1/4   cup (1/2 stick) chilled margarine or butter
      1   cup packed brown sugar
      1   cup chopped pecans
  1 1/2   cups sour cream

Preheat oven to 350 degrees. Grease and then flour a 12x8x2-inch baking pan.

Topping

Reserve 2/3 cups of dry cake mix and place in large bowl. Place remainder in medium bowl. Cut in butter. Mix in brown sugar and nuts.

Batter

Using a large bowl and electric mixer, make a topping by beating 3 eggs and then adding sour cream, blending well. Add reserved dry cake mix and beat about 5 minutes until very creamy.

Pour half of batter into prepared pan. Sprinkle with half of the topping mix. Pour remaining half of batter over topping. Sprinkle remaining half of topping over second layer of batter.

Bake for 40 to 45 minutes until cake is done and golden brown on top. When a toothpick inserted in center of cake comes out clean, the cake is done.

Cut into 24 2-inch square servings. It is best served warm, but may be served at room temperature.

FROSTINGS

BROWN BUTTER FROSTING

Makes 1 cup

A delicious frosting that has long been forgotten. Give it a try and enjoy a new taste treat!

- 1/4   cup (1/2 stick) margarine or butter
- 2   cups confectioners' powdered sugar
- 2   tablespoons skim milk
- 1 1/2   teaspoon vanilla
- 1-2   tablespoons water

Over medium-high heat, melt margarine until *golden brown*. Remove from heat. Blend in powdered sugar. Add milk and vanilla and mix until well blended. Add 1 tablespoon water and mix again. If mixture is too stiff to spread, add additional tablespoon of water.

Spread frosting over baked cake layers.

CREAMY CHOCOLATE FROSTING

Makes about 1 1/2 cups

- 4   (1 ounce each) squares unsweetened baking chocolate
- 1/4   cup hot water
- 4   cups confectioners' powdered sugar
- 1/2   cup (1 stick) margarine or butter
- 1   egg
- 1 1/2   teaspoons vanilla

In glass measuring cup or bowl, place water and chocolate squares. Microwave on Defrost (30% power) for 6 to 8 minutes until chocolate is melted.

With electric mixer, blend sugar and butter. Pour in chocolate and water mixture, and beat 1 minute. Add egg and vanilla and beat another 2 to 3 minutes until well blended and of spreading consistency. Frosts tops and sides of two 9-inch layers.

If refrigerated, this will keep for several weeks in an air-tight container.

DECORATOR'S CAKE FROSTING

I received this recipe at a cake decorating class. It is excellent for frosting wedding and birthday cakes. It is also a perfect consistency to use with a pastry tube for making cake decorations.

- 1 1/2 cups shortening
- 1/2 cup hot water
- 2 boxes confectioners' powdered sugar
- 1/8 teaspoon salt
- 1 teaspoon butter flavoring
- 2 teaspoon **colorless** vanilla flavoring

Using electric mixer, cream shortening until very soft. Add salt, a little powdered sugar and flavorings. Then alternately add water and powdered sugar, beating on medium speed until frosting is smooth after each addition. (Do Not mix on a high speed as it will cause air bubbles in frosting).

This frosting can be used to frost a cake, with enough to use in a pastry bag to make decorations for the cake.

Decorations can be made and frozen on waxed paper placed on a cookie sheet and covered with plastic wrap. These will keep several weeks. To use: thaw decorations and use on frosted cake. Do not put brightly colored decorations on cake **before** freezing cake as color will bleed into frosting when thawed.

VARIATIONS: Chocolate: Add 3 tablespoons cocoa to powdered sugar mixture.

Lemon: Omit butter and vanilla flavorings and add 3 teaspoons lemon flavoring.

Wedding Cake Frosting

Five recipes of frosting will ice and decorate a wedding cake as follows: one 6-inch layer (top tier), one 14-inch layer, and one 18-inch layer, making three tiers, suitable for a small wedding. Will serve 50 to 60 people.

MOCHA FROSTING   *Makes about 1 cup*

This is a very creamy "chocoffee" frosting that sets on top, yet remains soft inside. It makes a great frosting for **Miracle Whip Chocolate Cake** (page 120).

1/4	cup hot water
2	tablespoons instant coffee
6	ounces semi-sweet chocolate chips
1/8	teaspoon salt
1/2	teaspoon vanilla
2	cups confectioners' powdered sugar

In microwave, heat water, coffee and chocolate chips on 30% power, stirring frequently, for 3 minutes or until chocolate is melted. Microwave powers vary, so time may need adjusting.

Add salt and vanilla and stir. Gradually add sugar and stir until well blended and frosting is stiff.

Spread on cake layers. After cake is frosted, let it sit open to the air until a thin nonsticky layer forms. Then place in cake box or air-tight container.

If used within 5 days, this frosting does not require refrigeration.

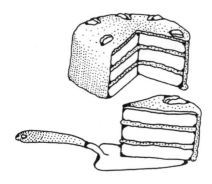

NO-FAIL BOILED FROSTING   *Makes about 1 to 1 1/2 cups*

This frosting is very creamy, neither fluffy nor stiff, yet it forms a thin nonsticky coating. It can be flavored with lemon, orange, peppermint or other flavoring.

       1   cup sugar
     1/2   tablespoon light corn syrup
     1/8   teaspoon salt
       6   tablespoons water
       1   egg white, stiffly beaten
       1   teaspoon vanilla
     1/2   cup margarine or butter
     1/2   package confectioners' powdered sugar

In small bowl, beat 1 egg white until stiff but not dry. In large saucepan, cook sugar, syrup, salt and water over low heat, stirring until sugar dissolves. Cover 2 to 3 minutes to dissolve sugar crystals on sides of pan. Uncover.

Continue to cook until soft-ball stage (236 degrees on candy thermometer) is reached. Remove from heat. Gradually add hot syrup to beaten egg whites, beating constantly with electric mixer. Add vanilla and beat until frosting is of spreading consistency.

Cream butter and powdered sugar, adding a little water if needed, until frosting is stiff but creamy. Add this mixture to the boiled mixture and cream with mixer.

This is enough frosting for a 2-layer cake.

VARIATIONS: Lemon or Orange: substitute orange or lemon juice for the water and vanilla. Coloring may be added according to the flavoring used.

Instant coffee (about 2 teaspoons) may be added to frosting after cooking while it is still hot.

Shredded coconut can be patted on top of icing before frosting sets.

SEVEN-MINUTE FROSTING   *Frosting for top and side of 9-inch two-layer cake*

This frosting is light, airy, and well worth the little extra time to whip it to perfection. It literally melts in your mouth.

    2   unbeaten egg whites
1 1/2   cups sugar
  1/4   teaspoon cream of tartar
  1/3   cup water
    1   teaspoon vanilla

In top of double boiler, place egg whites, sugar, cream of tartar, and water. Beat with electric mixer for 1 minute to blend. Place over boiling water and cook, beating constantly, until mixture forms stiff peaks. This will be approximately 7-minutes, as the name suggests (Do Not Overcook). Remove from boiling water. Add vanilla, and continue to beat until spreading consistency (approximately 2 minutes).

Spread frosting on layers. When cake is completely frosted, let it stand uncovered until a thin, nonsticky crust forms on top. Then cover cake or place on covered cake plate. Melt 1 ounce unsweetened chocolate (see page 120). With spoon drizzle chocolate in swirls onto top of cake and let drip down side like "icicles".

THIS FROSTING SHOULD NOT BE MADE ON A VERY HUMID OR RAINY DAY, AS IT WILL NOT WHIP CORRECTLY!

VARIATIONS: **Chocolate**: Add 1 tablespoon cocoa to mixture after removing from heat.

Brown Sugar: Substitute brown sugar for regular sugar. Also, if desired, substitute 1/2 teaspoon maple flavoring for vanilla.

Peppermint Stick: Add vanilla and a few drops of food coloring to make pink frosting. Beat until spreading consistency - about 2 minutes. After cake if frosted, sprinkle top and sides of frosted cake with crushed peppermint-stick candy.

8

Chicken/ Poultry

CHICKEN AND POULTRY

CHICKEN AND POULTRY

Chicken is one of the least expensive, yet most versatile, foods available. It can be baked, roasted, grilled, stewed, braised, fried or cooked in a crockpot or microwave. The different ways to cook and serve chicken are limited only by your time and imagination.

Because chicken has fewer calories per ounce than beef or pork, it is popular with the calorie-conscious. Most of the fat of a chicken is located in and just under the skin; therefore, if you are cutting down on calories and fat, remove the skin and all visible fat from the chicken before cooking or eating it.

Although chicken is usually a very tender and juicy meat, occasionally it is tough and stringy, regardless of how it is cooked. Some brands are more tender than others; therefore, find a tender brand and rely upon it for preparing these recipes. In some recipes, a good canned chicken, such as Valley Fresh, can be substituted for stewed frying chicken.

If cooked chicken is to be removed from the bone, first remove skin and then remove chicken from bones. Next, cut chicken into bite-sized pieces or leave in large pieces and place them in a colander. To lower calories and fat, rinse under warm water for thirty seconds. Drain well.

By using the recipes in this section, you can serve chicken often and delight your family and friends with a variety of tasty, inexpensive meals.

BRUNSWICK STEW

Makes 6 to 8 servings

A hearty meal for a cold winter day.

3	pounds meaty chicken pieces: thighs, breasts, drumstick OR 24 ounces canned chunk chicken
1	pound lean pork, cubed
1	tablespoon chicken bouillon
1	cup chopped onion
1/2	cup chopped celery
10	okra pods, thinly sliced
1	tablespoon dried, chopped chives
2-4	cups water (used for cooking chicken)
1	(16 ounce) can tomatoes, cut into pieces
2	medium potatoes, peeled and diced
1	(10 ounce) package frozen lima beans or butter beans
1	(17 ounce) can whole kernel corn
1	tablespoon worcestershire sauce

In large dutch oven, cook chicken and pork with bouillon, onion, celery, okra and chives in the water until meat is tender. Remove skin and bones from chicken. Cut into bite-size pieces. Place in colander and rinse with warm water to remove any excess fat.

Pour liquid from dutch oven and remove fat by pouring into a liquid/fat separating pitcher. Discard any fat. Return broth to dutch oven. Add tomatoes, potatoes, lima beans, corn and worcestershire sauce. Cook over medium-low heat for about 1 hour until flavors are well blended.

Serve hot with **Sour Cream Corn Bread** (page 91) and a salad.

CHEESY CHICKEN SANDWICHES

Makes 3 to 6 servings

On muffins, this makes a quick lunch. Or cut into wedges and serve as an appetizer.

- 4 ounces (1 cup) grated cheddar cheese
- 1 (6 ounce) can chunk chicken, drained
- 1 (4 ounce) can green chili peppers, drained
- 1 (3 ounce) package cream cheese, at room temperature
- 6 English muffin halves

Preheat oven to 350 degrees.

Mix cheese, chicken, chili peppers and cream cheese until well blended. Place about 2 tablespoons of mixture on each muffin half. Place each muffin half on a cookie sheet.

Bake until cheese melts, about 15 minutes.

Place each sandwich on a plate and cut in half. Serve with 1 dill pickle wedge and potato chips.

CHICKEN AND DRESSING

Makes 5 to 6 servings

- 8 chicken breast halves, cooked, deboned, skinned, cut in large pieces
- 1/2 cup (1 stick) margarine, melted
- 1 (8 ounce) package of cornbread stuffing mix
- 1 can cream of chicken soup
- 1 can cream of celery soup or cream of mushroom soup
- 2 cups water
- 2 teaspoons chicken bouillon granules

Preheat oven to 350 degrees. Grease 9x12x2-inch casserole dish.

Put half of dry stuffing mix into casserole. Place pieces of chicken on top. In frying pan, melt margarine and toss with remaining half of stuffing. Place this mixture on top of chicken.

Heat soups, water and bouillon until well blended. Pour soup mixture on top of stuffing.

Bake about 30 minutes or until hot and stuffing is slightly browned on top.

Serve hot with green beans and **Cranberry Orange Salad** (page 211).

VARIATION: Use 16 ounces of stuffing - 8 ounces dry in casserole and 8 ounces mixed with the sauteed vegetables. Saute 1 cup diced celery and 1 cup chopped onion in margarine until tender. Mix with second half (8 ounces) of stuffing and continue with directions above.

CHICKEN AND DUMPLINGS

Makes 4 servings

A traditional Southern dish that's an all-time favorite!

3	boneless, skinless chicken breasts	1/4	teaspoon Italian seasoning
	OR 3 cups cooked chicken	1/2	teaspoon Morton's Nature's Seasoning
3	cups water	1	teaspoon Mrs. Dash seasoning
2	medium potatoes, peeled,	2 1/2	cups chicken broth or water
	cut into chunks	2	teaspoons chicken bouillon granules
1	medium onion, diced	1	(16 ounce) can peas and carrots
2	stalks celery, diced		**Fluffy Dumplings** (recipe follows)
1/4	teaspoon basil		

In large pot, add water and chicken breasts and gently boil for about 30 minutes or until tender. Remove chicken to cool. Strain broth and reserve 2-1/2 cups. Cut chicken into bite-sized pieces. Return to pot.

Add 2-1/2 cups of chicken broth, potatoes, onion, celery, basil, Italian seasoning, Nature's Seasoning, and chicken bouillon. Simmer for about 20 minutes. Add peas and carrots. Simmer about 10 minutes longer.

Heat chicken mixture until it bubbles; immediately add large spoonsful of **Fluffy Dumpling** mixture on top. Immediately cover with lid and cook over low heat for 15 minutes. **DO NOT REMOVE LID from pot during this 15-minute cooking time.**

When cooking is complete, gently remove lid. Serve hot with **Leaf Lettuce and Feta Cheese** or **Pickled Beet Salad** (page 217).

Fluffy Dumplings

The dumplings are as light and fluffy as a cloud! However, if **anyone** peeks during the cooking time, the dumplings will be heavy and tough (see Cooking Tip below).

1	cups biscuit baking mix
1/3	water or skim milk
1	teaspoon fresh minced parsley

In small bowl, add biscuit baking mix. Add water and mix well.

Cooking Tip
PLACE A "NO-PEEK" REMINDER ON TOP OF THE POT!

CHICKEN CREPES SUPREME   *Makes 4 servings*

Although this recipe requires a little extra preparation time, you can prepare it in advance. Your efforts will be rewarded with compliments from guests!

6	deboned, skinned, chicken breasts, cut into 1/2-inch cubes (about 3 to 4 cups of cooked meat)
3	tablespoons margarine or butter
1	medium (1/2 cup) finely diced onion
2	stalks (1/2 cup) diced celery
1/3	cup finely diced green pepper
1/2	teaspoon fresh minced garlic
1/3	cup semi-dry white wine or cooking sherry
1/8	teaspoon dill weed
1/8	teaspoon ground nutmeg
1	teaspoon Mrs. Dash or seasoned salt
3	tablespoons flour
1/2	cup sour cream
1/2-1	cup skim milk
	Chicken Dinner Crepes (page 137)
1/2	cup sour cream, for topping
1/2	cup mozzarella cheese
1/2	cup sliced almonds, toasted

Preheat oven to 325 degrees.

In margarine, saute chicken, onion, celery, green pepper, and garlic. Add 1/3 cup wine, dill weed, nutmeg, and Mrs. Dash. Continue cooking until chicken is tender, about 5 minutes.

Sprinkle flour over chicken mixture, stirring to mix well. Gradually add milk, stirring constantly until the thickness of a medium white sauce. Remove from heat and stir in sour cream.

Place scant 1/2 cup filling along center of crepe. Fold 1 edge over filling and roll up in jelly-roll fashion. Place in a 9x12-inch casserole. Continue with each of the remaining crepes, making about 8 filled crepes. Spread remaining 1/2 cup sour cream over top of crepes and sprinkle with paprika. Sprinkle with 1/2 cup mozzarella cheese; scatter almonds on top.

Cover and bake 20 to 30 minutes or until hot. Uncover and bake 5 additional minutes.

CHICKEN DINNER CREPES
Makes 16 small crepes or 8 large crepes

A tender, delicate pancake-like crepe that can be filled with any desired filling (see pages 136 or 170).

1	cup flour
1/8	teaspoon salt
3	eggs
1 1/2	cups skim milk
2	tablespoons margarine or butter, melted, or cooking oil

Mix flour and salt. Add eggs, one at a time, beating thoroughly with each addition. Gradually add milk, mixing until well blended. Then add melted margarine and stir until smooth. Let batter stand, at room temperature, for 1 hour before cooking crepes. See Cooking Tip below.

Place prepared filling on one end of cooked crepe and then roll up, jelly-roll fashion, and place in lightly greased baking dish.

Cooking Tip

Pour 1/8 cup (2 tablespoons) crepe batter into hot frying pan that has 1 teaspoon oil, turning pan immediately so that batter spreads and covers as much of the bottom of the pan as possible. This should make a paper-thin layer. Cook until lightly browned on one side and top appears almost dry. Loosen edges while you are browning crepe, so that you can turn it immediately when lightly browned, as these cook quickly. Turn crepe and brown other side, cooking about 20 seconds. Cool crepes. Stack crepes, separating with a layer of waxed paper between each crepe. To keep crepes from drying out, cover with soft cloth.

Crepes, which are separated with waxed paper, may be placed in a sealable plastic bag and frozen for several weeks. Thaw before filling.

CHICKEN PIE *Makes 4 to 6 servings*

A chicken dish that is tasty and makes its own crust on top. An easy, yet delicious, way to have a variation of chicken pot pie.

     6   chicken breasts, deboned, skinned (5 to 6 cups) OR
         2 (12-1/2 ounces each) cans chunk white chicken, undrained
1 3/4   cups chicken broth
     1   teaspoon chicken bouillon granules
     1   can cream of celery soup or cream of chicken/mushroom soup
   1/2   cup (1 stick) margarine or butter, melted
     1   cup self-rising flour
   3/4   cups skim milk
     1   teaspoon parsley
         salt and pepper to taste

Preheat oven to 350 degrees. Lightly grease 9x13x2-inch casserole dish.

Place chicken in single layer in casserole dish. Sprinkle bouillon over casserole. Pour 1-1/2 cups broth over chicken. Mix 1/4 cup broth with soup. Spread soup mixture over chicken and broth. Mix melted margarine, flour, milk and parsley together and spread evenly over soup.

Bake for 40 to 50 minutes or until golden brown crust forms. Serve hot.

VARIATIONS: Add 1 (16 ounce) can peas and carrots to casserole before adding chicken. Continue directions.

If you like a thicker crust, use 3/4 cups (1 1/2 sticks) margarine, 1 1/2 cups self-rising flour and 1 cup plus 2 tablespoons skim milk.

If using canned chicken, do not drain. Use only 1 1/4 cups additional broth. Pour only 1 cup broth over chicken and mix remaining 1/4 cup broth with soup.

CHICKEN SPAGHETTI
Makes 5 to 6 servings

This is a delectable spaghetti but very different from the conventional spaghetti with meat sauce. From Hallie Townsend.

1	teaspoon chicken bouillon
1	(2 to 3 pound) frying chicken, cooked, skinned, deboned (about 4 cups cooked chicken) chicken stock reserved from cooking chicken above, strained
6	ounces vermicelli (thin spaghetti), drained but not rinsed
3	tablespoons light olive oil
1	medium onion (3/4 cups diced)
3-4	stalks celery (3/4 cup diced)
1/4	cup chopped green pepper
1	(16 ounce) can tomatoes, undrained
1	(2 ounce) jar sliced mushrooms, drained
1	(15-3/4 ounce) can cream of mushroom soup
1	teaspoon basil
1/2	teaspoon oregano
1/2	teaspoon Italian seasoning
1	teaspoon Morton's Nature's Seasoning
1/4	pound (1 cup) grated cheddar cheese
1	cup canned green peas, drained

Cook vermicelli according to package directions, using reserved chicken stock and adding water for the remaining liquid required. Drain, but do not rinse, vermicelli. Place in a large bowl and add bouillon. Stir to mix well.

In large frying pan, add oil, onion, celery and green pepper. Saute over medium heat until vegetables are tender. Add tomatoes, mushrooms, soup, basil, oregano, Italian seasoning, and Nature Seasoning. Mix and simmer about 30 minutes.

While tomato mixture is cooking, cut cooked chicken into large bite-size pieces. In large bowl, mix vermicelli, chicken, soup mixture and cheese. Then add green peas and gently stir to mix well.

Serve immediately while hot. **Heavenly Fruit Salad** (page 212) and toasted garlic bread make a perfect flavor combination.

VARIATIONS: This mixture can be placed in greased 9x12x2-inch casserole, covered and baked in a 325 degree oven for 20 minutes. Lower temperature and keep dinner warm while enjoying cocktails.

CHINESE SWEET AND SOUR CHICKEN DINNER   *Makes 4 servings*

Reminiscent of China Town in San Francisco, California, this is an especially delicious version of a classic Chinese dish.

4-5	deboned, skinless chicken breasts, uncooked
1/4	cup flour
1/4	teaspoon salt
1/8	teaspoon pepper
	oil for frying
2 1/2-3	cups cooked white rice
	Chinese Red Sweet and Sour Sauce (page 40)

Cut each chicken breast into bite-sized pieces. Put flour, salt and pepper into a plastic bag. Add chicken, a few pieces at a time, and shake to coat. Repeat with remaining chicken. Fry chicken nuggets in hot oil until they float to the top of the oil and are lightly golden brown. Remove from hot oil and drain on paper towels (see inset below).

Add chicken to sweet and sour sauce and serve in bowl. Serve rice in bowl. On each plate, spoon chicken and sauce over rice. Complete the meal with a tossed green salad and **Blue Cheese Supreme** dressing (page 219).

* * * * * * * * * *

How to Drain Fried Foods

When draining food on paper towels, place a brown paper bag under the paper towels. This will help absorb more grease and will make clean-up easier. This technique works for any meat that needs to be drained, especially bacon or fried foods.

CORDON BLUE   *Makes 4 to 6 servings*

Because this is covered and cooked at 225 degrees, the chicken is fork-tender. It can be prepared in the morning, refrigerated, and then baked later in the day.

6   boneless chicken breasts, skin removed
3   rectangular slices Swiss cheese, cut in half
6   slices thinly sliced lean ham or Canadian bacon
1   envelope Lipton Cup-A-Soup mix, cream of chicken flavor
1   can cream of mushroom soup
1/2 cup skim milk
1/2 cup sour cream
1   tablespoon dried minced onion or 1/4 cup fresh minced onion

Preheat oven to 225 degrees.

Place each chicken breast between 2 sheets of plastic wrap. Pound each chicken breast with meat mallet or other heavy object to flatten and tenderize chicken.

On each chicken breast, place 1/2 slice of cheese and 1 slice of ham. Roll up each chicken breast, jelly-roll fashion, and secure end with a toothpick. Mix soups, sour cream and milk. Pour over chicken breasts.

Cover and bake 2 hours. Uncover and bake 30 minutes longer until sauce thickens.

Serve hot with rice or noodles, steamed broccoli and a salad.

VARIATION: After placing chicken in casserole dish, sprinkle 1 1/2 cups instant rice around chicken. Add 1 cup of water to casserole. Cover with soup mixture and continue with above instructions.

To reduce fat and calories, omit cheese and ham, but still roll-up chicken. Using a 3-ounce jar of dried smoked beef, place a layer of beef in bottom of casserole dish before adding chicken.

Cooking Tip

While using the oven for 2 hours to bake the chicken, why not bake a batch of **Crunchy Croutons** (page 221). Since they both require a long cooking time, this will conserve energy and your time.

CRUNCHY CHICKEN CASSEROLE   *Makes 5 to 6 servings*

When you're really in a hurry and want a delicious meal, try this casserole. It can be prepared in advance and placed into the oven 30 minutes before mealtime. The original recipe was shared by Dot Edmunds.

2-3	cups cooked chicken, chopped
1/2	cup chopped celery
1/2	cup low-calorie mayonnaise
1/2	cup sour cream
1	egg
1	can water chestnuts, drained and diced
2	cups **cooked** rice
2	tablespoons chopped onion
1	can cream of chicken soup, undiluted
1/2	teaspoon salt
1/2	teaspoon pepper

Preheat oven to 350 degrees. Lightly grease 2-quart casserole.

Mix all ingredients together and put in casserole. Bake in preheated oven for 25 to 30 minutes, until bubbly and hot. Then add topping (below) and bake another 5 to 10 minutes.

Topping

Sprinkle with 1 cup crushed potato chips or crushed corn flakes.

VARIATIONS: Add 1/2 tsp. cayenne pepper OR a small green pepper, diced (1/2 cup) OR 1 (16 ounce) can peas and carrots OR top with sliced almonds, lightly toasted OR 1 (4 ounce) jar sliced mushrooms, drained.

Heavenly Chicken on Rice

Make the following modifications to the **Crunchy Chicken Casserole** recipe above:

(1) Use 5 to 8 large raw, boneless, skinless chicken breasts in place of cooked chicken.

(2) Omit sour cream and cooked rice.

(3) Mix remaining ingredients together. Add 2 teaspoons basil, 2 teaspoons Italian seasoning, 1/2 teaspoon garlic salt, 1 1/2 cups raw white rice, and 3/4 cup water. Mix well.

(4) Put mixed ingredients in casserole. Place chicken breasts on top. Bake at 250 degrees for 30 minutes. Cover casserole and bake for an additional 45 minutes to 1 hour until rice is done.

CRUSTY CHICKEN DIVAN *Makes 5 to 6 servings*

 2 (10 ounces each) packages of frozen broccoli spears
 7-8 chicken breast halves, uncooked, skinned and deboned OR
   2(12 1/2 ounce) cans boneless white chicken meat (3 cups)
 1 can cream of chicken soup
 1/2-1 cup low-calorie mayonnaise
 1/2 cup chicken broth (from cooking chicken breasts)
 1 (2 ounce) jar diced pimento
 2 teaspoons Morton's Nature's Seasoning or seasoned salt
 2 teaspoons Italian seasoning
 2 teaspoons basil
 2 stalks (1/2 cup diced) celery
 1 very large onion, diced (1 cup)
 4 ounces (1 cup) grated cheddar cheese
 1 teaspoon fresh minced garlic
 1 1/2 cups stuffing mix

Preheat oven to 325 degrees. Grease 9x12x2-inch casserole dish.

Thaw broccoli and drain well. Arrange in the bottom of prepared casserole dish.

Place small colander inside of a saucepan. Add 1 cup of water. Place chicken breast in colander and cover saucepan. Steam about 15 minutes until chicken in done. Remove chicken breasts and drain. Measure 1/2 cup of water from saucepan and use as chicken broth. Cut chicken into large bite-sized pieces. Place cooked chicken on top of broccoli.

Mix soup, mayonnaise, 1/2 cup broth, pimentos, Nature's Seasoning, Italian seasoning, basil, celery, garlic and onion. Pour mixture over chicken breasts. Sprinkle cheese on top and then sprinkle stuffing mix on top of cheese.

Cover and bake about 25 minutes or until hot. Uncover and cook about 15 minutes longer or until stuffing is browned on top.

Remove from oven and serve hot with a salad and **Baked Curried Fruit** (page 249) for a well-balanced, nutritious meal.

EASY CROCKPOT CHICKEN DINNER   *Makes 4 to 6 servings*

  1   (3 to 3 1/2 pound) whole frying chicken
  1   envelope dry onion/mushroom soup mix, uncooked
  1   teaspoon basil
  1   cup water or dry white wine
  4   large carrots, peeled and cut into 3-inch pieces
  6   medium whole potatoes, peeled

In crockpot, place whole chicken. Pour dry soup mix over chicken and add basil and water or wine. Add carrots and potatoes. Cover and cook on high for about 4 to 6 hours or on low for 8 to 10 hours, until chicken is easily removed from bones.

Remove chicken from crockpot. Remove bones from chicken and place pieces of meat on a large platter. Add potatoes and carrots to platter.

Serve with **Leaf Lettuce with Feta Cheese Salad** (page 213), **Whole Wheat Bread** (page 99) and **Chicken Gravy** (recipe follows).

Chicken Gravy

For each cup of liquid left in crockpot after removing chicken and vegetables, mix:

  1 1/2   teaspoons corn starch and
  1   tablespoon water

Pour corn starch mixture into hot liquid in crockpot and continue to cook, stirring constantly, until mixture thickens. Pour into gravy pitcher and serve.

FLUFFY CHICKEN CASSEROLE
Makes 4 to 6 servings

Since this can be prepared a day or two in advance, your last minute preparations will be minimal when company's coming for dinner. Very light!

1	(3 pound) frying chicken, boiled, skinned and deboned OR
	2 (12 1/2 ounce) cans chunk chicken, drained and broth reserved
1	(8 ounce) package herb stuffing mix
1 1/2	cups chopped green onion and green onion tops, sauteed
2	stalks (1/2 cup chopped) celery, sauteed
1	teaspoon Morton's Nature's seasoning
1/2	cup Miracle Whip salad dressing
1 1/2	cups chicken broth (reserved from cooking chicken)
2	eggs
1 1/2	cups skim milk
1/4	teaspoon pepper
1	can cream of mushroom soup

Preheat oven to 325 degrees. Lightly grease large 9x13x2-inch casserole.

Cook chicken and drain, reserving cooking liquid. Strain cooking liquid and remove any fat. Use 1 1/2 cups for chicken broth. Cut chicken into large bite-sized pieces.

Sprinkle half of the stuffing mix in the bottom of casserole. Mix onions, celery, Nature's seasoning, Miracle Whip and chicken together. Evenly spread the chicken mixture on top of stuffing. Pour chicken broth over chicken mixture. Mix eggs, milk, pepper and soup together. Pour this mixture over the chicken mixture.

If desired, refrigerate up to 24 hours. Remove from refrigerator about 1 1/2 hours before cooking. Just before baking, sprinkle other half of stuffing mix on top.

Bake for 50 minutes or until bubbly hot and slightly browned on top.

VARIATIONS: Add 1 (16 ounce) can peas and carrots over first layer of stuffing mix.

Add 1 can sliced water chestnuts, chopped, to chicken mixture.

GARDEN BASKET DINNER   *One serving per basket*

A complete meal in individual baskets. Ingredients are listed for one person. Increase ingredients for any number of people. Select cooking temperature that suits your life-style.

Quantity Per Person

1-2	chicken breasts, boneless or bone-in	1	teaspoon water
2-3	tablespoons instant rice, uncooked	1-2	teaspoons worcestershire sauce
1/2	cup canned green beans, drained	3/4	teaspoon salt
1	tomato, peeled and cut into wedges	1/8	teaspoon pepper
1	small onion, whole or diced	1/8	teaspoon paprika
1	potato, peeled and diced	1	tablespoon margarine or butter substitute
1	small green pepper, cut into strips	1/8	teaspoon basil
6	whole canned mushrooms, drained	1/8	teaspoon oregano

OPTIONAL:

- 1/4 cup sliced zucchini
- 1/8 teaspoon Texas Pete hot sauce
- 1   tablespoon parmesan cheese

Place all ingredients, except parmesan cheese, in center of aluminum foil. Fold aluminum, drug-store fashion, to completely seal foil packets. Place foil baskets, not touching, in single layer on cookie sheet.

Variable Baking Chart

250 degrees	3 to 4 hours
325 degrees	1 hour 45 minutes
350 degrees	1 to 1 1/2 hour
450 degrees	45 minutes to 1 hour

Serve by either placing aluminum baskets on plate or remove ingredients from foil and place on individual plates. Sprinkle each basket with parmesan cheese.

A salad and **Homemade French Bread** (page 95) complete the meal.

STORAGE: Uncooked foil-wrapped chicken baskets can be frozen. On serving day, place frozen chicken package in shallow baking dish. Add 20 to 30 minutes to baking times listed above.

GRILLED BARBECUED CHICKEN
Makes 4 servings

Enjoy the great outdoors while cooking!

1   (3 to 4 pound) frying chicken, cut up
2   cups **Prime Time Barbecue Sauce** (page 35)

Preheat oven to 350 degrees. Place chicken in a single layer in large casserole dish. Add 1 cup barbecue sauce. Bake for 45 minutes.

With tongs, remove chicken, drain and place on a HOT charcoal or gas grill. Cook for 30 minutes, basting with remaining 1 cup of barbecue sauce, turning frequently, until well done and skin is browned.

Serve chicken hot with additional barbecue sauce, **Holiday Potatoes** (page 184), **Dutch Red Cabbage** (page 253) and a **Green Bean Casserole** (page 254).

HAWAIIAN GRILLED CHICKEN BREASTS
Makes 4 to 6 servings

6-8   boneless, skinless chicken breasts
1/4   cup San-J teriyaki marinade
1/4   cup soy sauce
1   teaspoon fresh minced garlic
1   teaspoon cream-style prepared horseradish
1   can pineapple slices, drained (juice used in marinade)

Using a meat mallet, pound each chicken breast to tenderize. Pound until breasts are about 1/2 -inch thick. In shallow glass casserole, mix teriyaki marinade, soy sauce, garlic, prepared horseradish, and reserved pineapple juice. Add chicken breasts in a single layer and marinade several hours, turning occasionally.

Remove chicken from marinade and place on HOT grill or in hot frying pan. Lower heat to medium high if chicken starts to brown too much. Cook until chicken is done, about 3 minutes on each side. To prevent burning, turn chicken often, basting with marinade each time chicken is turned. After turning chicken the last time, place a slice of pineapple on each breast. Continue to cook until pineapple is warm.

Remove from grill or frying pan. Serve with **Simple Microwave Rice** (page 190) and **Peas and Water Chestnuts** (page 257) or **Summer Vegetable Medley** (page 259).

VARIATION: **To Cook Indoors**

Spray griddle or frying pan with nonstick cooking spray or a little olive oil. After marinating chicken, place breasts and pineapple slices on **hot** griddle or frying pan and cook for 3 minutes. Turn chicken and cook an additional 3 minutes. Turn pineapple as needed to heat and gently brown on each side. Do not over-cook chicken.

HOT CHICKEN SALAD SANDWICHES   *Makes 6 sandwiches*

If you are feeding a crowd for lunch, double the recipe. Prepare in advance and refrigerate until time to bake. A great change from cold chicken salad. This recipe is a modified version of one shared by Kitty Windham, Aiken, SC.

12	slices white sandwich bread
1/2	cup (1 stick) margarine or butter
2	(6 1/2 ounces each) cans chunk chicken, chopped
3	boiled eggs, chopped or grated
1/2	cup salad olives, chopped
1/2	cup finely chopped celery
2	tablespoon instant dried onion
3/4	cups low-calorie mayonnaise
4	ounces (1 cup) cold pack sharp cheese

Trim crust from bread, and spread margarine on 6 slices of bread. Spread the cheese mixture evenly over the buttered slices. Mix chicken, eggs, olives, celery, onion and mayonnaise. Cover each sandwich with another piece of bread, forming the top of each sandwich.

Blend remaining margarine with cheese to form a smooth paste. Spread on top of sandwiches. Place sandwiches on a large cookie sheet. Cover with waxed-paper. Place in refrigerator.

Thirty minutes before serving, preheat oven to 400 degrees. Heat sandwiches, uncovered, for about 20 minutes until hot, cheese melts and bread is toasted.

VARIATION: This filling can be used for cold sandwiches. Omit the cheese on top and do not heat. Serve cold.

OVEN-BAKED FRIED CHICKEN   *Makes 6 to 8 servings*

This is the perfect way to have "fried chicken" without all the fat! You may even like it better!

     1 1/2   cups herb stuffing mix, crushed into small crumbs (see inset below)
       1/4   teaspoon basil
       1/4   teaspoon Morton's Nature's seasoning
       1/2   teaspoon paprika
       1/8   teaspoon pepper
         1   envelope Lipton Cup-A-Soup, cream of chicken flavor
       1/3   cup hot water
       6-8   boneless, skinless chicken breasts
       2-3   tablespoons margarine, melted

Add basil, Nature's seasoning, paprika and pepper to crushed stuffing mix. Stir to mix well. Set aside. Mix water and soup mix together. Let sit for 5 minutes to thicken.

Dip each piece of chicken in soup mixture and then roll in stuffing mixture. Place chicken in shallow casserole dish so that pieces are not touching. Drizzle melted margarine over the top of each chicken breast.

Preheat oven to 350 degrees. Bake for 45 minutes to 1 hour until chicken has a golden brown crust.

Oven-Baked Fried Chicken (Second Method)

         1   cup seasoned bread crumbs (see inset below)
       6-8   boneless, skinless chicken breasts
       1-2   tablespoons light olive oil or margarine

Rinse chicken breasts. Place each breast in a small sandwich bag. Pound with a meat mallet to about 1/2 inch thickness. Roll each breast in bread crumbs. Place on the rack of a baking pan. Dot each breast with oil or butter. Bake at 350 degrees about 35 to 45 minutes until golden brown.

* * * * * * * * *

How to Make Seasoned Bread Crumbs

For the best Seasoned Bread Crumbs, make crumbs from **Crunchy Croutons** page 220. Process croutons about 30 seconds in food processor. Or use **Crunchy Seasoned Bread** (page 89) to make bread crumbs.

RUSSIAN SWEET AND SOUR CHICKEN   *Makes 8 servings*

A deliciously tender recipe of unknown origin.

          2 (2-3 pounds each) frying chicken, cut in pieces
          1 (12 ounces) jar apricot preserves
        1/4 cup water
          1 envelope dry onion soup mix
          1 (8 ounce) bottle Russian salad dressing

Preheat oven to 350 degrees.

Make sauce by mixing preserves, water, soup mix and Russian dressing together. Place chicken in 9x12x2-inch baking dish. Cover with sauce.

Bake uncovered for 1 hour, basting 2 or 3 times.

Remove from sauce and serve hot with **Twice Baked Stuffed Potatoes** (page 188)**, Tangy Cauliflower** (page 260), and **Spinach Salad Delight** (page 218).

This freezes well, either baked or unbaked. Thaw before baking or increase cooking time about 30 minutes.

VARIATION: One (16 ounce) jar of apricot preserves could be substituted for the 12 ounce jar of apricot preserves. This will make sauce a little sweeter.

SEASONED TURKEY   *Makes 10 to 12 servings*

A tender, juicy method for cooking a turkey. This is perfect for serving as a main course or making turkey sandwiches. The cooking juice is delicious when thickened and served as a **Seasoned Gravy** (recipe follows).

- 1 (5 1/2-6 pound) turkey breast with bone
- 2 teaspoon minced fresh garlic
- 1/2 teaspoon each: marjoram, rosemary, Cajun seasoning mix, chili powder
- 1 teaspoon each: Old Bay Seafood Seasoning, ground dry mustard and cream-style horseradish
- 1 large onion, diced or 3 tablespoons dried minced onion
- 1/2 cup water
- 1/4 cup worcestershire sauce

Wash turkey, drain, and place in 3-1/2 quart or larger crock pot, making sure that the lid will fit securely after turkey is added to crockpot. Place all seasonings, garlic and onion around the sides of the turkey. Pour water and worcestershire sauce over the top of the turkey. Place lid on crockpot.

Turn temperature control to HIGH and cook 3 to 4 hours or until done. When the turkey is done, the bone will gently release from the meat. Remove turkey from crockpot, drain, and place on a large cutting board. If gravy is desired, reserve liquid in crockpot for making **Seasoned Gravy**. Let turkey cool for 5 minutes, while making gravy. Cut into thin slices. Place slices on a serving platter. Garnish with fresh parsley, if desired. Serve with mashed potatoes and gravy.

Turkey Gravy

Strain liquid in crockpot. For each cup of liquid, mix the following:

- 1 1/2 teaspoon corn starch
- 1 tablespoon water

Pour corn starch mixture into hot broth mixture in crockpot, stirring constantly until thickened.

Storage Tips

Left over turkey retains its flavor better if it is refrigerated in a large piece rather than slices; however, slices may be refrigerated and used quickly. To store, place in sealed plastic bag so that turkey will retain its moisture. A turkey breast will keep in the refrigerator for 4 to 5 days; slices should be used within 3 days.

SPANISH RICE WITH CHICKEN AND SAUSAGE   *Makes 6 to 8 servings*

An all-time favorite that combines sausage and rice, topped with chicken. This rice is absolutely the best!

1	tablespoon olive oil or other cooking oil
3	pounds of meaty chicken pieces
2	cups chopped onion
1	tablespoon fresh minced garlic
2	green peppers, chopped
1 1/2	pounds Kielbasa sausage, cut in 1/2 -inch pieces
4	cups water
1	teaspoon basil
4	teaspoons chicken bouillon
1/8	teaspoon curry powder
1	tablespoon paprika
2	cups uncooked long-grain white rice
1	(10 ounce) package frozen green peas
1	(4 1/2 ounce) jar sliced mushrooms

Preheat oven to 350 degrees. Grease 9x12x2-inch casserole.

In frying pan, add oil and heat 2 minutes on medium-high temperature. Add chicken pieces, a few at a time, and brown each piece. Remove from frying pan and drain on two layers of paper towels.

To the frying pan, add onion, garlic, peppers and sausage in skillet. Cook over medium-high heat until vegetables are lightly browned. To remove grease, pour ingredients into a colander and run under hot water for 1 minute. Drain well. Add to casserole dish.

Spread mushrooms evenly over vegetable and sausage layer. Add rice, chicken bouillon, basil, curry powder, paprika, rice and green peas. Gently stir ingredients to mix well. Place chicken pieces on top of casserole. Cover casserole.

Bake 35 to 40 minutes. Reduce oven temperature to 300 degrees, uncover casserole, and continue baking another 20 to 30 minutes until rice is tender. Remove from oven and serve.

If prepared in advance, cover and refrigerate until just before baking. Add 10 to 15 minutes to the baking time.

SPECIAL EVENT CHICKEN TETRAZZINI   *Makes 8 servings*

A dish named after Louisa Tetrazzini, the famous Italian operatic soprano (1874-1940). This has been such a favorite with friends and relatives that I take it to covered dish suppers. It can be prepared in advance and freezes well. Contributed by Beth Lynn, Aiken, SC.

3-5   pound fryer (boiled, skinned, deboned and drained) (4 to 5 cups cooked chicken chunks) reserve liquid to use for cooking noodles

8   ounce package narrow noodles
(cooked in chicken broth from above and well drained)

1   cup chicken broth

1   medium onion, grated

1   can cream of mushroom soup

1/4   cup (1/2 stick) margarine or butter

1-2   ounces (1/4-1/2 cup) grated cheddar cheese

Topping

1/4   cup (1/2 stick) margarine, melted

2   cups bread crumbs or crushed corn flakes

Preheat oven to 350 degrees. Lightly grease a 3-quart casserole or a 1-quart casserole and a 2-quart casserole.

Cut chicken into large, bite-size pieces. Melt cheese and margarine. Add chicken broth, onion, and soup to cheese mixture. In casserole dish, alternate layers of noodles, chicken and cheese sauce in casserole, starting with chicken layer, making 2 layers of each and ending with sauce.

Combine topping ingredients and place on top of casserole. Bake for 30 to 40 minutes until hot in center.

VARIATIONS: Add 1 small green pepper, diced.

Add 2 to 3 pounds fresh shrimp, peeled and boiled, instead of the chicken.

9

Desserts

DESSERTS

DESSERTS

No matter how delicious the meal, everyone looks forward to the conclusion: dessert! Pies and cakes have been listed in their own separate sections. All other desserts are presented here.

Want a simple dessert for your family? Try **Your Choice Cobbler** in their favorite flavor: Apple, Blueberry, Cherry or Peach. Having a business dinner? Impress your guests with sinfully delicious **Elegant Strawberry Crepes** or **Martha Washington Candy**.

If there are children, young or old, at your house, keep the cookie jar full of **Super-Duper Chocolate Chip Cookies** or **Old-Fashioned Ginger Snaps**.

CANDIES

MARTHA WASHINGTON CANDY *Makes 120 candies*

My family always made this candy to give to, and serve to, friends during the Christmas holidays. This candy looks, and tastes professional. A perfect gift-giver. This may sound like a lot of candy, but it disappears so quickly.

1 1/2	cups (3 sticks) margarine or butter
2	(16 ounces each) boxes powdered sugar
2	teaspoon vanilla flavoring
1-2	tablespoons water
1	2-inch cube paraffin
6	(1 ounce each) squares unsweetened baking chocolate
60	(2 cups) pecan halves

Cream margarine, sugar and vanilla together until well mixed and creamy. Add water, a little at a time, if needed to make dough form into balls. Roll into balls about 3/4 inches in diameter. Cover a cookie sheet with waxed paper. Place balls on waxed paper, about 1/2 -inch apart. Refrigerate about 30 to 45 minutes.

In glass container, heat chocolate and paraffin in microwave on 30% power for 7 to 9 minutes, until melted. Place each candy ball on a fork and dip, one at a time, into melted chocolate, rolling with fork to completely cover candy ball with chocolate. Drain a few seconds until chocolate stops dripping.

Remove from fork by putting fork down on waxed paper, place pecan on top, pressing to gently flatten ball. Slide fork from under ball before removing fingers from pecan. Repeat procedure with each ball. Let candy stand until chocolate is set and hardened, about 2 to 10 minutes.

These may be kept at room temperature in an air-tight container for several months.

VARIATIONS: Add 2 cups chopped pecans to creamed mixture. To decorate, substitute a candied cherry for each pecan half.

Other flavorings, such as mint, orange, lemon, rum or brandy, may be substituted for vanilla.

A few drops of coloring may be added to represent the flavoring used.

Storage Tip

> If using mint flavoring, do not store any other candy in the same container, as it will absorb the mint flavor.

MICROWAVE FUDGE   *Makes 32 small pieces*

This oh, so creamy dessert is ready in 15 minutes or less.

- 1/2   cup (1 stick) margarine or butter, melted
- 1/2   cup cocoa
- 1/4   cup evaporated skim milk
-   1   (16 ounce) box confectioners' powdered sugar
- 1/2   cup chopped pecans
-   1   teaspoon vanilla flavoring

Line the bottom of an 8-inch square dish with waxed paper.

In large bowl, melt margarine 2 minutes on 30% power. Add cocoa and milk. Stir. Add powdered sugar. Stir and cook for 2 minutes on high in the microwave. Remove and quickly stir to mix ingredients well. Add nuts and vanilla, stir well. Pour into prepared dish.

Cool and cut into small squares.

VARIATION: Use an additional 32 pecan halves. Make 8 rows of 4 pecans, spacing pecans evenly on top of hot fudge. Cool and cut into rectangles with one pecan on each piece.

PULLED BUTTER MINTS   *Makes about 3 dozen*

In my family, pulling mints or taffy was a very special family occasion enjoyed by all.

2	cups sugar	1/4	cup (1/2 stick) margarine or butter
1	cup water		few drops of oil of peppermint or other flavoring

Combine sugar and water. Cook slowly, stirring constantly until mixture bubbles rapidly. Add butter. Boil slowly on high for about 10 minutes, without stirring, to the hard ball stage (248 to 264 degrees on candy thermometer). (see insert below).

Immediately remove from heat and pour in a circle on a cold, lightly greased slab of marble, trying to make the circle an even thickness. When candy is brittle on surface, yet soft in the center, loosen the slab. Begin stretching candy.

To stretch candy, fold candy and pull gently, but firmly, with tips of fingers. Smear a few drops of food coloring and flavoring in center of candy. Continue folding and pulling candy until the color is evenly distributed.

Stretch into a long rope, continually turning, which gives a pillow effect. With kitchen scissors, cut off pieces into desired lengths (1/2-inch to 3/4-inch long). Place pieces on a cloth to dry overnight. When hard and dry, put into an air-tight container and mint will become soft and creamy.

SUGARED PEANUTS   *Makes about 4 cups*

Place in a candy dish and serve for an appetizer or dessert.

2	cups sugar	4	cups raw, shelled peanuts
1	cup water		

Preheat oven to 250 degrees. Grease 9x12-inch (or larger) cookie sheet.

In large saucepan, add sugar, water and peanuts. Over medium heat, bring to a boil, stirring constantly until all liquid is absorbed. Spread evenly in a single layer on greased cookie sheet.

Bake for about 1 hour or until they look dried out. Separate peanuts.

Store in air-tight container or sealable freezer plastic bags.

* * * * * * * * *

How to Test Candy Temperature

To test temperature without a candy thermometer, pour some of the hot mixture into a cup of cool water, removing spoon to form a coil of candy. At hard ball stage, coil should be brittle.

TAFFY   *Makes about 2 pounds of candy*

An old Virginia recipe. This is so much better than any taffy you can buy! Great for gift-giving during the holidays.

2	cups sugar
1 1/2	cups light corn syrup
1/4	teaspoon salt
1	tablespoon vinegar
1/2	cup evaporated skim milk

Grease or butter a large baking pan.

Mix sugar, syrup, salt and vinegar. Cook slowly until sugar is melted and mixture is boiling. Slowly add milk, keeping candy boiling the entire time. Boil briskly to firm ball stage (244 to 248 degrees on candy thermometer). Immediately pour into large buttered pan.

When cool enough to handle, but not too cool, pull until candy is light and no longer sticky to the touch. Place candy on waxed paper or in buttered pan. Using scissors, cut into 1 inch pieces.

Store, unrefrigerated, in air-tight container. This keeps for weeks.

VARIATIONS: 1/2 teaspoon flavoring of your choice may be added.

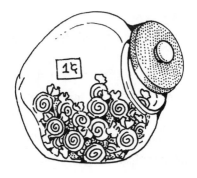

COOKIES

CHILDREN'S PAINTED COOKIES   *Large batch*

Start a tradition at your house - painted cookies! This recipe is excellent for making children's cookies, because they taste great and each young child can "paint" his own creations.

- 1 1/4 cups flour
- 1/2   teaspoon baking soda
- 1/2   teaspoon salt
- 6   tablespoons margarine or butter
- 1   egg, divided into yolk and white (reserve egg white for painting)
- 1/2   teaspoon vanilla flavoring
- 1/2   cup sugar

Preheat oven to 350 degrees.

In medium bowl, mix flour, baking soda, and salt together. Cream margarine, egg yolk, sugar and vanilla together. Gradually add flour to creamed mixture, beating until dough is well mixed, but not too stiff.

On a heavily floured surface, place dough and knead in enough flour so that dough is just stiff enough to roll out with rolling pin. Roll to 1/4-inch to 3/8-inch thickness, depending upon design of cookie cutter used. Dough should be thick enough to take the imprint of the cookie cutter if it has a surface design.

Cut cookies into shapes with cookie cutters and place cookies on ungreased (no-stick) cookie sheet. Paint cookies (recipe and instructions follows).

Bake about 8 to 10 minutes until cookies just start to brown. Remove from oven. Using spatula, remove cookies and place on flat surface to cool. Paint or decorate cookies as directed below with pastry tube.

Store cooled cookies in an air-tight container.

VARIATION: After cookies are cooled, use a pastry tube of frosting and decorate.

How to Paint Cookies

- 1 egg white (reserved from above)
     food coloring—any color—just a few drops
- 3 or more small water color paint brushes (NEW)

In a small cup, combine the egg white with 1/4 teaspoon water and mix well. Divide mixture between several custard cups or other very small containers. Add one color of food coloring to each cup to make "paint". Blend the color into the egg white.

Place a paint brush into each color and let children decorate the cookies.

CHOCOLATE FUDGE COOKIES   *Makes 24 large cookies*

Are these candies or cookies? Taste them and decide for yourself. A simply delicious recipe shared by Yvette Sanders, Barnwell, SC.

2	cups sugar
1/2	cup skim milk
1/4	cup (1/2 stick) margarine or butter
3	tablespoons cocoa
1/2	cup peanut butter
2	cups miniature marshmallows
1/2	cups chopped pecans
1	teaspoon vanilla

Melt margarine, sugar, milk, and cocoa. Over medium-high heat, cook until mixture comes to a rolling boil. Remove from heat. Stir in peanut butter until smooth. Then stir in marshmallows, nuts, and vanilla.

Drop by spoonsful on waxed paper. Let sit until hardened.

Store in air-tight container.

HALL OF FAME COOKIES   *Makes about 4 dozen cookies*

Although these cookies are great when just cooked, they are better if made 1 day in advance and stored in an air-tight container.

3/4	cups (1-1/2 sticks) margarine or butter
1/2	cup sugar
	Juice of 1/2 lemon (about 2 to 3 tablespoon juice)
1	lemon peel, grated (see insert below) or 1-1/2 teaspoon dried lemon peel
1	egg yolk (save egg white for another recipe—see page 171)
1 1/2	cups self-rising flour
48	pecan halves

Preheat oven to 325 degrees. If the oven is too hot, the cookies will brown before they are done.

With electric mixer, cream margarine, sugar and lemon peel in large mixing bowl. Add egg yolk and mix well. Gradually add flour, mixing well after each addition.

Drop by teaspoons on an ungreased (no-stick) cookie sheet. Place a pecan half on each cookie and press gently to flatten dough slightly. Place cookies about 2 inches apart.

Place cookie sheet on a shelf in the middle of the oven and bake 10 to 12 minutes until the cookies just start to brown on the bottom. If cookies brown too quickly, move them to a higher shelf. Cookies are done when they are a very pale golden brown on top.

VARIATIONS: Add 1 cup chopped pecans to the batter before adding the flour. The pecan half on top is optional.

* * * * * * * * * *

How to Grate Lemon Peel

With sharp knife or peeler, remove the outer yellow rind of lemon. Use about 2 tablespoons of sugar from the recipe. Place peel and sugar in a mini-food processor and turn on for a few seconds.

The sugar keeps the peel from sticking to the sides of the processor and grates it more quickly and easily.

OATMEAL MUNCHIES   *Makes 3 dozen cookies*

1	cup flour
1/2	teaspoon baking soda
1	teaspoon salt
3/4	cup salad oil
1	cup packed brown sugar
1/2	cup sugar
1	egg
1/4	cup water
1	teaspoon vanilla flavoring
2	cups uncooked quick-cooking (not instant) oatmeal
1	cup chopped pecans
1	cup chocolate chips

Preheat oven to 350 degrees. Combine flour, soda and salt. Mix well and set aside.

With electric mixer, cream oil, sugars, egg, water and vanilla. Gradually blend in flour mixture and mix well. Add oatmeal, nuts and chocolate chips and stir to mix well. Drop by small spoonfuls onto greased (or no-stick) cookie sheet.

Bake for 12 to 15 minutes. Cool. Store in air-tight container. These keep for weeks.

ALTERNATE: Coconut or raisins may be substituted for the chocolate chips or nuts. 1 cup of Kellogg's Just Right cereal can be substituted for 1 cup of oatmeal.

OLD-FASHIONED GINGER SNAPS *Makes 5 dozen 3-inch cookies*

This recipe is a modern version of a 1930s recipe. The cookies are very tasty and have a real crunchy 'snap' to them. These can be cut into gingerbread men shapes and decorated with frosting.

1/2	cup vegetable oil
1/2	cup sugar
1/2	cup molasses
1	teaspoon ground ginger
1/4	teaspoon cinnamon
2 1/4	cups self-rising flour or
	2 1/4 cups regular flour and 1/2 teaspoon baking powder

Preheat oven to 400 degrees.

In a large mixing bowl, using electric mixer, combine oil, sugar, molasses, ginger and cinnamon and mix until creamy. Blend in self-rising flour and mix well. Divide dough in half.

On floured surface, roll out each half of dough, one half at a time, until very thin (about 1/8 -inch). Cut with a cookie cutter, choosing a shape of your choice. Place cookies on nonstick coated cookie sheet about 1/4 inches apart to allow room for expansion.

Bake about 5 to 6 minutes until cookies appear dry on top and just begin to brown around the edges. Do not let them brown too much. Remove cookies and cool.

Store in air-tight container. These will keep for weeks.

VARIATIONS: Before baking, sprinkle top of cookies with sugar and bake.

Bake cookies. Cool. Then decorate with **Decorator's Cake Frosting** (page 127).

* * * * * * * * *

How to Measure Molasses and Corn Syrup

To keep sticky ingredients from sticking to the measuring spoon or cup, and thereby causing an inaccurate measurement, spray measuring utensil with Pam (no-stick cooking oil) before measuring molasses or corn syrup.

SUPER-DUPER CHOCOLATE CHIP COOKIES
Makes 14 dozen 2-inch diameter cookies

These are better than ever and have plenty of fiber.

3 1/2	cups flour		1	egg
1	tablepoon baking soda		1	tablespoon skim milk
1	teaspoon salt		2	teaspoons vanilla
1/2	cup (1 stick) butter		1	cup cooking oil (canola)
1/2	cup (1 stick) margarine		1 1/4	cup crushed corn flakes
1	cup firmly packed brown sugar		12	ounces chocolate chips
1	cup granulated sugar			

Preheat oven to 325 degrees.

Mix flour, baking soda and salt together in a small bowl. In large mixing bowl, beat butter, margarine, brown sugar, sugar, egg, milk, vanilla, and oil in a bowl until mixture is creamy and well blended.

To this mixture, alternately add flour mixture, mixing after each addition, until batter is well mixed. Stir in corn flakes, and chocolate chips. Drop by heaping teaspoonsful on an ungreased cookie sheet, placing cookie dough about 2 inches apart.

Bake about 12 minutes or until cookies start to very lightly brown on edges. Remove from oven and let cool slightly, about 2 minutes. Remove cookies from pan and place on paper towels to cool completely.

Store cookies in air-tight container. These keep for several weeks without refrigeration.

VARIATION: Spread dough into a 15x11x2 -inch baking pan. Bake for 20 to 30 minutes, until set in middle. Cut into squares and let cool in pan.

Omit corn flakes and substitute 1 cup quick-cooking oatmeal.

OTHER DESSERTS

APPLESAUCE BARS

Makes 24 to 36 bars

Lusciously moist and tasty. You must try these!

Bars

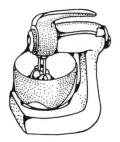

1	cup firmly packed brown sugar
1/2	cup margarine or butter, at room temperature
1	cup unsweetened applesauce
1	egg
1 1/2	cup flour
1	teaspoon baking soda
1	teaspoon cinnamon
1/4	teaspoon each: salt, cloves, nutmeg
2	cups Kellogg's Just Right cereal
	Glaze (recipe follows)

Preheat oven to 350 degrees. Grease and flour 13x9-inch pan.

In large bowl, cream brown sugar and margarine until light and fluffy. Add applesauce and egg; blend well. Stir in flour, baking soda, cinnamon, salt, cloves and nutmeg until well mixed. Stir in cereal. Spread mixture into prepared pan.

Bake for 25 to 30 minutes or until toothpick inserted in center comes out clean. While **Glaze** is still hot, drizzle it over warm bars. Cool completely. Cut into squares.

Glaze

2	tablespoons margarine or butter
1/4	cup firmly packed brown sugar
1	teaspoon powdered sugar

Melt margarine over low heat. Stir in brown sugar. Cook about 1 minute or until mixture bubbles, stirring constantly. Remove from heat. Stir in powdered sugar.

BUTTERSCOTCH SAUCE   *Makes about 2 cups*

This is luscious served over vanilla ice cream.

    1 1/2 cups packed brown sugar
      2/3 cups light corn syrup
      1/3 cup water
      1/4 cup (1/2 stick) margarine or butter
      2/3 cups evaporated skim milk
      1/8 teaspoon salt
      1/2 teaspoon vanilla flavoring
      1/2 cup chopped pecans or walnuts

Put sugar, corn syrup, water, and margarine into a saucepan. Bring to boil and boil to the soft ball stage (230 to 238 degrees on a candy thermometer). Cool. Then beat in the evaporated milk, salt and vanilla. Stir in the pecans.

Serve warm over vanilla ice cream (or ice milk), bananas or your choice of pudding.

DATE CHEWS   *Makes about 64 squares*

      1   cup sugar
      1   teaspoon baking powder
      3/4 cups flour
      1/4 teaspoon salt
      1   cup chopped pecans or other nuts
      1   cup chopped dates
      1/4 cup skim milk
      2   eggs

Preheat oven to 350 degrees. Grease and flour two 8-inch pans.

In a large bowl, add sugar, baking powder, flour and salt and mix. Add eggs and mix. Add nuts and dates and stir to mix well. Pour into prepared pans.

Bake 12 to 15 minutes until batter springs back when touched and is lightly browned on top.

When cool cut into small squares and roll in powdered sugar. Stored in air-tight container, these will keep unrefrigerated for a week or more.

VARIATION: Add 1/2 teaspoon instant coffee and 1/2 cup shredded coconut.

DELICATE LEMON SQUARES   *Makes about 36 squares*

A modified version of Yvette Sander's recipe, this rich pastry dessert has a delicate lemon flavor. It is easy to prepare and will stay fresh for several days.

Bottom Crust

- 1/2   cup margarine or butter, room temperature
- 1   cup flour
- 3/4   cup confectioners' powdered sugar

Preheat oven to 350 degrees. Mix margarine, flour and sugar to make the bottom crust. Pat into a 9-inch square baking dish. Bake for 15 minutes. While this layer is cooking prepare the **Top Filling** (recipe follows).

Top Filling

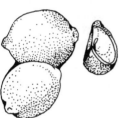

- 2   tablespoons flour
- 1/2   teaspoon baking powder
- 1   cup sugar
- 3   tablespoons lemon juice
- 2   eggs, slightly beaten
- 3   tablespoons powdered sugar, reserved

In a medium bowl, stir baking powder and flour into sugar. Add the lemon juice and eggs and beat with electric mixer for 1 minute on medium speed. Pour this mixture over the bottom crust.

Bake for 25 minutes. While still warm, sprinkle with the 3 tablespoons of powdered sugar. Cut into 1-1/2-inch squares.

Serve warm or at room temperature. Store in air-tight container, separating each layer with waxed paper or plastic wrap.

VARIATIONS: 1 cup of shredded coconut can be added to top layer before baking.

ELEGANT STRAWBERRY CREPES   *Makes 24 crepes (12 servings)*

An elegant dessert fit for a king! Most of the preparation can be handled in advance.

Dessert Crepes

1	cup flour	3	eggs
1/8	teaspoon salt	1 1/2	cups skim milk
2	tablespoons sugar	2	tablespoons margarine, melted

Put flour, sugar and salt into a bowl. Add eggs, one at a time, beating thoroughly with each addition. Gradually add milk, mixing until well blended. Add margarine; beat well. Let batter rest for 1 hour at room temperature.

Over medium high-temperature, heat frying pan. Using 2 tablespoons of batter for each crepe, pour batter onto heated surface. Immediately lift pan from burner and gently swirl to make a larger, thinner crepe. Loosen edges and flip over. Cook each side for about 30 seconds, until batter is dry on each side and lightly browned. Stack crepes on a plate and cover with a clean cloth, which will keep them moist, while you prepare sauce and filling. (see **Cooking Tip** on page 137).

Cream Sauce

6	ounces cream cheese
8	ounces (1 cup) sour cream
2	tablespoons lemon juice

In medium bowl, with electric mixer, blend cream cheese, sour cream and lemon juice until creamy and well mixed. Set aside.

Strawberry Filling

3	(16 ounces each) packages frozen strawberries, thawed
3	tablespoons corn starch

Preheat oven to 350 degrees. Grease two 9x9-inch baking dishes. Place colander over a saucepan. Fill colander with thawed strawberries, letting juice drain into saucepan. Reserve strawberries. Place corn starch in small custard cup. Blend in enough strawberry juice to make a paste. Then add 2 tablespoons more strawberry juice. Stir cornstarch mixture into saucepan with drained strawberry juice. Heat over medium heat, stirring constantly, until thickened. Remove from heat. Add strawberries.

To Assemble Crepes: Place 1 tablespoon **Cream Sauce** on each crepe, spreading almost to edges. Top with 1/2 tablespoon of **Strawberry Filling.** Roll up each crepe, jelly roll fashion, and place in baking dishes. Spread any remaining **Cream Sauce** evenly over top of the crepes. Drizzle remaining **Filling** on top. Heat 15 minutes in oven.

MERINGUE TOFFEE STICKS

Makes 50 to 70 small bars

One of Mother's special recipes which I fondly remember from early childhood. These are delicate cookies which are slightly sweet with a crisp texture and a delicate cinnamon flavor.

- 1 cup (2 sticks) margarine or butter
- 1 cup sugar
- 1 teaspoon cinnamon
- 1 egg yolk
- 2 cups flour
- 1 teaspoon vanilla flavoring
- 1-1 1/2 cups chopped pecans
- 2 egg whites (see page 163 for extra egg white)

Preheat oven to 350 degrees. Grease and flour 11x15-inch pan.

With electric mixer, blend margarine, sugar and cinnamon until creamy. Add egg yolk and vanilla. Mix until blended. Gradually add flour and continue beating until well blended. Pat out into pan. Sprinkle pecans on top and press firmly into dough.

In small bowl, beat egg whites until frothy but not stiff. Brush top of bars with beaten egg whites.

Bake 30 minutes. While still hot, cut cookies into small sticks about 3/4 x 2-inches long. Leave in pan until cooled completely. Gently remove with a spatula and place in an air-tight container.

Cooking Tip

To make spreading egg whites easier, place hand in a small plastic bag and then use hand to spread egg whites.

PECAN COCOONS

Makes 4 dozen

A tender, dainty cookie that is luscious enough for the most formal occasion.

1	cup (2 sticks) margarine or butter
1/3	cup sugar
1	tablespoon water
2	teaspoons vanilla flavoring
2	cups flour
1	cup chopped pecans
1/2	cup confectioners' powdered sugar (for rolling Cocoons)

Preheat oven to 325 degrees.

Mix margarine and sugar until creamy. Add water and vanilla and mix well. Add flour and pecans and stir to mix completely, forming a dough. If dough is too soft to handle, chill 3 to 4 hours. Shape into small balls or oblong fingers. Place 1/2-inch apart on ungreased cookie sheet.

Bake 20 to 30 minutes until they just start to brown. While warm, roll in powdered sugar and place on cake rack to cool completely.

Store in air-tight container. These will keep a week or more.

VARIATION: Substitute 1/4 cup confectioner's powdered sugar for granulated sugar.

PRALINE CREPES

Makes 8 servings

	Dessert Crepes (page 170)		
1	cup packed brown sugar	1	tablespoon water
1/4	cup (1/2 stick) margarine or butter	1/8-1/4	teaspoon rum extract
1/4	cup skim milk	1/2	cup chopped pecans
1/2	teaspoon corn starch	1	pint vanilla ice milk or ice cream

Prepare **Dessert Crepes** and set aside while making sauce. In small saucepan, add brown sugar, margarine and milk and heat until boiling. Reduce heat and simmer for 3 minutes. Mix corn starch, water and rum extract together. Pour into hot mixture and cook, stirring constantly, until sauce is thickened. Remove from heat. Stir in pecans.

To Assemble:

Place a scoop or two of ice cream in center of each crepe and fold sides over. Place seam side down on plate. Pour about 2 tablespoons of sauce over each crepe. Serve immediately.

SUPER-MOIST BROWNIES   *Makes about 54 brownies small squares*

Calling all chocolate lovers! These will disappear in a hurry. Contributed by Helen Killion, Aiken, SC.

     4   squares (1 ounce each) unsweetened baking chocolate
   1/2   cup (1 stick) margarine or butter
     4   eggs
   1/4   teaspoon salt
     2   cups sugar
     1   teaspoon vanilla
     1   cup flour
     1   cup chopped pecans

Preheat oven to 325 degrees. Grease and flour one 9x13-inch pan.

Melt chocolate and margarine by cooking on 30% power in microwave for 3 to 4 minutes. Cool. Beat the eggs, salt and sugar until ingredients are light and creamy. Fold in the melted chocolate mixture and the vanilla. Add flour and beat until batter is smooth. Fold in nuts.

Bake between 25 and 35 minutes until set. Using serrated knife, cut into small squares (see insert below). Cool.

VARIATIONS: Before cutting. Cover with marshmallow cream and then cover with a layer of fudge frosting. Leave uncovered until frosting sets. Cut into small squares, as this is very rich.

* * * * * * * * * *

How to Avoid Cookie Crumble

When cutting any type of bar cookie or dessert, try using a serrated knife after bars are cool to prevent crumbling the top layer of cookie bars.

YOUR CHOICE COBBLER   *Makes 4 to 6 servings*

- 1/4 cup (1/2 stick) margarine or butter
- 3/4 cup self rising flour
- 2 teaspoons baking powder
- 1/2 cup skim milk
- 1/2 cup sugar plus 2 tablespoons
- 1 (16 ounce) can pie filling - peach, cherry, apple OR blueberry

Preheat oven to 350 degrees. Place margarine in 8x10-inch casserole dish, and microwave on 50% power for 2 minutes or until margarine is melted. Make a batter by mixing flour, baking powder, milk and 1/2 cup sugar. Mix well and pour over margarine. Evenly spread pie filling over batter.

Bake about 25 minutes. Then sprinkle with 2 tablespoons of sugar (this will be after batter comes to top). Continue to bake an additional 10 to 15 minutes until done and toothpick inserted in center come out clean.

Serve warm or hot with a scoop of vanilla ice cream.

VARIATIONS: When using apple or peach pie filling, add 1/4 teaspoon cinnamon or apple pie spice to pie filling.

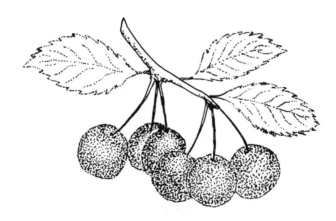

10
Pasta, Potatoes & Rice

PASTA, POTATOES AND RICE

PASTA, POTATOES AND RICE

These popular grain products are a good source of vitamins   Although these starches have been blamed for being fattening, this is a misconception. The foods themselves are not so high in calories; it's the cream sauces, butter, gravy, and other trimmings that make these dishes fattening.

Because our bodies process starches more slowly than sugar, grain products provide more long-lasting energy and delay hunger. We use rice, potatoes and pasta as fillers, but they are really tasty in their own right.

Because pasta, potatoes and rice can be cooked in many various ways and with many assorted foods, these are multipurpose foods that add variety to meals.

PASTA

CREAMY MACARONI AND CHEESE

Makes 4 servings

Because this dish is not baked in the oven, it is very creamy, unlike most oven-baked macaroni and cheese. Its cheesy flavor is enhanced by the addition of prepared mustard (see insert below).

1 1/2	cups uncooked elbow macaroni, cooked according to package directions
2	tablespoons margarine or butter
2	tablespoons flour
1-2	cups skim milk
1-2	tablespoons prepared mustard
12	ounces (3 cups) shredded cheddar cheese

Pour macaroni into colander and rinse 30 seconds with hot water. Drain well.

In frying pan over medium-high heat, melt margarine and stir in flour with wire whisk to form paste. Gradually add milk, stirring constantly to make a smooth sauce. Cook until mixture boils and thickens, adding more milk as needed to make a medium white sauce. Reduce heat to medium. Add mustard and cheese, stirring well to mix. Continue heating and stirring until cheese melts. Reduce heat to low. Pour macaroni into skillet. Stir until macaroni and cheese are well mixed.

Serve immediately or leave on low until serving time, adding a little milk occasionally to thin sauce if it becomes too thick.

This reheats well in the microwave using 80% power. Microwave until hot.

* * * * * * * * *

How to Increase Cheese Flavor

When you want to increase the flavor of cheese in cooked dishes, try adding or increasing the amount of prepared mustard. This will increase the cheese flavor without increasing the calories.

HOT GERMAN NOODLES   *Makes 6 to 8 servings*

5 slices bacon, cooked crisp & crumbled	1/2 cup chopped celery
4 ounces (2 1/2 cups) uncooked egg noodles, cooked according to package directions	1/4 teaspoon salt
	1/8 teaspoon pepper
1/3 cup chopped onion	2/3 cup water
1/3 cup sugar	1/2 cup vinegar
2 tablespoons flour	2 tablespoons chopped fresh parsley or 2 teaspoons dried parsley flakes

Rinse noodles with hot water and drain well.

In large skillet, fry bacon until crisp. Drain and crumble. Remove all except 1 tablespoon of bacon drippings. Add onion to skillet and cook until tender. Stir in sugar, flour, celery, salt and pepper. Add water and vinegar. Cook until mixture boils and thickens, stirring frequently. Add cooked noodles and parsley. Cook over low heat until thoroughly heated.

Serve with **Oven Baked Fried Chicken** (page 149) and collard greens.

MACARONI CROWD PLEASER   *Makes 16 servings*

Designed to feed a large crowd, this can be served hot or cold.

1 can cream mushroom soup	1 teaspoon HOT Mrs. Dash seasoning
1 (4 oz) can mushroom, slices or stem & pieces	1 teaspoon Morton's Nature's Seasoning
1 cup low-calorie mayonnaise	8 ounces macaroni, cooked according to package directions
1 pound (4 cups) grated cheddar cheese	
1 (4 ounce) jars chopped pimentos	1-2 (10 oz.) packages frozen broccoli spears, thawed & drained
1/4 cup chopped onion	1 cup bread crumbs (see page 73)
1/4 cup chopped green pepper	2 tablespoons margarine, melted

Preheat oven to 375 degrees. Lightly grease a large 3-quart casserole dish.

Mix first 9 ingredients together. Rinse macaroni and drain well. Then stir broccoli and macaroni into soup mixture. Pour into prepared casserole and sprinkle with bread crumbs. Drizzle with margarine.

Bake about 30 to 45 minutes until bubbly hot.

This freezes well before it is baked.

RAINBOW PASTA SALAD

Makes 6 to 8 servings

Rainbow Rotini is a blend of multicolored, vegetable-flavored pasta twists. It makes a beautiful salad with lots of flavor. Because it is best prepared in advance, it is a great salad for a covered-dish or buffet supper.

- 8 ounces Rainbow Rotini pasta, cooked according to package directions, drained and cooled
- 1/2 cup diced green pepper
- 1/2 cup diced onion
- 1/2 cup zesty Italian salad dressing
- 1/4 cup pickle relish
- 1 teaspoon celery seed
- 1 teaspoon seasoned salt
- 2 tablespoons prepared mustard

While pasta is cooking, dice green pepper and onion and place in large bowl. Add Italian dressing, pickle relish, celery seed, salt, and mustard. When pasta is drained and cooled, add to large bowl. Mix well to evenly coat pasta and vegetables with dressing mixture.

Serve immediately or chill until serving time.

VARIATIONS: Add 4 hard-boiled eggs, diced. Add 2 fresh, ripe tomatoes, diced and drained.

NOODLE CHEESE BAKE

Makes 6 servings

A delicious change from rice and potatoes.

4	eggs	2	cups cottage cheese
3/4	cup sour cream	5	cups cooked fine noodles
1	teaspoon salt	1/4	cup bread crumbs (page 73)
2	tablespoons sugar	3	tablespoons margarine, melted

Preheat oven to 375 degrees. Lightly grease 2-quart baking dish.

Beat eggs, sour cream, salt and sugar together until well blended. Add the cheese and noodles. Pour into prepared dish. Sprinkle with bread crumbs and margarine.

Bake about 40 minutes.

Use the oven to bake the entire dinner by serving this with **Oven-Baked Fried Chicken** (page 149) and a fresh green salad.

ZESTY MACARONI SALAD   *Makes 8 servings*

This popular salad can be made in advance and served at picnics and pot-luck suppers.

- 1 (8-ounce) package of small elbow macaroni
- 2 medium tomatoes, diced and drained
- 1 green pepper, diced (1/2 cup)
- 1 medium onions, diced (1/2 cup)
- 3 stalks celery, diced (1/2 cup)
- 2 tablespoons prepared mustard
- 1 teaspoons celery seed
- 1/2 teaspoon seasoned pepper
- 1/2 cup low-calorie mayonnaise
- 1/4 cup pickle relish
- 1/2 teaspoon salt or Morton's Nature's seasoning

Cook macaroni according to package directions. Drain well for at least 5 minutes. Drain diced tomatoes. In large bowl, mix green pepper, onion, celery, mustard, celery seed, seasoned pepper, mayonnaise, pickle relish, and salt. Stir to blend well. Add drained macaroni and stir to coat well.

Add tomatoes and toss gently just until well mixed. Refrigerate.

Serve cold or at room temperature.

POTATOES

BAKED HOME FRY WEDGES   *Makes 4 servings*

A good alternative to french fries without all the calories! These are delicious!

> 2 very large baking potatoes
> Italian seasoning
> Garlic salt
> Cayenne pepper
> Dried minced basil
> No-stick cooking spray

On terry cloth dish towel, place potatoes on one end and roll up towel, folding in ends of towel, so that potatoes are completely enclosed. If preferred, wrap in plastic wrap.

Microwave 5 minutes on high. Turn potatoes 90 degrees. Microwave another 5 minutes. Test potatoes. They should be firm yet yield slightly when firmly squeezed.

Let wrapped potatoes rest for at least 10 minutes to complete cooking. Uncover and cool until they can be handled.

Cut each potato lengthwise into eight spears. Place skin side down on baking sheet, not touching. Spray each potato generously with no-stick cooking spray. Sprinkle the seasonings generously over the spears.

Bake in 350 degree oven for about 20 to 30 minutes, or until golden brown. Serve hot.

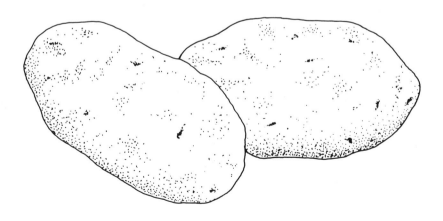

GERMAN POTATO SALAD   *Makes 6 servings*

If you've never tried hot potato salad, give this luscious German version a try.

4	slices bacon, diced
8	medium potatoes, cooked, drained, peeled and chopped
2	eggs
1/3-1/2	cup sugar
1/2	cup vinegar
1/4	teaspoon dry mustard
1/4	teaspoon pepper
1	tablepoon salt
1	tablespoon diced green pepper
1/2	cup pickle relish
4	stalks (1 cup diced) celery

In 3-quart saucepan or frying pan over medium heat, cook bacon until browned and crisp. Remove from pan, drain on paper towels and blot any excess fat (see page 140).

Cook potatoes until tender; drain well. Peel potatoes and chop into small pieces. In small bowl, mix eggs, sugar, vinegar, pepper, mustard and salt. Leave 1/4 cup bacon drippings in pan. Discard any excess drippings. Add egg mixture to saucepan, stirring constantly until sauce thickens, but does not boil. Remove from heat.

Stir in potatoes, green pepper, onion, pickle relish, celery and bacon. Gently toss to coat all ingredients. Serve warm.

GRANDMOTHER'S POTATO SALAD *Makes 6 to 8 servings*

Before commercial mayonnaise was available, my grandmother made her "special" **Homemade Dressing** for potato salad. It only takes a few minutes to make the dressing, which is the secret to this potato salad's wonderful flavor.

  6-8   medium potatoes, peeled, cooked, drained and diced (5 cups diced potatoes)

     1   tablespoons fresh minced parsley

     3   tablespoons pickle relish, drained

     3   tablespoons finely minced onion

         Homemade Dressing (recipe follows)

After draining diced potatoes, mash some of them with a fork or potato masher. Add parsley, relish and onion to potatoes. Pour half of the dressing over potato mixture and stir until well mixed. Add more dressing if needed and refrigerate any remaining dressing. If desired, add salt and pepper to taste.

Serve potato salad cold or at room temperature. Store in refrigerator.

VARIATION: Add 2 boiled eggs, diced or grated

Homemade Dressing

2	tablespoons flour	1/2	cup vinegar
1/4	cup sugar	1/2	cup water
1	teaspoon dry mustard	1	egg, beaten
1	teaspoon salt	1/2	teaspoon pepper (optional)

Mix flour, sugar, dry mustard and salt together in a saucepan. Then gradually add water, vinegar and egg, stirring with a wire whisk. Heat on medium heat, stirring constantly until sauce thickens to the consistency of mayonnaise.

Use as dressing for potato salad or refrigerate until needed. This keeps for up to 5 days.

HOLIDAY POTATOES
Makes 8 to 10 servings

Because this classic recipe can be prepared in advance and is delicious with so many meals, it is the most-often requested potato casserole.

- 1/2 cup (1 stick) margarine, room temperature
- 1/2 cup chopped onion
- 2 (8 ounce each) cartons sour cream
- 1 teaspoon salt
- 1 can cream of chicken soup
- 8 ounces (2 cups) grated sharp cheddar cheese
- 2 pounds frozen hash brown potatoes, thawed and drained
- 1 recipe **Crunchy Topping** (recipe follows)

Preheat oven to 350 degrees. Spray 9x12x2-inch casserole with no-stick cooking spray.

In large bowl, add margarine, onion, sour cream, salt, soup and cheese. Stir to mix. Add potatoes and mix well. Pour potato mixture into casserole dish. Cover.

Bake 30 minutes. Uncover, add **Crunchy Topping** and continue baking for another 30 minutes.

VARIATIONS: **To Lower Calories**:

> Omit sour cream and 1/2 cup margarine. Add 1/2 cup low calorie mayonnaise and 1 teaspoon black pepper. Use only 1 cup grated cheese.

Crunchy Topping

- 1/2 cup margarine, melted
- 2 cups crushed corn flakes

Mix margarine and corn flakes. Use as a topping on casseroles.

MASHED POTATOES WITH GRAVY *Makes 5 to 6 servings*

A classic without which no Southern cookbook would be complete.

4-5	large potatoes
1/4	cup (1/2 stick) margarine or butter
1/4-1/2	cup skim milk
1/4	cup sour cream
1/2	teaspoon salt
1/4	teaspoon pepper

Boil potatoes until tender. While potatoes are boiling, place margarine, 1/4 cup of milk, sour cream, salt and pepper in mixing bowl. Mix until blended. When potatoes are done, cool slightly and peel while they are still rather hot. Cut potatoes into large hunks and place in bowl. With electric mixer, cream potatoes and other ingredients until well blended and smooth. Add remainder of milk for a thinner consistency.

Serve hot. Or place in greased casserole and microwave until hot, about 3 minutes, before serving. Serve with **Chicken Gravy** (recipe follows), if desired.

Chicken Gravy *Makes 1 cup*

1	cup water
1 1/2	teaspoons chicken bouillon
1-2	drops gravy browning and seasoning sauce
1 1/2	teaspoons corn starch

Heat 3/4 cups water, bouillon and seasoning sauce until bouillon dissolves. Dissolve corn starch in remaining 1/4 cup water. Pour corn starch mixture into hot bouillon mixture, stirring constantly, until thickened, about 1 minute.

To make 2 cups of gravy, double all recipe ingredients. If more thickening is needed, use 1 1/2 teaspoons corn starch to each tablespoon water.

Cooking Tip

Because so many nutrients of a potato are just under its skin, boil potatoes before peeling. Also, since the cooked skin can be removed without losing any potato, it is more economical to boil before peeling.

SCALLOPED POTATO CASSEROLE   *Makes 4 to 6 servings*

4	ounces (1 cup) grated cheddar cheese	1	cup skim milk
1	can cream of mushroom soup	6	medium potatoes, peeled and sliced
1/4	teaspoon pepper	4	medium onions, sliced
1	teaspoons salt		

Preheat oven to 350 degrees. Lightly grease a 2-quart casserole dish.

Mix soup, pepper, salt and milk together. In the prepared casserole dish, place half of the potatoes in a layer, then half of the onions. Pour half of soup mixture over potatoes and onions. Repeat layers with the remaining potatoes, onions and soup. Sprinkle grated cheese on top.

Bake uncovered for about 1-1/2 hours.

SIMPLE POTATO CASSEROLE   *Makes 4 servings*

Designed for the calorie conscious, a delectable potato dish without any sauce.

2	large onions, peeled and thinly sliced	1/4	teaspoon salt
4	large potatoes, peeled and thinly sliced	1/8	teaspoon pepper
2	tablespoons margarine or butter, melted		

Preheat oven to 350 degrees. Spray a 9x12x2-inch casserole with no-stick cooking spray.

Place 1/2 of potatoes in layer in casserole dish. Place 1/2 half of onions evenly over potato layer. Sprinkle 1/2 of salt and pepper over casserole. Place remaining 1/2 of potatoes in casserole. Then add remaining onions. Sprinkle remaining salt and pepper over casserole. Pour margarine evenly over casserole.

Cover with lid or aluminum foil and bake for 20 minutes. Uncover and bake an additional 40 to 50 minutes until potatoes are tender and casserole is golden brown on top. The casserole is done when a fork can be easily inserted into center of casserole.

VARIATIONS: If you like a creamy sauce, sprinkle 1 tablespoon corn starch over first layer of potatoes. Pour 1 cup skim milk over top of casserole. Dot with 3 tablespoons margarine. Bake as directed above.

Served with **Pickled Beets** (page 258), a green salad and toasted **Crunchy Seasoned Bread** (page 89).

Ham and Potato Casserole

To the **Simple Potato Casserole** recipe, add the following:

One (6 to 7 1/2 ounce) can ham or 8 ounces cooked ham or smoked pork shoulder may be added after the first onion layer.

Bake as directed above.

SPEEDY BAKED POTATOES
Makes 4 servings

If you think cooking a potato in the microwave dries it out, try this recipe. The potatoes are soft and moist every time!

    4 medium to large Idaho baking potatoes
    plastic wrap, as needed

Wash potatoes and drain. Wrap each potato in plastic wrap. Place potatoes in microwave. Microwave on High for 10 minutes. Let rest 5 minutes. Turn potatoes 90 degrees. Microwave on High again for 10 minutes. Let rest again for 5 minutes. Test potatoes for doneness by squeezing on sides of potato. If potatoes are done, they will "give" when squeezed. If potatoes are large, you may need to repeat process and cook 5 more minutes and let rest.

When potatoes are done, leave them in plastic wrap until ready to serve. Remove from plastic wrap before serving.

Serve hot and pass the butter and sour cream. Or use artificial butter granules. They are a delicious way to reduce fat and cholesterol, yet give a wonderful butter taste to potatoes.

For Two Servings

Wrap 2 potatoes in plastic wrap as directed above. Microwave for 5 minutes. Let rest 5 minutes. Test for doneness. If potatoes don't pass the squeeze test, repeat process of cooking 5 minutes and resting 5 minutes. Test for doneness.

TWICE-BAKED STUFFED POTATOES

Makes 15 to 20 servings

When Idaho potatoes are plentiful and prices are lowest, purchase a large bag, prepare these potatoes and freeze for later use. It's great to have these in the freezer for unexpected company.

      12 medium to large Idaho baking potatoes
     1/2 cup (1 stick) margarine or butter
   3/4-1 cup of skim milk
       2 teaspoons salt
       1 teaspoon pepper
       4 ounces (1 cup) grated cheddar cheese
           paprika

Preheat oven to 350 degrees. Cover bottom of two (2) 9x12-inch baking pan with aluminum foil. Wash potatoes and dry. Place on baking pan so that potatoes are not touching. Bake for 1 to 1 1/2 hours or until done. When potatoes give a little when firmly squeezed, potatoes are done. Remove from the oven.

In large mixing bowl, place margarine, salt and pepper. Cut each potato in half to make two long potato halves. With a spoon, scoop out most of the potato, leaving a thin shell of potato attached to the skin, and place in the mixing bowl on top of the margarine. Reserve skins.

With an electric mixer, cream all ingredients together, adding milk a little at a time. With a spoon, stir in the cheese until well mixed. Fill each potato half by stuffing the shell with creamed potato mixture.

Return to oven and bake about 20 minutes until slightly browned on top and cheese is melted. Serve hot. Stuffed potatoes may be microwaved to heat and melt cheese.

Potatoes may be stuffed and refrigerated until ready to bake the second time.

To Freeze:

Cover stuffed potatoes with plastic wrap and freeze. When solidly frozen, remove potatoes from pan and store in a plastic bag. When ready to serve, remove the desired number of potatoes, place in pan, cover with foil and bake as above, adding about 25 to 30 minutes to cooking time (total 45 to 50 minutes).

Serve with steak, ribs, roast or grilled chicken and a green salad.

Cooking Tip

Because the outer skin needs to be a little crusty so that you can remove inner potato meat easily, it is not recommended that you microwave these potatoes during the first cooking, before stuffing.

RICE

EASY ONION RICE

Makes 4 servings

Rice with taste appeal!

3/4	cup long-grain rice, uncooked	3/4	cup water
1	(10-1/2 ounce) can French onion soup	1/4	cup (1/2 stick) margarine or butter, melted

Preheat oven to 350 degrees. Lightly grease a 2-quart casserole. Mix rice, soup, water, and margarine. Pour into prepared casserole.

Bake 45 minutes to 1 hour until rice is tender, stirring once after baking 30 minutes.

Easy Onion Rice—Version #2

1	cup uncooked rice	1	can beef consomme
1	package dry onion soup mix	1	soup can of water

Prepare and bake as directed above.

HOT SEASONED RICE MOLD

Makes 4 to 6 servings

Tired of plain rice? Try this colorful, tasty rice!

- 3 cups cooked rice
- 4 ounces (1 cup) grated cheddar cheese, divided
- 1 (4 ounce) can diced green chilies
- 1 (2 ounce) jar diced pimentos, drained
- 1/3 cup skim milk
- 2 eggs, beaten
- 1/2 teaspoon salt
- 1/2 teaspoon pepper
- 1/2 teaspoon cumin

Combine rice, 1/2 cup cheese, chilies, pimento, milk, eggs, salt, pepper, and cumin. Evenly divide mixture into 12 muffin cups sprayed with no-stick cooking spray. Sprinkle with remaining cheese.

Preheat oven to 400 degrees. Bake for 15 minutes or until set. Remove from mold and serve.

These may be cooked and frozen and reheated on high in the microwave.

VARIATIONS: Add 1/4 cup finely diced, cooked ham or canadian bacon.

Substitute 1/3 cup liquid egg substitute in place of 2 eggs.

SIMPLE MICROWAVE RICE   *Makes 4 servings*

Never worry about rice burning or sticking to the pot again. In the microwave, it cooks to perfection every single time.

    2   cups water
    1   cup long-grain, white rice

Add water and rice to 2-quart, covered glass dish, suitable for use in the microwave. Microwave on high for 3 minutes. Continue to microwave, using 50% power, for 15 minutes. Do not remove cover. Let stand, covered, for 15 minutes.

Remove cover and stir gently to fluff rice. Serve hot.

WHITE AND WILD RICE CASSEROLE   *Makes 12 servings*

1/2	cup (1 stick) margarine	1	cup long grain white rice
1	large onion, diced (1 1/2 cups)	5	cups chicken broth
2	green peppers, diced (1 1/2 cups)	1/2	teaspoon salt
3-4	stalks celery, diced (1 cup)	1/8	teaspoon pepper
12	ounces mushrooms, sliced	2	teaspoons parsley flakes
1	package wild rice with seasonings (1 cup rice)	1	can sliced water chestnuts

Preheat oven to 350 degrees. Lightly grease 12x16-inch (3-quart) casserole.

In frying pan, melt margarine. Saute onions, peppers, celery and mushrooms until tender. Add wild rice, white rice, broth, salt, pepper, parsley and water chestnuts. Stir to mix well. Pour into prepared casserole.

Bake 1 to 1 1/2 hours until all moisture is absorbed and rice is tender.

VARIATION: In place of 5 cups broth, use 5 cups water and 5 to 7 teaspoons chicken bouillon.

* * * * * * * * * *

How to Reheat Rice in the Microwave

Rice reheats well in a microwave. To insure perfect results, cover rice and reheat on 80% power for 1 to 4 minutes, depending upon the quantity of rice being reheated. Three cups of cooked rice takes about 2 minutes.

Rice can be cooked in advance and refrigerated until needed, up to 5 days. Then reheat when ready to serve. Fluff rice before serving.

11

Pickling & Canning

PICKLING AND CANNING

PICKLES

If either you or a friend has a small garden, invariably it will produce an over-abundance of fresh cabbage, cucumbers, peppers and tomatoes. If you don't want to eat cabbage every day, yet you can't stand to see any of those luscious vegetables over-ripen, age or spoil, what do you do?

Select a recipe from this section and make pickles to be enjoyed all year long. Don't let the number of days required to prepare some of the pickles make you hesitant to try these recipes. Although many pickles are prepared in several steps on consecutive days, each step requires only a few minutes. Hot pepper jelly can be made in one afternoon and enjoyed throughout the year.

Although pickles are often served with sandwiches, barbecue and other meals, these pickles also make a delightful appetizer when served layered with cheese on crackers.

ELLA'S CHOW CHOW

Chow-Chow was a specialty of my mother-in-law, the late Ella Weeks. When served as a condiment, its mustard base enhances the flavor of cooked, leafy green vegetables, such as collards, kale and mustard greens.

The proportions below are recommended, but may be adjusted according to the fresh vegetables available in your area.

6 quarts chopped vegetables: (any combination of the following)

- 2 quarts chopped cabbage or chopped cauliflower
- 1 quart chopped green tomatoes
- 1 pint grated carrots
- 1 pint chopped green peppers
- 1 quart chopped, peeled pears
- 1 quart chopped onions

Chow Chow Syrup

Make a syrup of the following ingredients:

- 1 quart vinegar
- 1/2 cup flour
- 2 cups sugar
- 1 tablespoon salt
- 1 1/2 tablespoons celery seed
- 1 tablespoon tumeric
- 1 1/2 tablespoons dry ground mustard

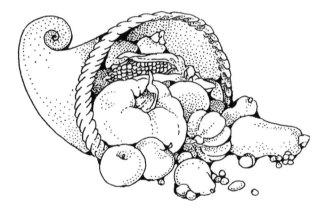

In a large pot, bring syrup to a boil, and boil until thickened. Add vegetables and cook about 5 minutes until good and hot. Pack in hot sterilized jars (pints or quarts) and seal with hot, sterilized canning lids and rims.

Store canned Chow Chow on your pantry shelves for up to 1 year. Chill before serving.

VARIATIONS: Substitute any of the following vegetables:

yellow summer squash
any mild pepper, such as banana peppers
fresh corn, cut from the cob

HOT PEPPER JELLY   *Makes about 4 pints or 8 half pints*

Pour this jelly over a block of cream cheese, serve with crackers, and you have a delicious appetizer.

      1/4   cup chopped green or red HOT peppers (see Preparation Tip below)
    1 1/2   cups chopped green pepper
    1 1/2   cups vinegar
    6 1/2   cups sugar
        1   bottle liquid pectin or Certo

In blender or food processor, add vinegar and then add all peppers and process until finely ground. To a large pot, add ground pepper mixture and sugar. Over high heat, bring to a brisk, continuous boil. Boil 3 minutes. Add pectin or Certo and boil 1 minute longer. Remove from heat and let rest 5 minutes. Pour mixture into hot, sterilized jars and seal. Cool. If well sealed, jelly will keep for 9 months to 1 year.

Preparation Tip

   Use all green or all red peppers, and the jelly will be a pretty red or green. If colors are mixed, the jelly will be an unpleasant brown color.

HOT-SWEET CUCUMBER PICKLES

Makes 8 to 12 pint jars

A sweet, crunchy pickle with a slight tangy bite! It makes an especially delicious **House Specialty Appetizer** (recipe follows). This pickle takes 3 days from start to finish; however, total time spent in the kitchen is less than an hour per day.

Soaking Solution

1	gallon (4 quarts) water
7 1/2	pounds of cucumbers, sliced
1	cup "pickling" lime

Day 1: Soak cucumbers in above solution of water and lime for 24 hours, making sure all cucumber slices are covered. Place plate on top and weight with a heavy, clean object, such as a gallon of water.

Day 2: Remove cucumbers, wash well until water is clear. Soak in clear water for 3 hours. Drain and wash again and place in the following solution and leave overnight.

Pickling Mixture:

2	quarts vinegar
4 1/2	lbs sugar (9 cups) (see insert below)
1/2	box pickling spices
1	tablespoon salt

Day 3: After soaking cucumbers overnight, pour vinegar mixture into large cooking pot. Bring to boil. Add cucumbers and bring to boil again. Boil 35 minutes. Seal in hot, sterilized, pint canning jars. CHILL before serving.

House Specialty Appetizer

Serve chilled, drained pickle slices in bowl. Serve a bowl of sliced Summer Sausage and a bowl of crackers. To assemble, each guest places a sausage slice on a cracker and tops with a pickle slice. Eat and enjoy!

* * * * * * * * *

How to Measure Large Quantities of Sugar

Five pounds of sugar contains approximately 10 cups of sugar. To easily measure 9 cups, remove 1 cup from a 5-pound bag and use remainder of the bag of sugar.

PICKLED HOT PEPPERS   *Makes 3 pints*

Preserve those hot peppers for year-round enjoyment by pickling them. This is quick and easy (less than 45 minutes). Suggestions for using this condiment are listed (see Serving Tip below).

- 48 fresh hot peppers, about 3 to 4 inches long and 1-inch in diameter at the stem end
- 1 quart vinegar
- 2 tablespoons sugar
- 1 teaspoon salt
- 3 clean pint jars with sealable lids

Wash peppers and remove the stem, leaving as much of the pepper as possible. Drain peppers in colander.

In large 3-quart pot, heat the vinegar, sugar and salt over high heat until the sugar is dissolved. Add the peppers. Bring to a boil and boil 2 minutes. Remove pot from heat.

With tongs, remove peppers from vinegar solution and pack into the pint jars, pressing gently to pack. Pour vinegar solution over peppers to within 1 inch from the top. Press peppers to submerge in vinegar solution. Wipe rim of jar, add top and seal.

Store in cool dry place. These peppers will keep for months.

Serving Tip

For those people who like spicy hot foods, slice peppers and use them as a condiment for the following:

| butter beans | stir-fry beef | string beans |
| taco salads | october beans (canned) | pizza topping |

STRAWBERRY FIG PRESERVES   *Makes 4 pints*

This tastes just like strawberry preserves.

- 6 cups mashed figs
- 6 cups sugar
- 1 box Sure-Jell or 1 package Pectin
- 3 small packages strawberry gelatine dessert mix

In large pot, place sugar and figs and boil for 20 minutes, stirring frequently. Add gelatine and Sure-Jell and boil for an additional 5 minutes.

Pour into hot, sterilized canning jars. Seal well.

12

Pies

PIES

PIES

Does the aroma of an apple pie baking make you think of a warm hearth, snow on the ground and family togetherness? With the modern convenience of frozen pie shells, both regular and deep-dish, making a pie is easier than ever.

For the chocolate lover, why not try French Silk Chocolate Pie, Fudge Pie or Chocolate Pecan Pie? When fresh strawberries are in season, make a Fresh Strawberry Pie.

To insure a tender crust, keep pie shell frozen or refrigerated until ready to bake. Refrigerator pies, such as Heath Bar Pie and Lemon Fluff Pie, need to be chilled several hours before serving.

When making pies, it is often just as easy to make two pies and freeze one for later. When pecans are in season, make several Southern Pecan Pies, freeze them and serve them later for special occasions. When you try these recipes, wonderful desserts await you and your family—and your lucky guests!

BUTTERMILK LEMON PIE

Makes one 9-inch deep dish pie

An old-family recipe of my Aunt Phil that's too delicious to be forgotten.

2	cups sugar	3	eggs
1/2	cup (1 stick) margarine or butter	1	cup nonfat buttermilk
1/4	cup flour	1 1/2	teaspoons lemon extract flavoring
1/8	teaspoon salt	1	nine-inch unbaked Deep Dish pie shell

Preheat oven to 350 degrees.

Beat sugar and margarine until creamy. Gradually add flour and salt, beating until blended. Add eggs and beat until fluffy. Continue beating and slowly add buttermilk and lemon extract. Beat until well blended. Pour into unbaked pie shell.

Bake for about 45 minutes until lightly browned on top and center of pie is set. Cool and serve at room temperature. Cut into wedges.

Because this is a large pie, it requires a deep-dish pie shell. **Do Not** substitute a smaller pie shell.

CHOCOLATE PECAN PIE

Makes 1 nine-inch pie

A pecan pie for chocolate lovers!

1 1/4	cups corn syrup
1/2	cup sugar
4	squares (1 ounce each) unsweetened baking chocolate, cut into pieces
1/2	cup evaporated skim milk
3	eggs, slightly beaten
1	cup pecan halves
1	nine-inch unbaked pie shell

Preheat oven to 350 degrees.

In saucepan, heat corn syrup, sugar, chocolate and milk, stirring constantly, until chocolate melts. Remove from heat. Slowly stir hot mixture into beaten eggs. Stir in pecan halves and pour into pastry.

Bake for 50 to 60 minutes. Cool several hours before serving. Cut into wedges. Top with a scoop of vanilla ice cream.

COCONUT PIE   *Makes 2 eight-inch pies or 1 (9 5/8") deep dish pie*

This pie makes its own crust.

1/3	cup (5 tablespoons) margarine
3/4	cup sugar
4	eggs
1	cup skim milk
1	cup nonfat buttermilk
1	teaspoon lemon flavoring
1/2	cup plus 2 tablespoons self-rising flour
1	(7 ounce) can shredded coconut (about 2 3/4 cups)

Preheat oven to 350 degrees.

Beat margarine and sugar together until well blended. Add eggs, one at a time, beating after each addition. Add milk and lemon flavoring, and beat until blended. Add flour and coconut and beat until well blended. Pour half of mixture into each pie shell.

Bake 30 to 40 minutes until crust forms and pie is lightly browned on top and set in the center. Cool.

Cut each pie into 6 to 8 wedges. Serve at room temperature.

VARIATION: Pour **Citrus Sauce Supreme** (page 104) over each slice of pie.

CREAMY PEACH PIE   *Makes one 9-inch pie*

Not the usual hot peach pie, this one is refrigerated.

1	(8 ounce) package cream cheese	1/4	cup lemon juice
2	eggs, divided into yolks and whites	1	(10 ounce) package frozen peaches, drained
1	(14 ounce) can sweetened condensed milk	1	nine-inch pie shell, baked

Preheat oven to 400 degrees.

In small bowl, beat egg whites until stiff. Set aside.

In large bowl, mix the cream cheese, egg yolks, condensed milk and lemon juice until well blended. Stir in the peaches. Pour into baked pie shell. Spread beaten egg whites on top of pie to form a meringue. Bake until meringue is browned on top. (about 15 minutes). Filling does not need to be cooked. Cool and then refrigerate.

VARIATIONS: Substitute 10 ounces of strawberries for peaches.

Substitute 1 can (16 oz) canned apple slices for peaches. Add 1/2 tsp. Apple Pie Spice.

CRYSTAL LIGHT LEMON PIE

Makes one 9-inch pie

Although there are many delicious drink mixes on the market, this particular pie was made with Crystal Light brand drink mix. If you have a favorite drink mix, try substituting it for the Crystal Light below.

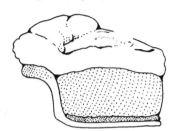

- 1 graham cracker pie crust, baked until golden browned, cooled.
- 2 envelopes of unflavored gelatine
- 1/2 cup sugar
- 3/4 cup boiling water
- 2 eggs, separated into yolk and white
- 1 tub (.55 ounces) dry Crystal Light Lemonade Mix (see inset below)
- 1 cup crushed ice

In food processor or blender, combine gelatine, 1/4 cup sugar and boiling water. Cover and process on High for about 40 seconds. Add egg yolks and process 10 seconds longer. With food processor or blender running, add Crystal Light Lemonade Mix crystals and cracked ice. Process until smooth.

In a small bowl using electric mixer, beat egg whites for 2 minutes until fluffy. Gradually add 1/4 cup sugar and beat until stiff.

Gently fold gelatine mixture into egg whites until well blended. Pour into baked pie crust. Chill several hours until set.

Cut into wedges, top with nondairy whipped cream and serve. Garnish with a few shavings of semi-sweet chocolate on top of whipped topping.

VARIATIONS: To make a lime pie, substitute 1 tub of Crystal Light Limeade mix for Lemonade mix. Pour pie into a baked graham-cracker crust.

Preparation Tip

One tub of Crystal Light Lemonade mix is the amount used to make 2 quarts of lemonade drink.

FLAKY PIE CRUST   *Makes one 8 or 9 -inch pastry*

When time permits, use this tender crust instead of a ready-made pie shell.

8-inch pie crust		**9-inch pie crust**	
1 1/2	cups flour	2	cups flour
1/4	teaspoon salt	1/2	teaspoon salt
1/2	cup shortening	2/3	cup shortening
4-5	tablespoons cold water	5-6	tablespoons cold water

In medium bowl, mix flour and salt. Add shortening and cut into flour mixture using a pastry blender or a fork.   Continue mixing until shortening is cut into pieces about the size of green peas or smaller. Add cold water and stir to make a stiff dough. Add additional water as needed.

Place dough on a clean, floured surface. Rub flour on rolling pin. Roll dough into a circle large enough to cover pie pan and hang over edges just a little. To remove pie shell from surface, start at one end and roll pastry around rolling pin. Place rolled pastry over pie pan and unroll. Press or crimp edges of pie shell, trimming as needed, until shell fits pie pan. Refrigerate immediately or add filling and bake.

Preheat oven to 400 degrees. With a fork, poke about 6 sets of tine marks into bottom of pie shell. Bake about 10 to 12 minutes, poking more tine marks into shell if it develops bubbles in the crust. Cool.

FOX HUNTER PIE   *Makes 1 pie*

For many years, Fox Hunter pie was served at the famous Fox Head Inn restaurant located in Manakin, Virginia, and owned by my aunt and uncle, Ethyl and Ralph Fields. Although the original recipe made 3 pies, this one has been modified to make only 1 pie and cocoa has been added.

1	unbaked pie crust	1	cup sugar
1/2	cups chocolate chips	1	tablespoon flour
3/4	cups finely chopped pecans	2	teaspoons cocoa baking mix
3/4	teaspoons vanilla	1/8	teaspoon salt
1/3	cup margarine or butter	3	eggs

Preheat oven to 325 degrees.

Pour 1/2 cup chocolate chips and 3/4 cup chopped nuts into pie shell. Beat vanilla, butter, sugar, flour, cocoa and salt together until creamy. Gradually add eggs, one at a time, and beat until mixture is well blended. Mixture will be thick. Pour mixture into pie shell.

Bake for 35 to 40 minutes. Cool. Cut into small wedges as this pie is very rich.

VARIATION: omit cocoa baking mix
                         substitute walnuts for pecans

FRESH STRAWBERRY PIE
Makes two nine-inch pie

During the fresh strawberry season, this pie will be especially delicious. The texture is light, creamy and brings out that fresh strawberry taste! This was shared by Carolyn Tucker, Aiken, SC.

2	nine-inch pie shells, baked and cooled
1	(4 ounce) package vanilla pudding and pie filling (not instant)
1	(3 ounce) package strawberry or wild strawberry gelatine
1 3/4	cups water
1	teaspoon lemon juice
8	ounces prepared nondairy whipped cream topping
2 1/2-3	cups sliced fresh strawberries

Combine pudding mix, gelatine, water and lemon juice. Stir and heat over medium heat until the mixture comes to a boil, and boil 30 seconds, stirring constantly. Pour into a bowl and chill in refrigerator for about 2 hours.

Fold in 1 1/2 cups whipped cream topping and blend well. Stir 2 1/2 cups strawberries into the mixture. Pour strawberry mixture into prepared pie shells. Chill 1 to 2 hours until set. Spread remaining whipped cream topping in a thin layer on each pie. Decorate topping layer with remaining sliced strawberries.

Refrigerate. Cut into wedges. Serve cold.

VARIATIONS: Use any flavor gelatine and any fresh fruit, such as orange gelatine and well-drained orange sections, OR Peach gelatine and fresh peach slices.

* * * * * * * * *

How to Store Fruit Pies

Fruit pies contain acids which will react with aluminum foil. Therefore, to protect pies after baking, cover with plastic wrap. If desired, place a layer of aluminum foil over the plastic wrap.

FRENCH SILK CHOCOLATE PIE   *Makes 6 to 8 servings*

With an unforgettably smooth texture and a light chocolate flavor, this is an all-time favorite chocolate pie!

- 1   nine-inch pie shell, baked until golden brown
- 1/2   cup (1 stick) margarine or butter
- 3/4   cups sugar
- 1   square (1 ounce) unsweetened baking chocolate, melted and cooled
- 1   teaspoon vanilla flavoring
- 2   eggs

With an electric mixer, place butter and sugar in large bowl and beat on medium speed for at least 5 minutes, until creamed thoroughly. Blend in melted chocolate. Add vanilla. Add 2 eggs, one at a time, beating 5 minutes after each addition until mixture is thick and creamy. Pour chocolate mixture into baked pie shell. Refrigerate. Chill 1 hour or more. Cut into 6 to 8 slices.

This may be garnished with dollops of whipped cream, chopped pecans or shavings of unsweetened baking chocolate.

It can be frozen and thawed in refrigerator 2 hours before serving.

VARIATIONS: **For a crowd or the freezer:**

Triple the recipe above and add 2 tablespoons coffee liqueur, 2 teaspoons instant freeze-dried coffee, and 1 teaspoon brandy flavoring. Makes 3 pies and serves 18-24 people.

To shave baking chocolate, grate chocolate with a hand grater

FUDGE PIE
Makes one 9-inch pie

Chocolate lovers will crave this sinfully delicious pie! This recipe was given to me so many, many years ago that the donor is unknown.

Nutty Crust

- 1/4 cup (1/2 stick) margarine, at room temperature
- 1/4 cup sugar
- 1 tablespoon flour
- 1 cup chopped pecans, walnuts or almonds

Mix margarine, sugar, flour and nuts until well blended. Press over bottom and sides of 9-inch pie pan.

Fudge Filling

- 1/2 cup (1 stick) margarine
- 1 cup sugar
- 3 eggs
- 2 (1 ounce each) squares unsweetened baking chocolate, melted and cooled (see page 120)
- 1/2 cup flour
- 1 teaspoon vanilla flavoring
- 1/2 teaspoon baking powder
- 1/8 teaspoon salt

Topping: 1 pint frozen vanilla ice milk or ice cream

Preheat oven to 325 degrees.

With electric mixer, beat margarine, sugar, eggs, chocolate, flour, vanilla, baking powder and salt until well blended and smooth. Pour chocolate mixture into prepared crust.

Bake for 35 minutes until set.

Let cool for 10 to 20 minutes before serving. Serve with a scoop of vanilla ice milk on top.

VARIATION: Serve whipped nondairy topping on pie instead of ice cream.

HEATH BAR PIE   *Makes one 9-inch pie*

If you like cheesecake, toffee, and chocolate, you will love this rich flavor combination.

    1   nine-inch pie shell, baked until golden brown
    1/2 teaspoon cream of tartar
    2   eggs, separated into yolk and white
    2   (8 ounces each) packages cream cheese
    1   teaspoon lemon juice or vanilla flavoring
    3/4 cup sugar
    4   Heath candy bars (1.4 ounces each), crushed into small pieces
    2   (1 ounce each) squares semi-sweet baking chocolate, melted

With electric mixer on high, beat egg whites until stiff. In large bowl, mix cream cheese, egg yolks, sugar and flavoring until mixture is very creamy. Gently fold in beaten egg whites.

Place 1/3 of creamed mixture into baked pie pastry and spread into a layer. Drizzle melted chocolate over this layer. Add another 1/3 of creamed mixture to pie, making another layer. Sprinkle crushed Heath bar candy over second layer. Top with remaining creamed mixture making a third layer.

Chill pie several hours or overnight. Cut into 8 small servings, as this pie is rich.

Preparation Tip

To crush candy bars: While candy is still wrapped, bend wrapper to break bars into smaller pieces. Place small pieces in a mini-food processor and chop until crumbs are formed.

Or place in a sealable plastic bag. Remove as much air as possible and seal. Place on a counter and strike candy with a heavy object, such as a meat mallet or the heavy end of a cooking spoon until candy is cracked into very small pieces.

LEMON FLUFF PIE
Makes two 8-inch pies or one deep-dish 9-inch pie

The texture is as airy as a cloud, and the filling is almost that high.

Pie Filling

1	envelope unflavored gelatine	1	cup sugar
1/2	teaspoon salt	4	egg yolks
2/3	cup lemon juice	1 2/3	cups water
1	teaspoon grated lemon peel	4	egg whites
1	nine-inch deep-dish pie shell, baked	1/2	cup sugar

In saucepan, place gelatine, 1 cup sugar and salt. Beat egg yolks, lemon juice and water together and stir into gelatine mixture. Cook over medium heat, stirring constantly, until mixture just begins to boil. Remove from heat. Stir in lemon peel. Chill, stirring occasionally, until partially set.

In mixing bowl, add egg whites and beat until soft peaks form. Gradually add 1/2 cup sugar, beating until stiff peaks form and sugar has dissolved. Fold this mixture into gelatine mixture. Pour into prepared pie shell. Refrigerate and chill until firm, about 2 hours.

Cut into small wedges and serve with a dollop of whipped cream on top.

OLD-FASHIONED LEMON CHESS PIE
One 9-inch pie or nine tarts

Lemon lovers will adore this old Virginia family favorite with a rich lemon taste! This was the lemon pie most cherished by my father.

2	eggs, separated into white and yolk
1	cup sugar
1 1/2	tablespoons corn meal
	Juice of 1 1/2 lemons (about 1/4 cup juice)
1/4	cup (1/2 stick) margarine or butter
1	nine-inch unbaked pie shell

Preheat oven to 400 degrees. In small bowl, with electric mixer, beat egg **whites** until stiff.

In large bowl, beat sugar, cornmeal, lemon juice, margarine and egg **yolks** for 5 minutes or until fluffy and creamy. Gently fold egg whites into egg yolk mixture. Pour into pie crust.

Bake in oven until the top browns, about 15 minutes. Then lower oven temperature to 300 degrees and bake about 25 to 30 minutes more until pie filling is set.

To store, cover with plastic wrap (see page 203). Store at room temperature and keep for up to 5 days. Pie may be refrigerated.

PECAN PIE
Makes two 9-inch pies

A Southern specialty! When pecans are plentiful, bake several and freeze them for later.

1/2	cup (1 stick) margarine, melted	2	tablespoons water
1	(16 ounce) box light brown sugar (2 1/4 cups)	1	tablespoon vanilla
2	tablespoons corn meal	2	cups chopped pecans
1/2	teaspoon salt	2	nine-inch unbaked pie shells
4	eggs, beaten		

Preheat oven to 350 degrees.

In large mixing bowl, beat margarine, brown sugar, corn meal, salt, and eggs until creamy. Add water and vanilla. Beat until mixed. Stir in pecans. Pour half of filling into each pie shell.

Bake for 15 minutes. Reduce temperature to 300 degrees and bake an additional 20 to 25 minutes until pie is set in the center.

Cool and cut into wedges. Garnish with a scoop of vanilla ice milk or ice cream.

STRAWBERRY PIE
Makes one 9-inch deep-dish

A wonderful way to enjoy strawberries when not in season. It is even better when made with fresh strawberries.

4	tablespoons corn starch
1	cup sugar
12	ounces (1 1/2 cups) "7-Up", regular or diet
6	drops red food coloring
2	(10 oz each) pkgs. frozen strawberries, thawed & drained OR 2 cups sliced fresh strawberries
1	nine-inch deep-dish pie shell, baked and cooled
1	package frozen nondairy whipped topping

If using frozen strawberries, thaw each package in microwave for 3 minutes on 30% power and set aside to drain. In medium pan, add cornstarch, sugar, "7-Up", and food coloring. Cook over medium heat until thickened. Cool. Add strawberries and mix well. Pour into baked pie shell.

Chill until set, several hours or overnight. Top with whipped topping before serving. Cut into 6 to 8 wedges.

VARIATION: add 1/4 teaspoon strawberry extract flavoring
Substitute an equal amount of frozen raspberries OR substitute frozen peaches and change food coloring to yellow.

13
Salads & Dressings

SALADS AND DRESSINGS

SALADS

Salads are visually appealing and add texture, variety and color to meals. They are a good source of fiber and low in calories. There are many variations of the congealed salad or tossed green salad.

A combination of different types of lettuce creates a more flavorful and colorful salad. Listed below are descriptions of the most common varieties of lettuce:

ICEBERG: A compact head of light green leaves with a very mild flavor. This is the most commonly-used head lettuce.

LEAF GREEN OR RED LETTUCE: This lettuce is darker green and grows in leafy bunches. The leaves have curly edges and are quite flavorful.

BOSTON: Also known as Butterhead, it has light green leaves which form a loose, rather than compact, head. It is very tender, yet crisp, and has a mild flavor.

BIBB: Also known as Limestone, it resembles Boston lettuce in shape and flavor; however, it is smaller and more delicate.

ROMAINE: It is a bunch of long, dark green, spoon-shaped leaves. It has a pungent flavor and coarser texture than most head lettuce.

SPINACH: Although this is not actually a lettuce, the tender green leaves give a delightful and unique taste and color to green salads.

Most salads can be made from any combination of lettuce varieties, with a mixture providing extra flavor, texture, and color.

Although many hundreds of bottled salad dressings are on the market, a homemade dressing adds that "something special" to any salad. Homemade croutons are like a cherry on a hot-fudge sundae, the crown to perfection.

SALADS

CHEF SALAD

Makes 4 salads

This salad is a fulfilling meal in itself, either for lunch or dinner. Increase quantities of ingredients to satisfy the heartiest appetites.

8-12	large leaf green lettuce leaves	4	ounces sliced cooked ham
1	small onion, thinly sliced	4	hard-boiled eggs, peeled
1	small green pepper, diced	2	tomatoes, cut into wedges
1	carrot, peeled and grated	4	ounces (1 cup) grated cheddar cheese
1	cucumber, unpeeled, thinly sliced	1	cup **Crunchy Croutons** (page 221)
4	ounces sliced cooked turkey		dressings of your choice

Wash lettuce and drain. Break lettuce leaves into bite-sized pieces. Place in salad bowls. Evenly distribute onion, green pepper, carrots, cucumber, turkey and then ham. Grate 1 egg over each bowl. Place tomato wedges around the edge of each bowl. Sprinkle with cheese and top with croutons.

Serve with a variety of different salad dressings, such as **Blue Cheese Supreme, KS Sweet and Sour Dressing,** or **Thousand Island Dressing** (pages 219 and 220).

VARIATIONS: Add 1/4 cup **Overnight Marinated Bean Salad** (page 216) to each salad.

Add 2 fresh mushrooms, sliced, to each salad.

CRANBERRY ORANGE SALAD

Makes 8 servings

1	pound whole cranberries
2	(3 ounce each) packages of lemon gelatine
2	cups boiling water
2	cups sugar
2	oranges, peeled, sectioned and chopped
1	cup chopped nuts, pecans or walnuts
2	cups shredded lettuce

Chop cranberries in food processor or blender. Set aside. Pour gelatine and sugar into large bowl. Add boiling water and stir until both are dissolved. Add cranberries, oranges and pecans. Stir to blend well. Pour into mold and refrigerate several hours or overnight.

To serve, unmold on serving plate. On each salad plate, shred 1/4 cup lettuce. Place a wedge of molded salad, and top with 1 teaspoon mayonnaise. Place a maraschino cherry on top.

CRANBERRY PINEAPPLE SALAD   *Makes 4 to 6 servings*

A beautiful salad to serve during the Christmas holidays, this belonged to my Great-Aunt Phil in Virginia.

1	envelope unflavored gelatine
1 1/2	cup water
2	tablespoons sugar
	juice of 1 lemon
1/2	cup cranberry sauce
1	cup raw chopped celery (3-4 stalks)
1/2	cup crushed pineapple, drained
1/2	cup chopped pecans

In bowl, add gelatine and 1/2 cup of cold water. Stir to mix well. Add 1 cup boiling water. Stir to dissolve gelatine. Add sugar and lemon juice. Add cranberry sauce and stir to dissolve, beating thoroughly to mix well.

Add celery, pineapple and pecans. Mix thoroughly and pour into mold. Refrigerate until congealed, several hours or overnight. Just before serving, unmold on plate.

HEAVENLY FRUIT SALAD   *Makes 1 quart*

To make salad, use equal amounts of the following:

> mandarin oranges, well drained
> miniature marshmallows
> shredded coconut
> bananas, peeled and sliced
> fruit cocktail, well drained

Mix fruit and drain well. Refrigerate, covered, for several hours or overnight. Drain again. Several hours before serving, make **Fruit Salad Dressing** (recipe follows) by mixing sour cream and sugar. Mix just enough of the dressing with the fruit to hold the fruit mixture together.

To serve, place on bed of shredded lettuce or lettuce leaves broken into pieces. Sprinkle with cinnamon and 1/2 teaspoon sugar for each serving.

Fruit Salad Dressing

1	pint of sour cream for every 4 cups of fruit
2	tablespoons sugar for each pint of sour cream

LEAF LETTUCE WITH FETA CHEESE

Makes 4 to 6 servings

A very light salad with a spectacular flavor.

1	bunch leafy green lettuce
1	purple onion, peeled and thinly sliced
4-6	fresh mushrooms, sliced
1	(4 ounce) package Feta cheese
1 1/2	cups **Crunchy Croutons** (page 221)
1/2	recipe **KC Sweet and Sour Dressing** (page 219)

Wash lettuce and remove any coarse stems. Place lettuce on paper towels to dry. Break lettuce into bite-sized pieces. Place on salad plates. Place onion slices on top of lettuce and top with mushroom slices. Crumble feta cheese and place on top. Sprinkle with croutons.

Shake salad dressing before pouring over salads.

VARIATIONS: Evenly divide 1 small can mandarin oranges, drained, among the salad plates.

Substitute 1 cup grated cheddar cheese.

LIME GRAPEFRUIT PINEAPPLE SALAD

Makes 4 servings

A delicious flavor combination, which is especially appropriate for a luncheon or dinner party. A delightful change from a green salad!

1	(8 ounce) can crushed pineapple, drained and juice reserved
1	(16 ounce) can grapefruit sections, drained and juice reserved
1/4	cup sugar
1	small (3 ounce) package lime gelatine dessert mix
1/2	cup low-calorie mayonnaise
6	maraschino cherries, quartered (optional)
1/4	cup chopped pecans (optional)

Grease a 9-inch square pan or 1 1/2 quart mold.

Add reserved grapefruit and pineapple juice to a small bowl and stir to mix. Pour 2/3 cups of reserved juice into saucepan. Add sugar and lime gelatine mix, heat until sugar is dissolved. Remove from heat. With wire whisk, stir in mayonnaise until well blended. Add pineapple, grapefruit, cherries and pecans. Pour into prepared 9-inch square pan or a mold.

Chill until set and firm. Unmold and serve on a bed of lettuce. If desired, top each serving with 1/2 teaspoon low-calorie mayonnaise and 2 teaspoons grated cheddar cheese.

MANDARIN ORANGE SALAD

Makes 6 to 8 servings

Perfect for a ladies' luncheon.

2	(3 ounces each) packages orange-pineapple gelatine mix
1	cup boiling water (including reserved mandarin orange juice)
1	(11 ounce can) mandarin oranges, drained and juice reserved
1	(13 ounce) can crushed pineapple, undrained
8	ounces (1/2 pint) sour cream
1	cup chopped pecans
1/4	cup shredded coconut
6-8	maraschino cherries

Lightly grease an 8-inch square dish or 1 1/2 quart gelatine mold.

Place gelatine mix in a heat-proof mixing bowl. Add reserved mandarin orange juice to a glass measuring cup. Fill cup to the 1-cup line with water. Microwave for 2 to 3 minutes on high until water boils. Pour boiling water over gelatine mix and stir until gelatine dissolves. Cool slightly. Add mandarin oranges, pineapple, and pecans to the gelatine mixture. Stir in sour cream and mix until well blended. Pour mixture into prepared dish.

Refrigerate until several hours or overnight. Cut into small rectangles. Place on bed of lettuce. Sprinkle each piece with coconut and top with a cherry.

MARINATED TOPPED SALAD

Makes 6 to 8 servings

The marinated vegetables can be eaten alone or placed on a bed of lettuce as a salad.

3	tomatoes, cut into wedges	1	head Iceberg lettuce, shredded
2	cucumbers, unpeeled, thinly sliced	4	ounces (1 cup) shredded cheddar cheese
1	purple onion, cut into thin wedges or slices	1 1/2	cups **Crunchy Croutons** (page 221)
1	(8 ounce) bottle zesty Italian salad dressing		salad dressings of your choice

In large glass or plastic bowl, add tomatoes, cucumbers and onion. Pour dressing over mixture. Refrigerate 24 hours.

Place lettuce on salad plates. Drain tomato mixture and place in center of each plate. Sprinkle cheese and croutons on top. Serve with salad dressing.

OVERNIGHT LAYERED SALAD
Makes 4 servings

Because this should be prepared in advance, it is a great salad for supper-clubs, covered-dish suppers, buffets and tailgating.

	fresh spinach, torn in small pieces, large stems removed
	green leaf lettuce, torn in small pieces
2	hard boiled eggs, chopped or grated
1	package frozen green peas, thawed & drained
1	small purple onion, cut in thin slices and separated into rings
6	fresh mushrooms, washed, dried and thinly sliced
4-5	pieces bacon, cooked crisp and crumbled
1/2	cup sour cream
1/2	cup low-calorie mayonnaise
1	tablespoon sugar
2	ounces (1/4 cup) grated Parmesan cheese or Swiss cheese

Place salad ingredients in glass bowl in layers, alternating colors to make it attractive, ending with layer of spinach. Mix sour cream, mayonnaise and sugar together. Spread over spinach like dressing. Sprinkle cheese and bacon on top. Do NOT toss or stir. Refrigerate overnight.

Can be served without tossing. If you prefer, it can be tossed just before serving.

VARIATION: Add 1/4 cup sliced celery or 1/4 cup water chestnuts.

OVERNIGHT MARINATED BEAN SALAD   *Makes about 1 quart*

This salad lets you combine the vegetables you like into a salad that keeps several weeks. Many restaurants use a similar marinated salad on their salad bars.

Use 4 to 6 cups of any mixture of the following drained vegetables:

Canned Vegetables	**Fresh Vegetables**
green beans	carrots, blanched
sliced mushrooms	purple onions, sliced
kidney beans	cabbage, finely shredded
green peas	green pepper strips
navy beans	
yellow wax beans	
chili beans	
corn	
butter beans	

A popular combination is: 2 cans green beans, 1 can waxed beans, 1 onion thinly sliced, 2 cups shredded cabbage, and 1 can sliced carrot.

Marinade

1 1/2	cups vinegar
1 1/2	cups sugar
2/3	cup cooking oil

Heat vinegar and sugar together until sugar is dissolved. Remove from heat and add oil. Pour over vegetables. Mix well. Refrigerate overnight.

Lower Cholesterol Marinade

1 1/2	cups vinegar
3/4	cups sugar
1/3	cup light olive oil or canola oil

PICKLED BEET SALAD
Makes 4 servings

Turn an ordinary vegetable into a delightful salad.

1	envelope unflavored gelatine
1/4	cup sugar
1/2	cup water
1/4	teaspoon lemon juice
1/2	teaspoon vinegar
1 1/2	teaspoon cream-style prepared horseradish
1/2	cup celery, finely diced
1/4	cup diced spring onions
1	(16 ounce) can julienne-style beets, drained, liquid reserved

Lightly grease 1-1/2 quart mold.

In saucepan over medium heat, cook gelatine, sugar and 1/2 cup water, stirring constantly, until gelatine is dissolved. Remove pan from heat.

Add enough water to beet juice to make 1 cup liquid. Pour into saucepan. Add lemon juice, vinegar and horseradish to gelatine mixture. Refrigerate until mixture is slightly thickened. Stir in celery, spring onions, and beets. Chill until congealed.

Serve on a bed of Iceberg or other variety of lettuce. Garnish with 1/2 teaspoon mayonnaise on top, if desired.

VARIATIONS: Substitute 1/2 cup grated carrots in place of the celery.

Preparation Tip

If you prefer to use "pickled" beets, omit the vinegar, lemon juice and sugar, as this is what "pickles" the salad.

SPINACH SALAD DELIGHT   *Ingredients per salad*

Try this for a change of pace from Iceberg lettuce.

- 6-8 fresh spinach leaves, washed and coarse stem removed
- 1 hard-boiled egg
- 1 fresh mushroom, sliced
- 1 teaspoon bacon bits
- 1/2 green onion, thinly sliced
- 2 tablespoons **KC Sweet and Sour Salad Dressing** (page 219) OR 2 tablespoons **Russian Salad Dressing** (page 220)

Break spinach leaves into bite-sized pieces. Either cut egg into wedges, chop or grate. Place egg and mushrooms on salad. Sprinkle with bacon bits and green onions. Pour salad dressing on top.

VARIATION: Add 1 tablespoon crumbled blue cheese to top of each salad.

WALDORF SALAD   *Makes 2 salads*

A classic fruit salad which is especially popular when apples are abundant.

- 8 large leaves Leaf Green lettuce
- 1 apple, pared and sliced
- 1 pear, pared and sliced
- 1 tablespoon raisins
- 1 tablespoon hot water
- 1/4 cup chopped pecans
  Fruit Salad Dressing (recipe follows)

Break lettuce into bite-sized pieces and place on salad plates. Place raisins in hot water for 5 minutes. Drain well. Mix apples and pears with dressing. Place on top of lettuce. Sprinkle with raisins and pecans. Lightly sprinkle top of each salad with curry.

Fruit Salad Dressing

- 2 tablespoons low-calorie salad dressing or low-calorie mayonnaise
- 2 teaspoons sugar
- 1 teaspoon lemon juice

Mix salad dressing, sugar and lemon juice. Let sit 5 minutes before mixing with fruit.

SALAD DRESSINGS

BLUE CHEESE SUPREME

Makes about 3 cups

Blue cheese lovers—this is absolutely delicious! After adjusting and modifying this recipe many, many times, it's finally superb!

1	(8 ounce) carton sour cream
1/2	cup non-fat buttermilk
1/2	cup low-cholesterol mayonnaise
2	teaspoons fresh minced garlic
1/2-1	teaspoon onion salt
2	tablespoons olive oil
8	ounces blue cheese, crumbled

Mix sour cream, buttermilk, mayonnaise, and garlic until well blended. Add oil and mix again. Crumble blue cheese and add to buttermilk mixture. Stir to mix well. Chill.

Serve on salads, as a dip with fresh vegetable strips, or with celery strips and **Buffalo-Style Chicken Wings** (page 23).

VARIATION: Add 1 teaspoon garlic salt

Preparation Tip

When this dressing is first made, it is very stiff. However, after it chills for several hours it thins out and becomes just the right consistency for pouring.

KC SWEET & SOUR DRESSING

Makes 1 cup

This is an excellent dressing for any vegetable salad.

1/2	cup vinegar
1/2	cup sugar
1/3	cup salad oil
1	teaspoon salt

Heat sugar, salt and vinegar over medium heat until sugar is just dissolved. Add oil. Cool.

Try this dressing over a lettuce salad with fresh orange slices, purple onion and feta cheese.

VARIATIONS: Add 2 tablespoons catsup to dressing mix.

Dietetic Version

Substitute 12 <u>packets</u> Equal, OR 8 packets Sweet and Low, OR 16 <u>tablets</u> of Equal for the 1/2 cup sugar.

RUSSIAN DRESSING   *Makes 2 cups*

1/4-1/2	cups sugar
1/4	cup vinegar
1	tablespoons worcestershire sauce
1	tablespoon soy sauce
1	tablespoon lemon juice
2	tablespoons water
1	teaspoon basil
1	teaspoon garlic salt
1 1/2	teaspoons prepared mustard
2	tablespoons finely chopped onion
1/4-1/2	cup olive oil
1/2-3/4	cup catsup

Combine all ingredients together, using smaller of two quantities if a variable amount is given, such as 1/4 cup sugar. Shake well. Taste. Increase to upper limit of each ingredient, such as 1/2 cup sugar, according to your taste and shake to mix well.

Refrigerate to chill.

Delicious served over **Spinach Salad Delight** (page 218).

THOUSAND ISLAND DRESSING   *Makes about 1 cup*

To make a quick salad, serve this on a wedge of lettuce topped with diced tomato or tomato wedges.

1/2	cup low-calorie mayonnaise
1/4	teaspoon paprika
1/4	cup diced sweet pickles, drained
1	tablespoon chili sauce
1	tablespoon minced onion
1	egg, chopped or grated

Mix the mayonnaise, paprika, pickles, chili sauce, onion and egg together. Stir until well blended. Refrigerate.

VARIATION: Add 1 tablespoon chopped green olives.

TOPPINGS

ADDITIONAL TOPPINGS

The following toppings add a little variety, and a lot of taste, to salads. Give each one a try and see how you like it!

roasted peanuts	croutons	raisins
sliced olives	shredded coconut	alfalfa sprouts
bacon bits		

Sprinkle a little of one or more of the above ingredients on a green salad.

CRUNCHY CROUTONS
Makes 2 1/2 to 3 quarts

These croutons, which are the larger-sized ones served in popular restaurants, make a great salad spectacular! This is an excellent way to use stale bread.

1	loaf thick-sliced Italian Bread or any stale bread	1 teaspoon oregano
1/2	cup cooking oil	1 teaspoon basil
1	teaspoon garlic salt	2 teaspoons Morton's Nature's seasoning

Preheat oven to 225 degrees.

Stack several slices of bread on a cutting board. Cut stack of bread into 5 strips. Turn cutting board 90 degrees, and repeat this cutting process, cutting each strip into pieces 1-inch squares. On each of two (2) 11x15-inch pans, place half of bread cubes in single layers.

In shaker bottle with holes in top, add oil, garlic salt, oregano, basil and Nature's Seasoning. Shake to mix well. Sprinkle mixture over bread cubes, and stir to mix well.

Place both oven shelves near the middle of oven. Place one pan on each shelf. Bake for 2 hours or until lightly golden browned and very crunchy. Remove pans from oven and cool. NOTE: Add crumbs from bottom of pan to toasted seasoned bread crumbs and use for breading chicken and pork chops - see page 149)

Serve as a garnish for vegetable salads. When cooled, place in air-tight container. These will keep unrefrigerated for 1 month.

VARIATIONS: If smaller croutons are desired, cut into smaller squares and reduce cooking time accordingly, but make sure that croutons are cooked until crunchy.
For spicier croutons, increase seasonings accordingly.

Preparation Tip

To sprinkle oil and seasonings evenly, place these in a large empty spice jar with a sprinkle top. Shake well to mix oil and seasonings. Sprinkle over bread cubes, stirring to distribute mixture.

14

Seafood

SEAFOOD

SEAFOOD

Whether you live near the ocean or many miles away, fresh seafood is available to you. Seafood is a variety of high-protein delicacies that taste great and are great for you. Another reason for the popularity of seafood is its quick cooking time, usually under 30 minutes.

Since crab and shrimp are the most versatile and readily available seafood, they are emphasized in this section. Crabs are usually cooked by steaming them for about 20 to 30 minutes. When done, they should be bright orange in color. Although most of the crab recipes were tested with meat from Atlantic Blue Crabs, any crab meat will produce delicious results. Shrimp lends itself to a variety of cooking methods: grilled, boiled, broiled, fried or baked in a casserole. Both crab and shrimp can be served hot or cold.

Treat your family to a special seafood meal and let them rave!

CRAB

CRAB IMPERIAL

Makes 4 servings

Seafood fit for a king!

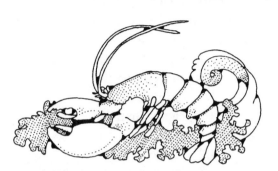

2	tablespoons margarine or butter
1	green onion, thinly sliced (1/2 cup)
3	stalks celery, diced (1/2 cup)
1	egg, beaten
1	tablespoon lemon juice
1/2	cup skim milk
3	slices white bread, crumbled (crust removed)
1	tablespoon chopped parsley
1/2	teaspoon Morton's Nature's seasoning
1	pound fresh lump crab meat

Preheat oven to 400 degrees. Lightly grease an 8x8-inch casserole.

Over medium-high heat, saute celery and onion in butter. Remove from heat. Add beaten egg, lemon juice and milk. Add crumbled bread, parsley and seasoning. Stir and mix well until bread is well moistened and separated into small pieces. Add crab and gently mix, leaving crab in hunks. Place in prepared casserole.

Bake 15 to 20 minutes or until hot.

* * * * * * * * *

How to Cook Blue Crabs

In a large pot, bring about 4 inches of water to a boil. Add 1 tablespoon Old Bay seafood seasoning. With burner on high, add crabs one at a time. Cover.

When pot comes to a boil, reduce heat to simmer and slowly boil for 20 minutes. All crabs should turn a bright orange color.

Remove crabs from water and cool. Remove flap, shell and 'dead man' (spongy tissue inside of shell). Remove all soft tissue and insides, leaving only hard shell filled with crab meat.

CRAB QUICHE
Makes 4 to 6 servings

A delicious and easy way to serve crab to a crowd.

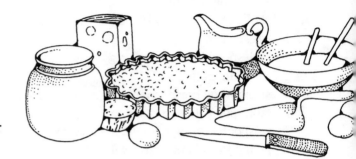

2	nine-inch frozen pie shells (not deep dish)
1	egg white
1	pound (16 ounces) crab meat
4-6	strips bacon
1/2	cup diced onion
1 1/2	cups skim milk
8	eggs
1/2	teaspoon salt
1/8	teaspoon coarse ground black pepper
1	teaspoon lemon juice
4	ounces (1 cup) grated Swiss cheese
2	teaspoons freeze-dried chives
1/8	teaspoon paprika
1	lemon, sliced for garnish

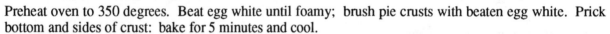

Preheat oven to 350 degrees. Beat egg white until foamy; brush pie crusts with beaten egg white. Prick bottom and sides of crust: bake for 5 minutes and cool.

Divide crab evenly between two (2) pie shells. Saute bacon until golden brown. Remove bacon and drain to remove grease. Cool. Then crumble bacon and place on top of crab. Beat milk, egg, salt, pepper and lemon juice. Pour over crab. Place cheese on top. Sprinkle with chives and paprika.

Place both pies on a cookie sheet and bake 35 minutes. Let sit 5 minutes and cut into wedges. Serve hot.

This quiche can be frozen. If frozen, bake while frozen for 40 to 45 minutes.

Serve with a sliced lemon, **Slow-Cooked Creamy Grits** (page 109), and a **Spinach Salad Delight** (page 218).

JOYCE'S CRAB SALAD

The cabbage adds that special something to the crab salad. It's one of the most popular seafood dishes.

2 1/2	cups (1-1/4 pound) crab meat
1	cup (packed) very finely grated cabbage
1/3	cup low-calorie mayonnaise
1/2	cup Thousand Island salad dressing
1/4	teaspoon salt
1/2	teaspoon pepper

Mix mayonnaise, dressing, salt and pepper. Stir in cabbage. Add crab and gently stir to mix well.

VARIATION: Use 2-1/2 cups (1-1/4 pound) imitation crab meat.

MOTHER'S DEVILED CRAB   *Makes 6 servings*

Made into a casserole, it's a delightful way to enjoy crab.

4	tablespoons (1/4 cup) margarine or butter
2	tablespoons flour
1	tablespoon chopped parsley
2	tablespoons lemon juice
1	teaspoon prepared mustard
1	teaspoon salt
1/2-3/4	teaspoon Texas Pete pepper sauce
1	cup skim milk
2	eggs, hard-boiled, grated
2	cups fresh lump crab meat

Crumb Topping

1	cup bread crumbs
2	tablespoons margarine, melted

Preheat oven to 425 degrees.

Melt margarine in saucepan, blend in flour with wire whisk. Add remaining ingredients (except crab) and mix well. Gently stir in crab meat. Place mixture into well-cleaned crab shells. Sprinkle bread crumbs on top; drizzle with melted margarine.

Bake for 15 minutes until hot and crumbs are golden brown. Serve hot with **Slow Cooked Creamy Grits** (page 109).

SAN FRANCISCO CRAB SANDWICHES   *Makes 8 to 10 sandwiches*

This recipe was inspired by the delicious crab sandwich served me at a historic Greek restaurant in downtown San Francisco.

1	loaf rye bread, sliced	8	ounces Thousand Island salad dressing
8-10	slices Swiss cheese		**Crab Filling** (recipe follows)
1	stick margarine, for grilling		

For Each Sandwich

With 2 slices of bread, spread Thousand Island dressing liberally on 1 side of each slice. Spread 1 slice of bread with **Crab Filling**, top with slice of Swiss cheese, then top with other slice of bread. Spread top of sandwich with margarine. Repeat process for each of sandwiches.

Over medium-high heat, melt a little margarine in frying pan or griddle. Place sandwich in pan, buttered side up, and cook until browned. Turn sandwich over, and cook until browned, and Swiss cheese is melted. Cut in half and serve.

Or place all sandwiches on large cookie sheet and bake at 350 degrees for about 20 minutes or until bread is browned on both sides and cheese melts.

Alternate Cooking Method for a Crowd

Spread Thousand Island dressing on each side of Hoagie bun, add crab and Swiss cheese slice. Cut in half. Wrap both halves in foil. Place on cookie sheet. Heat 15 to 20 minutes until cheese melts.

To Serve Cold

After putting sandwich together, cut in half and serve.

Crab Filling

1	(8-ounce) package low-cal cream cheese
1	tablespoon skim milk
2	tablespoons low-calorie mayonnaise
2	teaspoons cream-style prepared horseradish
2	tablespoons chopped onion
1/4	teaspoon salt
1	pound imitation crab meat or fresh crab meat, drained

Cut crab crosswise into 1 inch pieces. This prevents pieces from being too large and stringy. Mix cream cheese, milk, mayonnaise, horseradish, onion, salt and crab together, flaking crab during mixing.

SEAFOOD SALAD BAKE

Makes 4 servings

Although this recipe has been slightly modified, the original was shared by Myrtle Anderson, Aiken, SC.

2	cups sliced celery
1/2	cup chopped onion
1	medium green pepper, finely chopped
8	ounces sliced water chestnuts, drained
6-8	ounces fresh crab meat, drained and flaked or 1 (6 1/2 ounce) canned crab meat
1/3	pound medium shrimp, cooked, peeled and deveined or 4 1/4 ounces canned shrimp
2 1/2	ounce jar of sliced mushrooms, drained
1	cup low-calorie mayonnaise or salad dressing
4	hard-cooked eggs, sliced
1/2	teaspoon Morton's Nature's Seasoning
1/8	teaspoon cayenne pepper
1/4	teaspoon seasoned pepper
1/2	teaspoon paprika
1/2	cup buttered bread crumbs
1	cup cooked rice

Preheat oven to 350 degrees. Spray 2-quart casserole with no-stick cooking spray.

In large bowl, combine all ingredients except, bread crumbs, shrimp and crab. Mix thoroughly. Add shrimp and crab and mix very gently. Pour mixture into casserole. Sprinkle with buttered bread crumbs.

Bake for 30 minutes or until bubbly hot. Serve with a salad, either fruit or vegetable.

VARIATION: Substitute 3 (6 1/2 ounces each) cans tuna packed in water for the crab and shrimp.

Preparation Tip

This is better if made the day ahead, refrigerated and cooked the day of serving.

TOM'S FAVORITE CRAB CAKES   *Serves 2 to 3 people*

With the abundance of fresh crab meat during the late summer and early fall months, this became the most popular way to serve crab at our beach house.

- 1   egg
- 1   slice white bread
- 3   tablespoons grated onion
- 1   teaspoon lemon juice
- 1/4   teaspoon Old Bay Seafood Seasoning
- 1   tablespoon self-rising flour
- 2   cups (loosely packed) fresh crab meat, all shell removed
- 3   tablespoons flour
- 1   tablespoon cooking oil

Sprinkle 2 tablespoons flour in thin layer on a 12-inch square sheet of waxed paper or plastic wrap. In a 2-quart mixing bowl, add egg, bread, onion, lemon juice, seafood seasoning and 1 tablespoon self-rising flour. Mix all ingredients until bread is in very small pieces and all ingredients are mixed well.

Add crab meat to bowl. Gently stir to mix, leaving crab in pieces as large as possible. With clean hands, form into five (5) patties about 4 inches in diameter and 1-inch thick, placing each on surface prepared with flour. Sprinkle last tablespoon of flour over top of patties and spread to cover top of each cake with flour.

Add oil to a 10 or 12 -inch skillet, and heat over medium-high heat until hot. With a spatula, gently remove crab patties from waxed paper and place in skillet. Cook about 3 minutes, until lightly browned. Lower heat and turn patties over. Brown second side, cooking another 3 minutes. Remove patties from skillet and place on serving platter.

Especially good served with **Slow-Cooked Creamy Grits** (page 109), a green salad and toasted garlic bread.

SHRIMP

BEAUFORT STEW, EDISTO STYLE

By using this recipe, the hostess has time to serve delicious, fresh shrimp to a crowd. The recipe can be adjusted to accommodate any number of people. Be sure to have plenty of extra napkins, or hand towels, available as each person peels his own shrimp while eating.

Quantity Per Serving

3/4	pounds fresh large or jumbo shrimp, unpeeled
2-3	frozen niblet ears of corn or 1 1/2 ears fresh corn, shucked
1/4-1/3	pounds Kielbasa sausage or smoked sausage, cut into 2 -inch pieces
1	teaspoon Old Bay Seafood Seasoning

The above quantity is generous for 1 serving. When serving more people, increase the quantity of each ingredient accordingly. Cooking time will increase slightly as the number of servings is increased. Fill a large pot half full of water. Add the Old Bay seasoning and sausage. Heat over high heat until boiling. Reduce heat to low and cook about 20 minutes.

Add the ears of corn and bring to a boil again, which will take about 5 minutes. Immediately add shrimp and bring to a boil again. Turn the heat off when shrimp are pink. Remove pot from burner. Drain, spoon into bowls and serve immediately.

VARIATIONS: Add 1/4 pound Snow Crab legs per person to the pot when the shrimp are added. If crab legs are added, reduce shrimp to 1/2 pound per person.

Serve with **Cocktail Sauce Edisto** (40). **Crunchy Seasoned Bread** (page 89) and a salad make a complete meal.

Quantity for 4 Servings

3	pounds fresh large or jumbo shrimp, unpeeled
10	frozen niblet ears of corn or 6 ears fresh corn, shucked and silked
1	pound Kielbasa sausage, cut into 2-inch pieces
4	teaspoons Old Bay seafood seasoning

HAWAIIAN SHRIMP

Makes 4 servings

Inspired by a trip to Hawaii! When coconut is fried, it takes on a deliciously different taste which is enhanced when shrimp is dipped into the **Honey Mustard Sauce** (recipe follows). I do not recommend these be served with the usual tomato-based cocktail sauce.

1-1 1/2	pounds large shrimp, peeled with tails intact
3/4	cup self-rising flour
2-4	tablespoons club soda
1/2	cup shredded coconut
1/4	cup flour

Devein shrimp and rinse in water. Drain. Place 1/4 cup flour in small bowl. Mix 1/2 cup self-rising flour and club soda to form a batter and place in small bowl. Place coconut in small bowl.

Holding each shrimp by the tail, dip in flour, then in batter and next in coconut. Place on waxed paper. Fry a few shrimp at a time in hot oil until lightly golden brown and shrimp is floating on top of hot oil. Remove and drain on paper towels. Repeat with remaining shrimp.

Serve with **Honey Mustard Sauce**. Dip each shrimp in sauce. Serve with **Joyce's Hush Puppies** (page 90), **Cole Slaw** (page 251), and **Scrumptious Tomato Pie** (page 258).

Honey Mustard Sauce

Excellent on Hawaiian Shrimp and fried chicken strips.

1/3	cup Dijon mustard
1/3	cup sour cream
1/3	cup honey
1	teaspoon cream-style prepared horseradish

Mix all ingredients together and refrigerate.

LAYERED SEAFOOD EDISTO
Makes 4 to 6 servings

When you have an assortment of seafood, this is an excellent dish. Quantity of each seafood can be adjusted so long as you use a total of 1 pound.

- 1/2 pound fresh medium or large shrimp, peeled
- 1/2 pound flounder fillets, skinless
  Seasoned Sauce (recipe follows)

How to Cook Shrimp

Steam shrimp in 1/2 cup water and 1 teaspoon Old Bay Seafood seasoning, until shrimp turn pink. Drain well.

How to Cook Fish

Steam fish fillets in 1/2 cup water until fish is opaque white and flakes easily with fork. Drain well and reserve liquid. Remove skin if present.

Assembling Casserole

In 2-quart casserole, place layer of fish, flaked into bite-size pieces. Cover with 1/2 of **Seasoned Sauce**. If shrimp are large, cut them in half. Add a layer of shrimp. Cover with remaining sauce. Cover and bake at 350 degrees for 30 minutes or until bubbly. Uncover, and bake 10 minutes longer.

VARIATION: Sprinkle 1 cup of grated cheddar cheese on top of casserole before baking.

Serve with fluffy white rice, a Caesar salad and garlic bread.

Seasoned Sauce

2	tablespoons margarine	1/4	teaspoon ground red pepper or cayenne pepper
2	tablespoons flour	1/4	cup low-calorie mayonnaise
2	well-beaten eggs	1/4	cup chopped parsley
1/2	teaspoon each: seasoned salt, celery salt, pepper, worcestershire sauce	1	tablespoons lemon juice
1	teaspoon dry mustard	1/2	pound cooked crab meat, cartilage removed

Make medium white sauce as follows: Over medium heat, melt margarine in frying pan, stir in flour with whisk to make paste. Gradually stir in all of reserved fish liquid and enough milk (about 1 to 1 1/2 cups total liquid) to make a sauce with the consistency of thin pancake batter, stirring constantly with whisk. Add 2 eggs, seasoned salt, celery salt, pepper, worcestershire sauce, mustard, red pepper, mayonnaise, parsley and lemon juice. Stir until well mixed and heated throughout. Gently stir in crab meat, leaving it in pieces as large as possible.

VARIATION: Add 2 tablespoons diced green pepper to sauce.

SHRIMP PRIMAVERA

Makes 4 to 6 servings

Easy to prepare. It has great taste and eye appeal which makes it a good choice for a dinner party.

12	ounce package egg noodles, cooked according to package directions, drained
5	tablespoons margarine or butter
1/2	cup finely chopped onion
2	teaspoons fresh minced garlic
1 1/2	pounds large fresh shrimp, cooked
1 1/2	cups skim milk
2/3	cups grated parmesan cheese
1/4-1/2	teaspoon salt
1/8	teaspoon pepper
1-1 1/2	teaspoons Italian seasoning
1	tablespoon lemon juice
2	(10 ounces each) packages broccoli florets, cooked and drained

In large frying pan, melt 3 tablespoons margarine and saute onion and garlic until tender. Add shrimp and saute until heated thoroughly, about 2 to 3 minutes. Remove shrimp and onions from frying pan, place in bowl and keep warm.

In large frying pan add 2 tablespoons margarine and milk, heating until margarine melts. Stir in parmesan cheese, salt, pepper, Italian seasoning, lemon juice. Add drained noodles and cooked broccoli, and cook until heated.

Place noodles on platter and spoon shrimp on top. Serve hot.

Serve with **Copper Penny Carrots** (page 252) and **Overnight Layered Salad** (page 215).

SHRIMP PURLEAU

Makes 6 to 8 servings

Since Roy never measures anything and left that up to me, the *quantity* of ingredients may vary from his original creation. However, the list of ingredients and cooking instructions were shared by Roy Beasley, Barnwell, SC.

- 1   cup raw long grain white rice
- 1   tablespoon powdered butter flavored granules (optional)
- 2   cups water
- 6-8   slices bacon
- 2-3   pounds medium or large raw shrimp, peeled
- 1   teaspoon salt
- 1/2   teaspoon pepper
- 3/4   cup flour
- 1   large onion, diced (1 cup diced)
- 1/2   cup diced celery (2 stalks)
- 3   tablespoons worcestershire sauce

Cook rice in 2 cups of water, seasoned with 1 tablespoon powdered butter flavored granules. Set aside while preparing bacon and shrimp.

In large frying pan, fry bacon until crispy. Remove from frying pan and place on paper towels to drain. When cooled, crumble bacon into small pieces.

Remove all bacon drippings, except 1 tablespoon, from frying pan. Place salt, pepper, flour and shrimp into medium-sized paper bag or a gallon size plastic sealable bag. Shake to cover shrimp.

In remaining bacon drippings, saute shrimp, onions and celery, until shrimp are browned and vegetables are transparent. Sprinkle remaining worcestershire sauce over shrimp mixture. Add cooked rice, bacon, and shrimp mixture. Heat for 1 minute on medium heat.

Serve hot with a salad or cole slaw.

SHRIMP VERONIQUE

Makes 3 to 4 servings

Excellent for company or a special family meal.

1/2	cup diced, Spring onions with tops (2-3 small onions)
1	dozen fresh mushrooms, sliced
1	small green pepper, diced
2	stalks celery, diced
3	tablespoons margarine or butter
1	(8 ounces) package cream cheese
3	tablespoons skim milk
2	tablespoons dry white wine
2	ounces (1/2 cup) grated Swiss Cheese
1/4	teaspoon pepper
1/4	teaspoon cayenne pepper
1/4	teaspoon fresh minced garlic
1/4	teaspoon cream-style prepared horseradish
1 1/2	pounds medium or large shrimp, shelled and uncooked
1/4	cup **Crunchy Croutons** (page 221)
3	cups cooked white rice

Saute mushrooms, green pepper and celery in margarine until tender. Add shrimp and cook 5 minutes until shrimp turn pink. Add cream cheese, milk and seasonings. Stir until cheese melts. Add wine and Swiss cheese and heat, stirring until cheese melts. Add croutons. Stir well. Serve over hot white rice.

SHRIMP WITH SPANISH RICE

Makes 8 to 10 servings

This can be prepared a day in advance and cooked the next day.

- 1 tablespoon olive oil
- 1 large green pepper, diced
- 1 large onion, diced
- 4 stalks celery, diced
- 1/4 teaspoon fresh, minced garlic (or garlic packed in water)
- 3/4 pound Kielbasa sausage, cut into 1/2 -inch pieces
- 1 (4 1/2 ounce) jar, sliced mushrooms, drained
- 1 teaspoon dried basil
- 1/8 teaspoon curry powder
- 1 tablespoon paprika
- 2 teaspoons seasoned salt
- 1/2 teaspoon seasoned pepper
- 1/4 teaspoon cayenne pepper
- 1 can sliced water chestnuts, diced
- 1 can cream of mushroom soup
- 3 pounds medium shrimp, cooked, shelled and deveined
- 4 cups cooked long-grain white rice

Lightly grease a 9x12x2-inch casserole dish. Preheat oven to 350 degrees.

In skillet, add oil, green pepper, onion, celery, garlic and sausage. Cook over medium-high heat until vegetables are lightly browned and sausage is slightly cooked. Pour sausage mixture into a colander and rinse 1 minute under hot water. Drain well.

In large mixing bowl, add mushrooms. Stir in vegetable mixture from colander. Add basil, curry powder, paprika, seasoned salt, seasoned pepper, cayenne pepper, water chestnuts and soup and mix well. Add rice and shrimp to mixture and gently stir until well mixed. Pour into prepared casserole.

Cover casserole with aluminum foil. Bake for 35 to 45 minutes until bubbly hot.

Serve with fresh steamed broccoli, pickled beets, a fruit salad and **Sour Cream Corn Bread** (page 91).

SPICY CAJUN SHRIMP

Serves 4 servings

A great change of pace for shrimp lovers!

1	teaspoon cayenne pepper
1	teaspoon worcestershire sauce
1/3	cup margarine or butter
1 1/2	teaspoon minced garlic
1/2	teaspoon oregano
1/2	teaspoon thyme
1/2	teaspoon crushed red pepper
1/2	teaspoon salt
1/2	teaspoon pepper
1	teaspoon basil
1	large (2 medium) tomatoes, peeled and coarsely chopped
1/4	cup beer, at room temperature
1-1/4	pounds jumbo shrimp, raw, peeled and deveined
3	cups hot cooked white rice

In frying pan, combine cayenne pepper, worcestershire sauce, margarine, garlic, oregano, thyme, red pepper, salt, pepper and basil. Heat until margarine melts. Add shrimp and tomato. Cook 2 minutes, stirring constantly.

Add beer and stir. Cook until shrimp turn pink and opaque (about 1 minute longer).

Serve over hot white rice.

VARIATION: Substitute 1-1/4 pounds deboned chicken breasts for shrimp. Cut chicken into small pieces.

TAILGATE GRILLED SHRIMP KABOBS

*Makes 20 to 30 appetizer servings or
10 to 12 large servings*

When the weather is perfect, my family looks forward to enjoying these kabobs before the Clemson football games.

1/2	teaspoon dry mustard
1/2	teaspoon cayenne pepper
1	teaspoon ground ginger
1	teaspoon fresh minced garlic
1	cup tomato-based barbecue sauce
1	tablespoon juice from jar of sliced Jalapeno peppers
1	tablespoon horseradish
2	teaspoons teriyaki sauce
2	tablespoons grape jelly
3-4	tablespoons honey
6	drops hickory flavored liquid smoke
3-5	pounds large, raw shrimp, peeled, deveined, washed and drained
	package 8-inch wooden skewers, soaked in water for 30 minutes

Mix first 11 ingredients together. Add shrimp and marinate overnight. Remove from marinade, saving marinade to baste shrimp during grilling. Place 3 to 5 shrimp on each wooden skewer, piercing each shrimp twice as you thread them on skewer.

To Cook Immediately

Grill over HOT grill (charcoal or gas) for about 2 minutes on each side, basting frequently.

To Freeze

Prepare as above. Place a single layer of skewers, with raw shrimp gently touching, in a flat covered container. Repeat layers, placing a layer of waxed paper between each layer of shrimp. Freeze. Remove from freezer 4 hours before cooking. Cook as directed above.

VARIATION: Use marinade for cubes of raw, deboned chicken breasts. Cook as directed above.

FISH AND OTHER SEAFOOD

CATFISH STEW
Makes 8 servings

A real Southern delight created by the late Ella Weeks!

4	ounces (6 to 8 slices) sliced bacon	3-4	pounds potatoes, peeled and diced
5	pounds catfish fillets	1/4-1	cup skim milk
3	pounds onions, chopped	1/4	cup margarine or butter, optional

In heavy frying pan, fry bacon until crisp. Remove bacon from frying pan and place on paper towels to drain. Remove all except 1 tablespoon bacon drippings. In REMAINING 1 tablespoon bacon dripping, saute onions until clear and soft. When cool, crumble bacon.

In large pot with a small amount of water (1/2 cup), steam catfish, over medium heat, until meat can be easily flaked with a fork. Save cooking water. Remove skin, if any, from fish.

Strain cooking water into large pot. Add potatoes and cook until tender, adding more water if necessary. Then, add fish, salt, pepper, crumbled bacon, and margarine.

Cover and simmer over low heat to blend flavors for an hour or more, adding water or skim milk if more liquid is needed. If using margarine, add now.

Serve hot, with crusty bread and a salad.

VARIATION: Substitute equal amount of any mild, flaky fish for the catfish.
To make seafood chowder, use 2 1/2 pounds fish, and 2 1/2 pounds of seafood: either shrimp, crab, clams or oysters (or any combination of these).
Add about 2 teaspoons worcestershire sauce.

GRILLED FISH FILLETS
Makes 4 to 6 servings

4-6	fillets of fish (catfish, flounder or any other mild fish)	1	teaspoon Cajun seasoning
2	tablespoons fresh lemon juice	1	tablespoon San-J teriyaki marinade
1	teaspoon hickory flavored liquid smoke	1/4	cup parmesan cheese

Mix all ingredients, except parmesan cheese and fillets, together. Marinate fillets in shallow glass pan for several hours or overnight. Remove fillets from marinade (reserve this), and place fillets in a shallow, wire fish grilling basket. If you like them spicy, sprinkle with additional Cajun seasoning.

Grill on high for about 8 to 15 minutes, depending upon thickness of fillets, marinating frequently with reserved marinade. When fish are done, they will flake easily with a fork, and the meat should be opaque.

When ready to serve, remove from wire basket, place on platter and sprinkle with Parmesan cheese.

HEARTY FISH GUMBO   *Makes 4 to 6 servings*

On a cold winter day, this makes a delicious and hearty meal.

4	slices bacon
1	cup chopped onion
1	cup coarsely chopped green pepper
1	teaspoon fresh minced garlic
1	(16 ounce) can tomatoes, drained and cut uᵣ
1	can tomato soup
2	tablespoon chopped fresh parsley
1/2	teaspoon dried thyme leaves
1/4	teaspoon pepper
1	cup water
1/4	teaspoon Texas Pete hot sauce
1	(10 ounce) package frozen cut okra
1	pound mild-flavored fish fillets, fresh or frozen

Fry bacon until crisp and drain on paper towels. In bacon drippings, cook onions, peppers and garlic, stirring often, until tender. Crumble bacon. Cut fish into 1-inch pieces. Set aside and add last.

Add remaining ingredients to large pot. To this, add cooked vegetables. Heat on medium heat and simmer for 30 minutes until vegetables are very tender and flavors are blended. Add fish and crumbled bacon. Cover and simmer 10 minutes. Add additional water if needed.

Serve in bowls with a generous serving of **Sour Cream Corn Bread** (page 91) or **Aunt Nell's Spoonbread** (page 87).

SALMON PATTIES WITH CREAMED PEAS

Makes 3 to 4 servings

The sauce sets these apart from the ordinary.

Salmon Cakes

1	(16 ounce) can salmon, drained, flaked (reserve 1/4 cup liquid)
1	cup mashed potato flakes
1/4	cup grated onion
2	teaspoons lemon juice
1/4	teaspoon pepper
2	eggs
	Creamed Pea Sauce (recipe follows)

Mix all ingredients together. Press firmly into greased muffin cups. Bake 350 degrees 30 to 35 minutes.

Place Salmon Patties on plate and spoon **Creamed Pea Sauce** over each.

VARIATION: Make into patties like hamburgers. Fry in skillet in a little oil, about 7 minutes, until golden brown on each side.

Creamed Pea Sauce

This sauce adds a delightful flavor and makes the salmon patties moist and tasty.

2	tablespoons margarine
2	tablespoons flour
1/2	teaspoon dill weed
1/4	teaspoon HOT Mrs. Dash
3/4	cup skim milk
1/4	cup reserved salmon liquid
1	(8 ounce) package frozen green peas
1	(8 ounce) package frozen snow peas

Defrost peas in microwave and cook just until crisp (about 1 minute). In saucepan or skillet, melt margarine. Stir in flour, dill weed, salt, pepper and Mrs. Dash. Gradually add milk and reserved salmon liquid, stirring with whisk to make a creamy sauce. Cook over medium heat stirring constantly until mixture gently boils and thickens. Stir in peas and heat until peas are hot.

SEAFOOD CHOWDER

Makes 6 servings

This hearty Boston-style chowder is cooked on the light side with skim milk, but has plenty of taste.

1	pound mild-flavored fish fillets, such as catfish or flounder
1	cup water
1	large onion, peeled and diced
2	tablespoons margarine or butter
3	potatoes, peeled and diced
1	teaspoon Morton's Nature's seasoning or seasoned salt
1/4	teaspoon pepper
1/2	teaspoon basil
1	cup skim milk

Place fillets and potatoes in 1 cup water and steam until fish is opaque and potatoes are done. Remove fillets and flake then return to pot. In frying pan add onion, saute in margarine until tender, and then add to fish. Add seasoning, pepper, and basil. Simmer for 30 minutes, stirring occasionally and adding more water if necessary to keep mixture from sticking. Mash some of the potatoes to slightly thicken mixture. When everything is tender, add 1 cup milk.

Serve in bowls with saltine crackers. If desired, add a salad, or serve as a first course to dinner.

VARIATIONS: Add clams, shrimp, lobster, or any other seafood of your choice.

If you like a thicker chowder, mix 1 1/2 teaspoons corn starch with 1 tablespoon water. Pour mixture into hot liquid and stir until thickened.

15

Tailgating

TAILGATING

Tailgating is a term which refers to eating food taken from the car before or after a ball game. It closely resembles a picnic, except that it takes place in a parking lot rather than a park.

Methods of tailgating range from an easy, casual lunch to an elaborate cocktail party with grilled shrimp. Since so many recipes from other sections are perfect for tailgating, they have been listed below:

VEGETABLES

16

Vegetables

VEGETABLES

Many people, especially children, think eating vegetables is like taking medicine. However, vegetables can add nutritious and delicious variety to your meals. They are a good source of vitamins and minerals.

Because leafy green vegetables are usually the least favored vegetables, yet can be the most tasty and nutritious, special instructions have been given for this category of vegetables. Kale, cabbage, spinach, collards, and turnips are included.

Although a tomato is technically a fruit, it is placed in this section because most people think of it as a vegetable. Once you try Scrumptious Tomato Pie (page 258), it will become a favorite.

If properly cooked and seasoned, vegetables will become a delightful, healthy and enjoyable part of your meals.

BAKED CURRIED FRUIT
Makes 4 to 6 servings

During the winter when the prices of fresh fruit soar, this is a delightful way to serve fruit with a meal.

Make a mixture of any combination of the following canned fruit:

pineapple chunks	mandarin oranges
peaches	grapefruit
apricots	cherries
pears	grapes

Use at least 3 different fruits. Cut fruit into slices. Drain all fruit, reserving 1/2 cup of juice.

Preheat oven to 350 degrees.

Place layer of mixed fruit in a shallow baking dish. Dot with 1 tablespoon margarine or butter. Sprinkle with curry powder (about 1 to 2 teaspoons). Sprinkle 2 tablespoons brown sugar over fruit. Add 1/2 cup reserved fruit juice.

Bake uncovered for 45 minutes to 1 hour.

Serve this with **Pork Chops** (page 73) or **Oven-Baked Fried Chicken** (page 149).

BROCCOLI-TOMATO CHEESE BAKE
Makes 6 to 8 servings

2	(10 ounce) packages frozen chopped broccoli, thawed and well drained
1	cup sour cream
1	cup creamed cottage cheese
1/2	cup biscuit baking mix
1/4	cup margarine or butter, melted
1/2	teaspoon dried basil
1/2	teaspoon Italian seasoning
2	eggs
2	tomatoes, peeled, thinly sliced
1/4	cup shredded parmesan or Swiss cheese

Preheat oven to 350 degrees. Spray 8-inch square baking dish with no-stick cooking spray.

Spread broccoli into prepared dish. Beat sour cream, baking mix, margarine, eggs, and cottage cheese until well mixed. Pour mixture over broccoli. Top with tomato slices. Sprinkle with cheese.

Bake about 30 minutes or until golden brown and knife inserted into center comes out clean. Cool 5 minutes before serving.

CARROT RING
Makes 6 to 8 servings

3/4	cup (1 1/2 stick) margarine or butter
1/2	cup sugar
2	eggs, divided into yolks and whites
1 1/2	cups grated carrots, tightly packed
1	cup flour
1/2	teaspoon salt
1	teaspoon baking powder
1	teaspoon lemon juice
	rind of one orange, grated
	rind of one lemon, grated
1	tablespoon cold water
1	(16 ounce) can green peas, heated and drained

Preheat oven to 350 degrees. Heavily grease oven-proof ring mold, such as a bundt or tube pan.

Beat egg whites until stiff, but not dry. Cream margarine and sugar. Add egg yolks and mix until creamy and well-blended. Add carrots. Stir in flour, salt and baking powder until well mixed. Add lemon juice, orange and lemon rind and water. Mix well. Fold in beaten egg whites. Pour into prepared mold.

Bake about 30 minutes until well set. Cool 5 to 10 minutes and then unmold onto serving plate. Place hot green peas in center of mold.

VARIATION: Add 1/4 cup chopped water chestnuts to peas before heating.

COLE SLAW *Makes 8 to 10 servings*

This slaw will keep in the refrigerator for at least 2 weeks when stored in an air-tight plastic or glass container.

3/4	cup sugar plus 2 tablespoons sugar
1	cup vinegar
1	head cabbage, shredded
1/4	cup cooking oil
1	teaspoon salt
1	teaspoon dry mustard
1 1/2	teaspoon celery seed or 1/2 teaspoon celery salt

In 1-quart saucepan, heat sugar and vinegar over medium-high heat until sugar is dissolved, about 5 minutes. Remove from heat.

While heating sugar/vinegar mixture, shred 1 head cabbage into a large bowl. Add cooking oil, salt, mustard and celery seed. Pour sugar/vinegar mixture over cabbage and stir well.

Refrigerate 6 hours or overnight, stirring several times to distribute dressing. To serve, drain slaw and place in serving bowl.

VARIATIONS: Add 1/2 teaspoon poppy seeds and 1/2 teaspoon pepper.

Cole Slaw (Second Method) *Makes 6 to 8 servings*

1	large head cabbage (8 cups shredded)
1/2	cup low calorie mayonnaise
1/2	cup sweet pickle relish, undrained
2	teaspoons prepared mustard
2	teaspoons sugar
1/2	teaspoon celery seed
1/8	teaspoon pepper

Mix all ingredients together. Refrigerate for several hours.

Serve with slotted spoon.

COPPER PENNY CARROTS   *Makes 12 servings*

A similar recipe appeared on the label of Speas vinegar many years ago. It is delicious.

      2   pounds carrots, pared and sliced
      1   small green pepper, thinly sliced (1/4 cup)
      1   medium onion, chopped
      1   (10 3/4 ounce) can condensed tomato soup
    1/2   cup cooking oil
    3/4   cup vinegar
      1   teaspoon prepared mustard
      1   teaspoon worcestershire sauce
      1   cup sugar

Cook carrots in water until medium done. Drain well. Arrange layers of carrots, green peppers and onions in a bowl.

Combine soup, oil, vinegar, mustard, worcestershire sauce and sugar. Mix until well blended. Pour soup mixture over vegetable layers. Refrigerate overnight.

Drain well and place vegetables in serving dish. Serve cold.

CORN PANCAKES   *Makes 8 to 10 servings*

These are good served with any meal, but especially seafood.

3/4	cup self-rising corn meal	1 egg
3/4	cup self-rising flour	1 medium onion, finely minced
1	teaspoon baking soda	1-1 1/2 cups skim milk or buttermilk
2-3	tablespoons sugar	1 can creamed corn or 1 cup fresh creamed corn

Mix flour, corn meal, soda and sugar together. Stir in onion, egg and creamed corn. Mix well. Gradually add milk, stirring until batter is the consistency of pancake batter.

Heat frying pan or griddle over medium heat. Add 1 teaspoon cooking oil to prevent cakes from sticking. Pour about 2 tablespoons batter into pan for each pancake. Brown on first side, until bubbles appear on top. Turn, and brown about 30 seconds on other side.

Place in stacks on serving platter. Serve with butter, if desired.

DUTCH RED CABBAGE   *Makes 4 to 6 servings*

A recipe with color and flavor - designed for company. It is unusual and delicious. This dish is better if left overnight and then cooked.

1 1/2-2	pounds red (purple) cabbage, coarsely shredded
1	pound apples, peeled and sliced
1	cup uncooked long-grain white rice
2-4	tablespoons dark brown sugar
1/4	teaspoon salt
1/4	teaspoon pepper
2-3	cups water
1/2	cup vinegar
2	tablespoons margarine

Preheat oven to 250 degrees. Lightly grease 2-quart casserole.

Remove coarse outer leaves of cabbage before shredding. Place ingredients in prepared casserole in the following layers: cabbage, apples, rice, sugar, salt and pepper.

Repeat the layers until all ingredients are used, ending with cabbage and apples. Mix water, vinegar and margarine. Pour over the casserole.

Cover and bake 3 hours. Serve hot.

EASY FRENCH ONION SOUP   *Makes 2 servings*

1	(10-1/2 ounce) can French Onion soup
3/4	cup water
2	slices French bread, toasted
1/2	cup shredded Swiss cheese
1/2	teaspoon worcestershire sauce

Heat soup and water together. Simmer 10 minutes. Pour soup mixture into 2 oven-proof bowls with straight sides.

Place 1 slice of toast in each bowl. Cover each bowl with half of cheese. Place bowls on baking pan and broil 3 to 5 inches from broiler for 1 to 2 minutes, or until cheese is melted and bubbly.

VARIATIONS: Substitute 1/2 can water and 1/4 can dry white wine or sherry for the 3/4 can water.

GREEN BEAN CASSEROLE   *Makes 4 to 6 servings*

    1   (10 1/2 ounces) can cream of mushroom soup
    1/4 cup skim milk
    1   teaspoon Morton's Nature's seasoning
    1/8 teaspoon pepper
    2   (16 ounce each) cans French-style green beans
    1   can French Fried Onion Rings

Preheat oven to 350 degrees. Lightly grease 2-quart casserole.

Mix soup, milk, seasoning, and pepper together. Add string beans and mix well. Pour into prepared casserole dish. Place onion rings on top.

Bake 35 to 45 minutes until onions are browned on top.

VARIATIONS: Substitute 1 cup sliced almonds for onion rings.
            Add 1 tablespoon dried minced onion to soup mixture.

HOW TO COOK DRIED BEANS   *Use for any dried beans*

1 pound makes 6 to 8 servings

    1   pound of beans: cranberry (October) beans, butter beans, navy beans, black beans, great northern beans, etc.
    1   tablespoon imitation butter flavored granules
    1   teaspoon salt
    1/2 teaspoon pepper
        water to cover

Draw a sink of water and add beans. Wash and place in colander. Repeat process once more. Pour beans in large bowl, with enough water to cover beans plus 2 inches of water. Soak overnight. Drain.

In saucepan, add drained beans, butter flavored granules, salt, pepper and enough water to cover beans plus 2 inches more. Bring to boil. Simmer for 1 1/2 to 3 hours until beans are tender when pierced with fork. Crush some of beans to thicken mixture before serving. Add more water if needed.

Drain and place in a bowl, using slotted spoon to serve. **Ella's Chow Chow** (page 193) and **Pickled Hot Peppers** (page 196) are delicious served on top of beans.

VARIATIONS: Use 1/2 pound of bacon, fried crisp, to season beans in place of butter flavored granules.
            Use 4 ounces of cooked ham to season beans. Omit butter flavored granules.
            If serving as a soup, add a little more water and ham.

HOW TO COOK LEAFY GREEN VEGETABLES

Cabbage, Collards, Kale, Spinach and Turnips

Leafy green vegetables provide an abundance of vitamins and minerals, such as Vitamin A and Vitamin E. They are good for us and they taste great if cooked and seasoned properly.

Purchase 1/4 to 1/2 pound cabbage, collards, kale, spinach or turnips and greens per serving.

If these are bought prewashed, rather than straight from the garden, they will require fewer washings to remove any sand. If purchasing greens from the grocery store, look for fresh, green leaves that are not wilted. The following instructions apply to all greens; special notes, where applicable, are made about specific varieties.

Draw a large sink of cold water. Add about 1 tablespoon salt to this first sink of water. (The salt will kill any bugs in the greens and they will wash away in the water). Separate and wash leaves. Remove and place in colander to drain. Drain sink. If sand is visible, repeat process until no sand or grit remains in sink.

Place greens in a stack on cutting board. Cut into strips and then cut strips in half to make large bite-sized pieces. Place in large pot with 1 cup of water. Add 2 teaspoons imitation butter flavor granules, 2 teaspoons chicken bouillon granules, 1 teaspoon sugar and 1/2 teaspoon salt. Cover and cook until greens wilt and are tender. Add more seasonings as desired.

CABBAGE: Cut cabbage into small wedges. Omit sugar.

TURNIPS: Peel turnips, dice into 1/2-inch cubes and cook with greens.

COLLARDS: Remove ends of any large stems before cutting into pieces.

Drain and place in bowls to serve.

Ella's Chow Chow (page 193) and **Pickled Hot Peppers** (page 196) are delicious served on top of cooked leafy greens.

VARIATION: Add about 1/4 cup of lean ham pieces to water before cooking greens.

JAPANESE SWEET AND SOUR VEGETABLES   *Makes 4 servings*

A zesty, flavorful vegetable.

1	medium onion, diced	2/3	cup vinegar
2	teaspoons light olive oil	1/4	cup sugar
1	(16 ounce) package Japanese frozen vegetables	2	tablespoons teriyaki sauce
	(green beans, broccoli, mushrooms & red peppers)	3	tablespoons corn starch
1	(16 ounce) can whole kernel corn	1/2	cup water

In a frying pan, saute onion in oil for about 2 minutes, add mixed Japanese vegetables and cook until tender yet still crisp. (Do Not Overcook). Add the corn. Add the vinegar, sugar and teriyaki sauce and stir well.

Mix the cornstarch and enough water to form a smooth paste. Add remaining water. Pour this mixture into vegetable mixture and cook, stirring constantly, until mixture thickens. Remove from heat and serve.

NAVY BEAN SOUP   *Makes 6 to 8 servings*

1   pound (16 ounces) dried navy beans
1   quart plus 2 cups water (6 cups)
2   tablespoons real bacon bits
1   tablespoon butter-flavored granules
1   teaspoon Morton's Nature's seasoning
1   teaspoon beef bouillon
1   (12 ounce) can ham chunks, do not drain
2   tablespoons Mrs. Dash seasoning

Wash beans several times. Add to crockpot. Add 1 quart water, bacon bits, butter granules, seasonings, bouillon, and ham chunks. Cook 6 to 8 hours on low. When beans are done, mash about half of them to thicken soup. Add 1 more cup of water if needed.

Serve in bowls or mugs with toasted Whole Wheat Rolls (page 99), Cheese Roll-Ups (page 88) or saltine crackers.

VARIATION: Add 2 medium onions, diced

2 stalks celery, diced

and 1 teaspoon pepper

PEAS AND WATER CHESTNUTS

Makes 8 to 10 servings

2 stalks celery, chopped
4 medium onions, chopped
1/4 teaspoon fresh minced garlic
1 cup (2 sticks) margarine or butter
1 (8 ounce) jar whole mushrooms, undrained
1 tablespoon flour
1/2 teaspoon salt
1/4 teaspoon pepper
2 tablespoons chopped pimentos
1 cup herb stuffing mix
2 (10 ounce each) packages frozen green peas, cooked and drained
2 (8 ounce each) cans sliced water chestnuts

Preheat oven to 350 degrees. Lightly grease 3-quart casserole.

In frying pan over medium-high heat, saute onion and celery in 1/2 cup (1 stick) of margarine until vegetables are tender. Stir in flour. Add mushrooms, including juice, and garlic, stirring constantly with wire whisk until sauce thickens. Pour vegetable mixture into casserole dish.

Add peas, water chestnuts, salt, pepper, and pimento in casserole. Gently stir to mix with cooked vegetables. Sprinkle stuffing mix over top of casserole. Evenly distribute remaining 1/2 cup (1 stick) of margarine, cut into patties, over top of stuffing mix.

Bake for 20 to 25 minutes or until lightly browned on top.

Serve hot, with a slotted spoon for serving.

PICKLED BEETS   *Makes 3 to 4 servings*

This is a colorful vegetable which has a zesty taste.

1/4	cup water	1/3	cup vinegar
1/4	cup sugar	1	(16 ounce) can sliced beets, drained

Pour water, sugar and vinegar into 2-quart saucepan. Heat over high heat until sugar is dissolved, about 5 minutes, stirring occasionally. Add beets to saucepan. Stir well. Remove from heat and let cool for 15 minutes. Pour into glass or plastic container and refrigerate until chilled thoroughly.

To serve, drain beets and place in serving dish.

When stored in refrigerator in a tightly covered glass container, Pickled Beets will keep indefinitely.

VARIATIONS: Use 5 times the recipe to make 1 gallon of pickled beets.

SCRUMPTIOUS TOMATO PIE   *Makes on 9-inch pie*

This is a delicious and unusual way to serve tomatoes during the summer months when tomatoes are plentiful and ever so tasty. It has a superb, but slightly sweet, flavor combination that everyone enjoys. It is excellent served for a brunch or as a side-dish with **Beaufort Stew, Edisto Style** (page 231).

1	nine-inch pie shell, baked	1/2	teaspoon basil
1	large, sweet onion, diced	1/2	teaspoon oregano
3-4	large, very ripe tomatoes, peeled & sliced	1/2	teaspoon Italian seasoning
1/4-1/2	cup low-calorie mayonnaise	1	tablespoon sugar
1-1 1/2	cups grated cheddar cheese	2	tablespoons flour

Bake pie shell and cool. Place a paper towel in the bottom of a glass bowl and then add tomato slices. Microwave on **high** for 2 minutes until just warm. Drain well. Microwave onion slices for 3 to 4 minutes until slightly transparent.

Place half of the tomato slices in pie shell. Sprinkle 1 tablespoon flour over pie. Place all of the onions in a layer over tomatoes. Gently spread mayonnaise over top. Evenly distribute 1/4 teaspoon each of basil, oregano, and Italian seasoning. Sprinkle sugar over the seasonings. Distribute half of cheese on top of seasonings. Make another layer by adding remaining tomato slices. Sprinkle with last tablespoon of flour, remaining seasonings and cheese. With clean hands, gently but firmly press ingredients to pack them into the pie shell.

Preheat oven to 350 degrees. Bake pie for 45 minutes to 1 hour or so, or until cheese is melted and slightly browned and onions and tomatoes are **fully** cooked and very tender. Do not under-bake.

Cool for 5 minutes and cut into 8 wedges.

SOUTHERN BAKED BEANS

Makes 4 to 6 servings

A great Southern specialty for casual entertaining.

  1   tablespoon prepared mustard
1/2   cup packed brown sugar
1/4   cup vinegar
  1   cup diced onion
  2   teaspoons worcestershire sauce
  2   (16 ounces each) cans pork and beans

Preheat oven to 350 degrees. Lightly grease a 2-quart casserole.

In large bowl, add mustard, sugar, vinegar, onion and worcestershire sauce. Mix well. Add beans, mix and pour into prepared casserole.

Bake uncovered for 45 minutes to 1 hour.

Serve with grilled hot dogs, hamburgers or chicken. Include a big bowl of potato salad and cole slaw for an easy backyard barbecue.

SUMMER VEGETABLE MEDLEY

Makes 3 to 4 servings

A marvelous way to enjoy a variety of fresh summer vegetables from the garden or local farmers' market.

  1   medium onion, diced or several spring onions with tops
1/2   green pepper, diced
3-4   ears fresh corn, cut from cob OR 1 can whole kernel corn
  3   medium yellow Summer squash, sliced
2-3   fresh, ripe tomatoes, peeled & diced
  2   tablespoons sugar
  1   tablespoon light olive oil

Saute onion, celery, green pepper and squash in oil until tender. Add fresh corn, tomatoes and sugar. Cover and cook on low until tender.

VARIATION: Add 2 stalks celery, diced.

To serve as a casserole: Double the recipe above. In a saucepan, add 1 can cream of mushroom or cream of chicken soup and 1/2 cup skimmed milk. Heat and stir until well blended. Place cooked vegetables in casserole dish. Pour soup mixture over vegetables. Bake uncovered for 45 minutes in oven preheated to 350 degrees. If desired, top with French fried onion rings during last 20 minutes of cooking.

SUPPER CLUB BROCCOLI CASSEROLE
Makes 6 to 8 servings

A vegetable casserole that can be made ahead and baked while guests are socializing.

2	(10 ounce each) packages of frozen, chopped broccoli	2	tablespoons chopped onions
1	cup grated sharp cheddar cheese	2	eggs, slightly beaten
1	cup low-calorie mayonnaise	1	can cream of mushroom soup or cream of chicken soup

Preheat oven to 350 degrees. Lightly grease a large 9x13x2-inch casserole dish.

In a saucepan, add water as directed on broccoli package. Bring to a boil, add broccoli, and cook 2 minutes. Drain well in colander. In large bowl, mix cheese, mayonnaise, onions, eggs and soup. Stir in broccoli and mix well. Pour into casserole. Place **Topping** (recipe follows) over casserole. Cover with aluminum foil.

Bake for 45 minutes until set in center. Do not over-bake.

Uncover and serve hot.

Topping

    1   cup crushed crackers
    2   tablespoons margarine or butter, melted

Mix melted margarine and crackers together. Sprinkle over casserole.

TANGY CAULIFLOWER
Makes 6 to 8 servings

The zesty sauce adds a delightful flavor to cauliflower.

1	head fresh cauliflower	1/2-1	cup shredded cheddar cheese
1/2	cup low-calorie mayonnaise or salad dressing	1	teaspoon prepared (not dry) mustard
1	tablespoon finely chopped green onion and tops or finely minced mild onion		

Wash cauliflower and shake off water. Cut off large stem, leaving mostly the top of the head. Cut into bite-size florets and place in single or double layer on serving platter or dish.

Cover with plastic wrap. Microwave on HIGH for about 6 to 8 minutes until tender crisp (do not overcook).

While vegetable is cooking, mix mayonnaise, onion and mustard. Spread sauce over the hot cauliflower. Sprinkle with cheddar cheese. Loosely recover with plastic wrap.

Microwave 1 minute on high to heat topping and melt cheese. Serve hot.

VARIATION: This is equally good with fresh broccoli.

VEGETABLE SOUP

Makes 6 to 8 quarts

Vegetable soup has been around since the beginning of time. It's a wonderful one-dish meal with a variety of vitamins and minerals from an assortment of vegetables. Soup can be planned and made according the following recipe, or it can be made by using just those vegetables you have in stock. The soup can be made with or without meat.

Select 1-1/2 pounds of any one or combination of meats from the following:

>   boneless chicken, cut into small pieces
>
>   whole fryer, cooked, skinned, deboned, cut into small pieces
>
>   lean beef, cut into small cubes
>
>   lean ham or smoked pork shoulder

Into the large soup pot, add the following:

	meat selected from above	3	cups water
	(cut into small pieces)	1/2	teaspoon basil
1	large onion, diced	2	teaspoons bouillon, chicken or beef
1/4	small head cabbage, shredded	12	small pods okra, sliced
2	stalks celery, sliced	3	medium potatoes, peeled and diced

Bring mixture to a boil on high. Lower temperature to medium, and boil until meat is very tender. Add the following vegetables and simmer for 1 or more hours, adding more water if needed, until flavors are well blended:

16	ounce can string beans, drained
16	ounce can butter beans, drained
16	ounce can tomatoes, mashed into pieces, undrained
16	ounce can whole kernel corn, drained

Making vegetable soup is very flexible. Adjust the quantity of meat and vegetables to suit what you have in stock. Vegetables can be fresh, canned or frozen; however, when using frozen vegetables, soup will need to cook longer to make sure vegetables are tender. Experiment by omitting some vegetables and adding others.

Serve with crackers or hot homemade bread.

Preparation Tip

When you have left-over vegetables, such as steamed cabbage, green beans, carrots, butter beans, place them in an air-tight freezable container, making layers of vegetables. When you want to make vegetable soup, thaw and add during the last hour of cooking.

YELLOW SQUASH CASSEROLE

Makes 4 to 6 servings

In the garden, Summer squash seem to multiply beyond one's ability to consume them. This is an unusual and delicious way to enjoy them.

2 1/2	pounds yellow squash, sliced
1	large onion, chopped
1/4	cup water (for cooking squash)
1/2	cup (1 stick) margarine or butter
1	large carrot, peeled and grated
1/2	cup sour cream
1	can cream of chicken soup, undiluted
1	(8 ounce) package herb stuffing mix

Preheat oven to 250 degrees.

Cook squash and onion in the water until tender. Drain well. Add margarine, carrots, sour cream, soup and 1/2 (4 ounces) of stuffing mix. Stir until well blended. Pour into large casserole dish. Sprinkle the remaining stuffing mix on top and pat gently.

Bake 25 to 30 minutes, until bubbly hot.

Preparation Tip

To prevent a bitter taste in cooked squash, especially in more mature squash, scrape the outside "skins" with a serrated knife, thereby removing the bitter outer layer of the squash without actually peeling them. Wash under cold water.

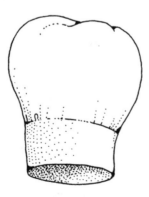

MEASUREMENTS AND EQUIVALENTS

1-1/2 teaspoons	1/2 tablespoon	2 pints	1 quart
3 teaspoons	1 tablespoon	4 cups	1 quart
4 tablespoons	1/4 cup	2 quarts	1/2 gallon
5-1/3 tablespoons	1/3 cup	4 quarts	1 gallon
10-2/3 tablespoons	2/3 cup	2 gallons	1 peck
16 tablespoons	1 cup	8 gallons	1 bushel
2 cups	1 pint	16 ounces	1 pound

1 ounce butter	2 tablespoons	1 pound grated cheese	4 cups
1 slice bread	1/2 cup crumbs	1/4 pound butter	1 stick
1 medium onion	1/2 cup chopped	1 ounce chocolate	1 square
1 lemon	2 to 3 tablespoons juice	5 pounds sugar	10 cups
1 cup raw rice	3 cups cooked rice	5 pounds flour	12 cups
1 stalk celery	1/4 cup chopped	2 tablespoons	1 fl. oz.

Emergency Substitutions

1 whole egg = 2 egg yolks
1 tablespoon corn starch = 2 tablespoons flour
1 cup milk = 1/2 cup evaporated milk plus 1/2 cup water
1 square (1 ounce) chocolate = 3 tablespoons cocoa plus 1 tablespoon butter

CANDY THERMOMETER TEMPERATURES

Soft ball	230-238 degrees	Very hard ball	254-265 degrees
Medium ball	238-244 degrees	Light crack	265-285 degrees
Firm ball	244-248 degrees	Hard crack	290-310 degrees
Hard ball	248-254 degrees		

MEAT THERMOMETER TEMPERATURES

Beef:	Rare	140 degrees	Medium-Rare	150 degrees
	Medium	160 degrees	Well-Done	170 degrees
Ham:	Precooked	140 degrees	Uncooked	160 degrees
Veal:		170 degrees		
Lamb:		170-180 degrees		
Fresh Pork:		185 degrees		
Poultry:		190-195 degrees		

APPENDIX A

The following is a listing of <u>HOW TO</u> sections that appear at the bottom of recipes throughout the book:

APPENDIX B

General Tips

1. When storing boiled eggs in the refrigerator, use a permanent magic marker and place a large "B" and date on each egg to distinguish it from the raw eggs.

2. To easily remove the silk from fresh corn, brush with a stiff brush, starting at the small end of the cob and brushing downward, BEFORE putting any water on corn.

3. To make cutting fresh parsley easy, use kitchen scissors and snip it into small pieces.

4. To measure shortening, add 1 cup of water to a large measuring cup. Add enough shortening in water to fill the measuring cup to the line that would equal the total quantity of 1 cup water plus the amount of required shortening. Pour out the water, leaving the correct amount of shortening.

5. To easily remove fat from cooked foods, place foods in a tall jar and chill until fat solidifies on top. A fat-separating pitcher works well for removing fat from liquids while the liquid is still warm.

6. To avoid washing all those measuring spoons and cups that are attached with a ring, remove the ring before using them so that only those needed for measuring need to be washed.

7. To reduce the gas that naturally occurs in cooked beans and onions, place 1 large peeled potato in mixture while it is cooking. When potato is done, discard it as it absorbs the gas.

Suggested Utensils and Appliances

In addition to those utensils and appliances that are in every kitchen, the following additions are very helpful:

> medium-sized wire whisk (for making sauces)
>
> electric mincer/chopper or mini-food processor (for chopping and mixing small quantities)
>
> crockpot
>
> electric mixer
>
> egg separator
>
> fat/liquid separating pitcher
>
> freezer

The following are really nice luxuries that take the time and effort out of preparing homemade bread and pasta:

> an electric bread machine and an electric pasta machine.

INDEX

BRUNCHES

CAKES

CHICKEN/TURKEY

COOKIES

CROCKPOT

DESSERTS

FRUITS

GRILLING

MARINADES

MEASUREMENTS

MEAT TEMPERATURES

PASTA

TAILGATING

VEGETABLES

VENISON

ENJOY EASY-TO-MAKE SOUTHERN DISHES

A versatile collection of family recipes for **Southern** cooking! Almost 300 easy-to-prepare recipes deliver delicious home-cooked flavor with ease. Written with clear instructions, these recipes use simple ingredients to bring exciting meals to your table. This is the *first* and *LAST* cookbook you will ever need!

I.S.B.N. 1-56875-094-3
$14.95
Cookbook

ABOUT THE AUTHOR

The author, Drew W. Weeks, was reared in Aiken, South Carolina and has lived in the South all of her life. She and her husband, Tom, live in Barnwell, South Carolina and have two grown children: Shannon and Warren.

Drew shares almost 300 one-of-a-kind, family-tested recipes for preparing delicious, home-cooked meals *with ease*. These Southern recipes range from Appetizers to Vegetables and are written with easy-to-follow directions, using basic ingredients.

Chicken & Dumplings, Best-Ever Meatloaf, Super-Moist Brownies, Lemon Chess Pie, Aunt Nell's Spoonbread, Grits Casserole and Beaufort Stew are just a few of the many mouth-watering recipes awaiting you inside, including some family-heirloom recipes.

The author gives many plan-ahead and cooking hints to help YOU prepare healthy meals with *maximum flavor* and *minimal effort*. This is the *first* and LAST cookbook you'll ever need!

WANT MORE GREAT COOKING??? SURE!

"True Southern Family Recipes by Drew W. Weeks. A versatile collection of almost 300 recipes, with clear instructions and simple ingredients, for easy, delicious home-cooked meals. Great for beginner and expert cooks! Price $14.95. Order Number 094-3.

"The Lowfat Mexican Cookbook: True Mexican Taste Without the WAIST" by Robert Leos and Nancy Leos. If you love Mexican foods as much as we do, but do not want the extra calories it contains, then this is just what the chef needs. Good eating as well as good health are here in this great little book. Price $6.95. Order Number 896.

"This For That: A Treasury of Savvy Substitutions for the Creative Cook" by Meryl Nelson. Meryl's cookbooks are nationally famous. *This For That* has been featured in Family Circle and many other national publications, TV and radio. Hints, Recipes, How-To's for using THIS when you're out of THAT, includes microwave directions. Price $6.95. Order Number 847.

"The Newlywed Cookbook" by Robin Walsh. Bet you have a wedding to go to soon—here is the perfect wedding gift to add to a set of hand towels or an appliance. *The Newlywed Cookbook* is the perfect kitchen gift along with our other titles listed here. The Famous *Chef Tell* says, "Amusing, creative ideas for the beginner cook. I highly recommend it!" Price $12.95. Order Number 877.

"Your One Year Diet Diary: An Easy-To-Keep Daily Record of Your Successes" by Diane J. Mentzer. If you're fed up with diets that don't work, then this special little book can help you to take control of your eating, and lose weight permanently. Price $6.95. Order Number 928-8.

SHIP TO:

(Please Print) Name: _____

Organization: _____

Address: _____

_____

YOUR ORDER

ORDER #	QTY	UNIT PRICE	TOTAL PRICE

PAYMENT METHOD

☐ Enclosed check or money order

☐ MasterCard   Card Expires _____   Signature _____

☐ Visa   ☐☐☐☐☐☐☐☐☐☐☐☐☐☐☐☐

Please rush me the above books. I want to save by ordering three books and receive FREE shipping charges. Orders under 3 books please include $2.50 shipping. CA residents add 8.25% tax.

R & E Publishers • 468 Auzerais Ave., Suite A, San Jose, CA 95126 • (408) 977-0691